2003

RELIGION AND POLITICS IN THE DEVELOPING WORLD: EXPLOSIVE INTERACTIONS

Contemporary Perspectives on Developing Societies

JOHN MUKUM MBAKU
Series Editor
Weber State University, Ogden, Utah, USA

Between 1989 and 1991, there were several changes in the global political economy that have had significant impact on policy reform in developing societies. The most important of these were the collapse of socialism in Eastern Europe, the subsequent disintegration of the Soviet Union, the cessation of superpower rivalry, and the demise of apartheid in South Africa. These events have provided scholars a new and challenging research agenda: To help the peoples of the Third World participate more effectively in the new global economy. Given existing conditions in these societies, the first line of business for researchers would be to help these countries establish and maintain transparent, accountable and participatory governance structures and, at the same time, provide themselves with more viable economic infrastructures. The *Contemporary Perspectives on Developing Societies* series was founded to serve as an outlet for such policy relevant research. It is expected that books published in this series will provide rigorous analyses of issues relevant to the peoples of the Third World and their efforts to improve their participation in the global economy.

Also in this series

Religion and Politics in the Developing World: Explosive Interactions

Edited by
ROLIN G. MAINUDDIN
North Carolina Central University, USA

Ashgate

Published by
Ashgate Publishing Limited
Gower House
Croft Road
Aldershot
Hampshire GU11 3HR
England

Ashgate Publishing Company
131 Main Street
Burlington, VT 05401-5600 USA

Ashgate website: http://www.ashgate.com

British Library Cataloguing in Publication Data
Religion and politics in the developing world : explosive
        interactions. - (Contemporary perspectives on developing
        societies)
        1. Religion and politics - Developing countries 2. Social
        conflict - Religious aspects 3. Social conflict - Developing
        countries
        I. Mainuddin, Rolin G.
        322.1'091724

Library of Congress Control Number: 2001095875

ISBN 0 7546 1507 3

Printed and bound by Athenaeum Press, Ltd.,
Gateshead, Tyne & Wear.

Contents R 382

322.109173+

About the Editor

Rolin G. Mainuddin (Ph.D., University of Kansas, 1992) is Assistant Professor of Political Science at North Carolina Central University, Durham, North Carolina. Although trained in European alliance politics, he has gradually shifted his research interest to the Middle East. While continuing to work on security issues, he has increasingly focused attention on the interaction between religion—particularly Islam—and politics. In addition to contributing a book chapter on democratization and human rights in the Gulf Cooperation Council countries (Paul J. Magnarella, ed., *Middle East and North Africa*, 1999), his articles have appeared in *Indian Journal of Asian Affairs*, *Journal of Third World Studies*, *Middle East Policy*, and *Military Review*. A past President (1998–1999) of the Association of Third World Studies, Dr Mainuddin is currently President-Elect of the North Carolina Political Science Association.

List of Contributors

Sylvia M. Jacobs (Ph.D., Howard University, 1975) is Professor of History at North Carolina Central University, Durham, North Carolina. Her research focus is on the history of the African diaspora. Among her books are *The African Nexus: Black American Perspectives on the European Partitioning of Africa, 1880–1920* (1981) and *Black Americans and the Missionary Movement in Africa* (1982). She has published numerous articles, essays, and biographical sketches on the relationship of African Americans with Africa and Africans, which have appeared in various journals, including the *Journal of Negro History*, *SAGE: A Scholarly Journal on Black Women*, and *Western Journal of Black Studies*. Aside from teaching and service awards, in 1984 Dr Jacobs won the best book award from the Association of Black Women Historians.

Gershon R. Kieval (Ph.D., The Johns Hopkins University, 1980) is a Senior Analyst at the United States Central Intelligence Agency. A former Adjunct Professor of Political Science and International Affairs at George Washington University, Washington, DC, he is the co-editor of *Israel Faces the Future* (1986) and co-author of *Israel: Land of Tradition and Conflict* (1993). In addition, Dr Kieval's numerous publications include *Party Politics in Israel and the Occupied Territories* (1983), *Israeli National Security Policy: Political Actors and Perspectives* (1988), and *Israeli Politics in the 1990s: Key Domestic and Foreign Policy Factors* (1991).

Robert Lawless (Ph.D., New School University, 1975) is Professor of Anthropology at Wichita State University, Wichita, Kansas. His research focuses on Southeast Asia (primarily the Philippines) and the Caribbean (primarily Haiti), with an interest in the integration of materialistic and cognitive approaches. Among his books and monographs are *The Concept of Culture* (1979), *Haiti: A Research Handbook* (1990), and *Haiti's Bad Press* (1992). Dr Lawless' articles have appeared in various journals, including *Anthropology*, *Journal of Anthropological Research*, *Journal of Ethnic Studies*, *Studies in Third World Societies*, and *Urban Anthropology*.

Alynna J. Lyon (Ph.D., University of South Carolina, 1999) is Assistant Professor of Political Science at Southeast Missouri State University, Cape Girardeau, Missouri. Her research focuses on the relationship between ethnic conflict and international politics. In addition, she has an interest in the United Nations, conflict resolution, and peacekeeping. Dr Lyon contributed a chapter on East Timor in *History Behind the Headlines* (2000). In 1999, she was winner of the International Studies Association Graduate Student Paper Competition for the Ethnicity, Nationalism, and Migration Section. She has served as the Chair of ENMISA Communications (1999–2000), a position she continues to hold.

Bernard Reich (Ph.D., University of Virginia, 1964) is Professor of Political Science and International Affairs at George Washington University, Washington, DC. A consultant to various agencies of the United States Government, he is Chairman of the Advanced Area Studies (Middle East—Fertile Crescent) at the Foreign Service Institute, United States Department of State. Dr Reich is the author or co-author of a number of books on the

Middle East, including *Quest for Peace: United States-Israel Relations and the Arab-Israeli Conflict* (1977), *The United States and Israel: Influence in the Special Relationship* (1984), *Israel: Land of Tradition and Conflict* (1985), *Securing the Covenant: United States-Israel Relations After the Cold War* (1995), and *Arab-Israeli Conflict and Conciliation: A Documentary History* (1995). His articles and reviews have appeared in many journals, including *AJAMES: Annals of Japanese Association of Middle East Studies, The Journal of Palestine Studies, The Korean Journal of the Middle Eastern Studies, Middle East Focus, Middle East Insight, The Middle East Journal, Middle East Review*, and *The New Middle East*.

Mohammad Rashiduzzaman (Ph.D., University of Durham, England, 1964) is Associate Professor of Political Science at Rowan University, Glassboro, New Jersey. His research focuses on Bangladesh, South Asia, and political Islam. He is the author of *The Central Legislature in British India* (1965), *Pakistan: A Study of Government and Politics* (1967), *Politics and Administration in the Local Councils: A Study of Union and District Councils in East Pakistan* (1968), and *Rural Leadership and Population Control in Bangladesh* (1982). Dr Rashiduzzaman has published articles in various journals, including *Asian Survey, Contemporary South Asia*, and *Journal of South Asia and Middle Eastern Studies*.

Debra Sabia (Ph.D., University of South Carolina, 1994) is Associate Professor of Political Science and Director of the Center for Latino Research and Outreach Services at Georgia Southern University, Statesboro, Georgia. Her publications include *Contradiction and Conflict: The Popular Church in Nicaragua* (1997) as well as articles in the *Journal of the Southeastern Council on Latin Amercian Studies, Journal of Third World Studies*, and *South Eastern Latin Americanist*. In addition to receiving teaching awards, Dr Sabia served as a Rotary Scholar to Ecuador in 1998.

Frank J. Trapp (Ph.D., The Florida State University, 1994) is Associate Professor of Political Science at the University of North Carolina at Pembroke. His research focuses on conflict theory, terrorism, and counter-terrorism. Currently, he is compiling a data base on anti-Israeli terrorism and Israeli counter-terrorism measures from 1968 to 2000. Among his various publications is a recently published article in the *Journal of the Peace and Sciences* on the potential for terrorism in the Balkans. Active in the Model United Nations, Dr Trapp had traveled with a delegation of United States college students to the European Model United Nations in the Hague, the Netherlands.

Michele Zebich-Knos (Ph.D., University of New Mexico, 1978) is Professor of Political Science and International Affairs at Kennesaw State University, Kennesaw, Georgia, where she also serves as Coordinator of the International Affairs major. Her research interests include democracy and development in developing countries, and global environmental issues. She has numerous publications, including a chapter on Ecotourism in *Latin American Development and Public Policy* (1994) and articles in the *Journal of Environment and Development, Journal of Peace Studies,* and *South Eastern Latin Americanist*. Dr Zebich-Knos is a member of the editorial board of the *South Eastern Latin Americanist*. During the 1990 and 1995 Haitian presidential elections, she served as an election observer for the Organization of American States.

Yahia H. Zoubir (Ph.D., American University, 1985) is Associate Professor of International Studies at Thunderbird (the American Graduate School of International Management), Glendale, Arizona. He is also the Director of Thunderbird Europe, French-Geneva Center in Archamps, France, and the editor-in-chief of the *Thunderbird International Business Review* (formerly *The International Executive*). In addition to publishing chapters in many books, he co-edited *International Dimensions of the Western Sahara Conflict* (1993) and edited *North Africa in Transition* (1999). Dr Zoubir's articles have appeared in a variety of journals including *Arab Studies Quarterly*, *Journal of Algerian Studies*, *Journal of North African Studies*, *Middle East Affairs Journal*, *Maghreb Review*, *The Middle East Journal*, *Middle East Report*, and *Middle Eastern Studies*.

Preface

This project was motivated by the skewed attention paid to political Islam in the literature on religion and politics. Yet, there is growing evidence of association of other religions with politics. To more fully understand the relationship between religion and politics, including violent interactions, warrants expanding the scope of research beyond Islam. Whereas the approach is not new, this study renews attention to that much needed research agenda regarding the behavior of a religious majority against the state. This multi-disciplinary work includes contributions by authors with expertise in different fields: anthropology, history, and political science. Except for two, however, all the contributors are political scientists. More chapters by anthropologists and historians and also participation by economists, psychologists, and sociologists would surely have added new insights. And case studies of Buddhism, Hinduism, and the Sikh religion—all three originating in South Asia—would have given the project a fuller comparative perspective. Unfortunately, that which is desirable is not always possible. An editor is circumscribed by both his contacts and time commitments of prospective contributors. However, all these chapters are original and written specifically for this book.

Every editor brings to a book his own biases, and I am no exception. Phrases such as 'Born again Christian' and 'Christian Professor' puzzled me. Also, I could not avoid noticing that in the West a ritual 'cleansing' of the body was not expected before reading (or touching) the Bible. Furthermore, I found that some people who identified themselves as Christians would immediately add that they were 'not practicing.' For someone who grew up in South Asia—Bangladesh (before 1971 the former East Pakistan)—those observations were confusing. Whether or not one practiced the religion, I was used to a person identifying oneself as a Hindu or Muslim. Subsequently, I came to appreciate the impact of the secular milieu on the Western thought process. Something else that perplexed me was the concept of 'Islamic fundamentalism'. Familiar with the five fundamentals of Islam, I could not accept associating that term with radicalism, militancy, and terrorism. Derived from 'Protestant fundamentalism', the term 'Islamic fundamentalism' illustrates the difficulty of finding a suitable functional equivalence. Interestingly, 'Islamic fundamentalism' is gradually being supplanted by Islamism in Western literature.

Technology is only a tool, and the benefits derived are contingent upon its use. With the ever-expanding frontier of digital communication, one no longer has enough computer skills. And limited knowledge, in failing to overcome a simple caveat, can be a cumbersome experience. Electronic mail both helped and hindered the publication of this book. On the one hand, it facilitated fast and convenient communication, both one-to-one and one-to-many, with the contributors. On the other hand, not knowing that endnotes do not transfer well, some of the files were corrupted. That delayed the completion of the manuscript. In the process, I was—to borrow a phrase—Baptized by fire. I only wish that it had been a lesson learned by reading and not through a painful and time consuming experience.

North Carolina Central University   Rolin G. Mainuddin
Durham, North Carolina

Acknowledgments

In putting together this collection of essays, I benefitted from the encouragement of various people: Choudhury Rafiqul Abrar, M. A. Aziz, Richard Bald, U. A. B. Razia Akter Banu, David Dabelko, Nader Entessar, Deborah Gerner, David Gilmartin, William Head, Gary Kline, Sung-Ho Kim, Jacob Kipp, Bruce Lawrence, Paul Magnarella, Talukder Maniruzzaman, K. M. Mohsin, Harold Molineu, Linda Norflett, Claude Rowland, Santosh Saha, Philip Schrodt, Donald Simmons, Tony Stewart, and Rudolf Zarzar. In particular, I would like to thank Ralph Braibanti, Carl Ernst, Ronald Francisco, Nicolae Harsanyi, Harold Isaacs, Laura Janda, Jaroslaw Piekalkiewicz, and David Williams. Jarvis Hall, my department chair, was generous in facilitating a suitable teaching schedule that allowed me to devote blocks of time to this project. Nurudeen Akinyemi and Sanford Silverburg provided contacts for the chapters on Mexico and Israel, respectively. I am indebted to John Mukum Mbaku and Freddie Parker for their invaluable advice in type-setting the manuscript. As the general editor of the *Contemporary Perspectives on Developing Societies* series, furthermore, Mbaku was a helpful guide at every step of the project.

I benefitted from Middle East panels at annual meetings of the Association of Third World Studies and the North Carolina Political Science Association. Also, I found it enriching to attend colloquia held by the Carolina Seminars on Comparative Islamic Studies and North Carolina Center for South Asia Studies (formerly Triangle South Asia Consortium). In particular, faculty seminars organized by the Center for Slavic, Eurasian, and East European Studies, University of North Carolina at Chapel Hill, were helpful in developing the idea for this book.

Libraries become a second home for the researcher and I owe special thanks to these institutions and staff. Bennie Daye, Debra Hazel, and Veola Williams were always eager to help at the Shepard Library, North Carolina Central University. Access to the D.H. Hill Library, North Carolina State University, and Davis Library, University of North Carolina at Chapel Hill, was very useful. In particular, I benefitted from resources at the Perkins and Lilly Libraries at Duke University. Other persons who facilitated the process included Anne Keirby of Ashgate who gave me gentle reminders from the United Kingdom; Kirsten Weissenberg and Rosalind Ebdon provided detailed and valuable feedback; and Ruth Peters was understanding and considerate at the other side of the Atlantic. Nazma Ali, my sister, never failed to surprise me with dinner invitations and delicious dishes just when I thought I was too pressed for time to cook. Marion Salinger was generous in readily agreeing to proof-read the entire manuscript. While I am grateful to all the aforementioned people, I am alone responsible for any errors remaining. Finally, I must thank the contributors, who waited patiently for a considerable length of time as I struggled to get the manuscript ready for publication.

List of Abbreviations

AIS	Islamic Salvation Army
AL	Awami League
BJP	Bharatiya Janata Party
BNP	Bangladesh Nationalist Party
CEB	Ecclesial base communities
CELAM	Latin American Bishops Conference
CHT	Chittagong Hill Tracts
CIA	Central Intelligence Agency
CONAI	National Mediation Commission
ERP	People's Revolutionary Army
EZLN	Zapatista Army for National Liberation
FBIS	Foreign Broadcast Information Services
FFS	Front of Socialist Forces
FIS	Islamic Salvation Front
FLN	Front de Liberation Nationale
FSLN	Sandinista National Liberation Front
GIA	Armed Islamic Group
GSPC	Salafist Group for Preaching and Combat
HAMAS	Harakat al-Muqawama al-Islamyya
JP	Jatiya Party
MAFDAL	Miflaga Datit Leumit
MIA	Armed Islamic Movement
MSP	Mouvement pour la Societe Pacifique
NAFTA	North American Free Trade Agreement
NGO	Non-government organization
NRP	National Religious Party
PAN	National Action Party
PDC	Christian Democratic Party
PLO	Palestinian Liberation Organization
PNA	Palestinian National Authority
PNC	Palestinian National Council
PRI	Institutional Revolutionary Party
SHAS	Sephardi Torah Guardians
TAMI	Tenuah LeMassoret Yisrael
UNC	Unified National Command
USSR	Union of Soviet Socialist Republic

Note on Translation

For a multi-disciplinary work with different contributors, with expertise in their specialized fields, it is not possible to follow any particular system of transliteration. The authors have taken responsibility for translations in their respective chapters. In providing translations in parentheses, they have tried to keep spellings of non-English words close to their pronunciation in the original language. However, words of non-English origin that are now generally accepted as part of the English language vocabulary have not been translated or italicized. As this book looks at religion from the perspective of the followers of the respective faiths, and not the secular notion of a collection of symbols or rituals, names of religions and holy books are capitalized. By the same token, a religion used as an adjective is also capitalized. This is my decision alone as the editor and should not be attributed to the individual authors.

List of Translations

Agudat Yisrael	Association of Israel
Ahl al-Da'wa	Members of the Proselytization
Al-Hijra wa al-Takfyir	Emigration and Excommunication
Al-Irshad wa'l Islah	Orientation and Reform
Aliyah	Immigration
Allah	God in Islam
Allah Akbar	God is Great
Al-Majd	Glory
Al-Mazdaqiya Hia'asl al-Ishtiraqiya	Mazdaqism Is the Source of Socialism
Al-Mujamma al-Islami	The Islamic Association
Al-Muwahiddun	Unifiers
Amar Shonar Bangla	My Golden Bengal
Amir	Commander
Ansar Allah	Supporters of God
Ashkenazi	European Jew
Bangali	The people of Bangladesh and the state of West Bengal in India
Bangalitva	Bangaliness
Bangla	The land of, and the language spoken in, Bangladesh and West Bengal
Bangobandhu	Friend of Bengal
Barrios	Neighborhoods
Boyevik	Fighter of the war
Caciques	Local political leaders
Campesino	Peasant farmer
Charter of Allah	Charter of God
Chiapanecos	Disaffected citizens of Chiapas
Communalism	Conflict between religious communities
Comunidades eclesiales de base	Ecclesiastical base communities
Conscientization	The development of a critical consciousness
Contra	Counter or against
Criollo	Mexican born Spaniards
Cristero	Follower of Christ
Datiim	Religious Zionists
Da'wa	Proselytization
Da'wa wa al-Tabligh	Proselytize and communicate
Degel HaTorah	Flag of the Torah
Eklesia Lanangwa	The Christianity of Freedom
El-Qiyam al-Islamyya	Islamic Values
Fatwa	Religious opinion or decree
Fitna	Disharmony

Front de Liberation Nationale	National Liberation Front
Gazavat	Holy war in Russian language
Gemeinschaft	Community
Geselischaft	Society
Ghadibun a'la Allah	Those Upset with God
Glasnost	Openness
Gush Emunim	Bloc of the Faithful
Hajj	Pilgrimage
Halachah	Law in Judaism
Halal	Ritually killed and prepared, or permissible in Islam
Hapoel Hamizrahi	Workers of the Spiritual Center
Harakat at-Mujtama' al-Islamiy ya	Islamic Resistance Movement
Harakat al-Nahda al-Islamyya	Movement for the Islamic Renaissance
Haredim	Ultra-Orthodox Jews
Hijab	Veil
Hiloniim	Secular Jews
Hindutva	Hinduness
Humanisme musulman	Muslim humanism
Iglesia popular	Popular church movement
Ijtihad	Interpretation
Imam	Religious leader
Intifada	Shaking off or uprising
Islah	Reform
Islamic Oikkya	Islamic Unity
Istish-had	Self-sacrifice
Iztema	Prayer congregation
Jahilyia	Pre-Islamic society
Jamaat al-lkhwan al-Muslimin	Association of Muslim Brothers
Jamaat al-Ulama	Association of Religious Scholars
Jamaat-i-Islami	Islamic Association
Jihad	Holy war in Islam
Joi Bangla	Victory to Bengal
Junud al-Allah	Soldiers of God
Kashrut	Dietary laws
Kazi	Religious judge
Knesset	Israeli parliament
Kofr	Blasphemy
Kosher	Ritually killed and prepared, or permissible in Judaism
Laicite islamique	Islamic secularism
Ley Reglamentaria	Reglamentary Law
Madrassa	Religious education institution
Majallat al-Ta'dhib al-Islamiy	Review of Muslim Education
Maktab	Community religious education facility

Maraboutic zawi'as	Akin to mystical brotherhoods
Maravi	Peoples of the Fire
Masjid	Mosque
Masortiim	Traditional Jews
Meimad	Dimension
Miflaga Datit Leumit	National Religious Party
Misnagdim	Non-Hasidic Jews
Mizrahi	Spiritual Center
Moetzet Gedolei Hatorah	Council of Torah Sages
Morasha	Heritage
Mouvement pour la Societe Pacifique	Movement for a Peaceful Society
Mujahidin	Holy warrior
Mulatto	A person of African and European mixed ancestry
Neturei Karta	Guardians of the City
Parastatals	State-controlled and state-owned corporations
Patronato	Royal patronage
People of the Book	Qur'anic phrase for Jews and Christians
Perestroika	Restructuring
Qital	Assassination
Rabindro Shongit	The genre of Rabindro Nath's songs
Rabita	World Muslim Congress
Rabitat al-Da'wa	League of Preaching
Sabbath	Holy day in Judaism
Sandinismo	Sandinista ideology
Secretaria de Gobernacion	Ministry of the Interior
Sephardi	Oriental Jew
Shahid Minar	Martyrs Tower
Shangshod	Bangladesh parliament
Shari'a	Law in Islam
Shari'a al-Islamyya	Islamic law
Shinui	Change
Shonar Bangla	Golden Bengal
Shongit	Song
Shurah	Council
Somocistas	Somoza National Guardsmen
Sunnah	Prophet Mohammad's examples
Tabligh	Communication with God through prayer
Tablighi Jamaat	Association of Communicators
Tamaddun Majlis	Cultural Forum
Tariqat	Path or way
Tenuah LeMassoret Yisrael	Movement for Jewish Tradition
Ti Legliz	Little Church
Ulama	Religious scholar
Um'ma	Community

Waqf	Endowment
Wataniyya	Nationalism
Weltanschauung	Worldview
Yeshiva	Religious seminary
Yisrael Ba'aliyah	Israel for Immigration
Zikr	A ritual intended to bring union with God

For my departed parents,
Rabia Khatoon and Abu Zafar Md. Shamsuddin

Introduction

What is the relationship between religion and politics? How are they associated in the developing world? When does the interface between them result in violence? This book attempts to address these questions. In particular, the objective is to understand the circumstances that lead to explosive interactions between religion and politics in the developing world. However, this focus does not imply a perpetual tension between the religious and political spheres. Rather, it explores those historical moments when the relationship does break down and often ends in violent conflicts.

With computer technology and the information revolution further demonstrating the significance of science, the very idea of assessing the relationship between religion and politics in the 21st century is striking. This is so because science has been identified with rationality, progress, and everything modern. In contrast, religion often has been perceived as irrational, backward, and traditional. In particular, the West—the epicenter of modernity—has relegated religion to the trash bin of the medieval period. With the hitherto marginalized *ulamas* (religious scholars) at the helm of state power, the 1979 Islamic Revolution in Iran was a shocking anomaly in that historical march. In inspiring the Shi'ite communities and domestic religious opposition, the Iranian Revolution posed a security threat for the regimes in the Middle East (Abi-Aad and Grenon, 1997, pp. 28–31, 65). For some in the West, the pain was three-fold. First, there is the memory of three waves of Muslim intrusion into Europe—beginning in the 8th century—by the Arabs from the southwest, Tartars from the northeast, and Seljuk and Ottoman Turks from the southeast (Lewis, 1995, pp. 11–12). Second, there is the perception that an orthodox Islamic 'Green Peril' has replaced the post-War Communist 'Red Menace' (Hadar, 1993, p. 27). Third, religious resurgence is a challenge to secularism. The first two points have received a lot of attention in the literature and an interesting debate has emerged around Samuel Huntington's (1993, pp. 31, 45; 1996) civilizational clash framework (Braibanti, 1999, p. 28; Gerges, 1999, pp. 16–18; Hunter, 1998, pp. 167–168; Lawrence, 1998, pp. 5, 9; Vincent-Barwood, 1998, p. 15) as well as issues of modernity, democracy, human rights, and gender (Baaklini, et al., 1999, pp. 33–43; Brynen, et al., 1998, p. 268; Euben, 1999, 20–25; Moghissi, 1999, pp. 52–54; Sayyid, 1997, pp. 99–120; Watt, 1988, p. 105). However, it is the third point that remains troublesome in the West.

Western civilization has its own memory of religious sufferings. In 1231, Pope Gregory IX established the Papal Inquisition to prevent the spread of heresy. Subsequently, in 1478, Pope Sixtus IV authorized the Spanish Inquisition and, in 1542, Pope Paul III blessed the Roman Inquisition. The Reformation by Martin Luther, which marked the Protestant Movement, was followed by the Counter-Reformation of the Roman Catholic Church which led to the establishment of the Society of Jesus (Jesuits). And the Catholic-Protestant struggle in (what is now) Germany—in which three-fourths of the German population perished (Crowther, 1995, p. 77)—pitted France and Sweden against Spain and the Holy Roman Empire and ultimately engulfed the rest of Europe in the Thirty Years War (1618–1648). In fact, it was during the Roman Inquisition that Pope Urban VIII presided over Galileo Galilei's persecution for disputing the Ptolemaic system and Aristotelian physics. Galilei's claim that the sun was rotating, and the resultant sun-spot controversy, earned him the wrath of the Jesuits. Earlier, Nicolaus Copernicus faced diatribes in Protestant circles, including those of Martin Luther, for debunking the macrocosm-microcosm doctrine that placed earth—and, by extension, man—at the center of the universe. As an illustration of changing times, later it was Isaac Newton who refused to honor a Royal mandate from King James II giving a Catholic monk a degree from the University of Cambridge. Given that both the Scripture and nature have God's blessings, Gelilei argued for coequal divinity of nature with the Scripture. In discovering the 'mechanics' of the cosmos, furthermore, Newton highlighted the role of human reasoning in demystifying the physical universe (Crowther, 1999, pp. 23–36, 71–73, 81–85, 122–124). Between 1700 and 1900, statistics—an invaluable tool for scientific investigation—permeated research from the physical sciences to the social sciences (Stigler, 1986, p. 4). Science has now become a fad and scientific methodology a badge of honor. Furthermore, in the 20th century the constant speed of light led Albert Einstein to reconsider the Newtonian static, absolute notion of time and space in his theory of relativity. He discarded the simultaneity of events. For Einstein, time and space were dynamic and relative. Thus, events were relative to the vantage points of the observers (Crowther, 1995, pp. 238–239), and that had implications for the very notion of truth.

While the Enlightenment did not reject God, the era paved the way for dissociating God from nature. Ultimately that culminated in some denying the very existence of God—often filling the void with science (Armstrong, 1993, pp. 344–345). The idea of Divine Intervention gave way to the modernist notion of universal principle. The latter, in turn, gave way to the postmodernist thought that truth is relative. In the social sciences, cultural assimilation—into the dominant culture—has been supplanted by cultural diversity. The principle of state sovereignty that has characterized the modern state-system since the 1648 Treaty of Westphalia at the end of the Thirty Years War in Europe—and entered into Article II, Section 7 of the United Nations Charter after World War II—has come under scrutiny. As the Balkan Crisis in the post-Cold War era demonstrates, minority rights are competing with state's rights (Krasner, 1999, ch. 3).The Bible and other holy books are now to be situated within the cultural context. And the cultural milieu addressed does not pertain to the time when the holy books were revealed but to contemporary societal power structures. At issue is the 'constructed' meaning of the religious texts themselves (Castelli, et al., eds., 1995, pp. 1–15; Lester, 1999, p. 44; Murphy, 1998, p. 46. Also, see Allen, 2001, p. 22). Scientific progress—which is traced back to the Enlightenment—has made secularism increasingly appealing in the West. The understanding of universal natural forces made human rationality autonomous and not subject to God's daily intervention during the modernist era. In challenging universalism, postmodernism propounded localism and relegated God to the infinity.

Yet, God did not die! At a time when the West has embraced secularism and worships science, the 1979 Iranian Revolution brought God back in full force. However, the *ulamas* in Iran were not trying to create an Amish society. Even though resentful of Western cultural infusion, they did not reject Western technology (Braibanti, 1995, p. 21; Esposito, 1999, p. 17; Lawrence, 1995, p. 221). While secularism has been accepted as the sine qua non for modernization and progress in the West, political Islam has relocated religion from the periphery to the central plain of scholarly discourse and policy analysis (Dekmejian, 1985; Eickelman and Piscatori, 1996; Esposito, ed., 1990; Hussain, 1985; Lewis, 1993; Roy, 1994). And that shift has continued with renewed attention to culture and identity in the postmodernist environment in the post-Cold War period (Huntington, 1993, p. 26; Moore, 2000, p. xiv; Smith, 2000, pp. 57–58. Also, see Inglehart, 1997, pp. 23–25; Harrison and Huntington, eds., 2000; Lapid and Kratochwil, eds., 1996).

Ironically, when God has been seemingly banished from the popular culture and academia in the West, God has been embraced as the solution to the crisis facing the *um'ma* (Muslim community). And this tide of religious resurgence has also touched Buddhism, Christianity, and Hinduism, observed a Roman Catholic theologian (Weigel, 1992, p. 173). One may also add Judaism to that list. Even in the West, which witnessed a *'privatization* of religion,' with political movements taking over some of the religious functions (Luckmann, 1991, pp. 170–176, emphasis original), the 'Christian Right' made a significant comeback in the United States in the 1990s (Green, Rozell, and Wilcox, eds., 2000; Rozell and Wilcox, eds., 1997; Rozell and Wilcox, eds., 1995).

Interestingly, in 1985 Jerrold Green (1985, pp. 317–20) had to argue that 'religio-politics' is a viable conceptual variable. Yet 15 years later, Scott Appleby (2000, p. 21) expressed optimism about 'religious peacebuilding' becoming a subfield of conflict resolution. Obviously circumstances have changed from the time when prominent scholars assigned religion a secondary or marginal role (Kedourie, 1961, p. 73; Smith, 1987, p. 35. Also, see Smith, 2000, pp. 59–65). Given the focus on minority groups, and exclusion of 'Islamist movements' from the study, the Minorities at Risk Project—by Ted Robert Gurr (2000, pp. 18, 232; 1993, pp. 18–22, 317; 1992, p. 59)—has found religious groups insignificant for conflict research. For greater insight into religious conflicts, however, the behavior of the majority groups warrants attention (Fox, 2000, pp. 423–424). This book addresses the behavior of majority religious groups. Instead of communal relations, the primary focus is on understanding, through case studies, the confrontation of religious resurgence—what Mark Juergensmeyer (1994) calls 'religious nationalism'—against the state. While most works on religious resurgence have been limited to Islam, The Fundamentalism Project—by Martin Marty and Scott Appleby (1995; 1994; 1993b; 1993a; 1991)—had directed attention to the need for a broader approach that incorporated other religious resurgence movements. Although this five-volume project was concluded with a better understanding of 'fundamentalism,' religious violence continues to demand scholarly attention.

Given the limited number of works addressing religious resurgence beyond Islam, and examining specific countries, this book redirects attention to the case study method. In assessing the impact of religion on politics, the latter is the dependent variable. The scope here is modest, however. This study compares the interactions between religion and politics for the three Abrahamic religions: Judaism, Christianity, and Islam. Beginning with Latin America, and moving from West to East, the task is undertaken through a case study of nine political units. While seven are nation-states, two—Chechnya and Palestine—involve entities that are struggling to carve out a statehood.

In Chapter 1, Debra Sabia notes the role of the Catholic Church in Nicaragua in opposing the brutal authoritarianism of the Somoza regime. Having facilitated the rise of the Sandinista regime to power, the church then found itself opposing the Marxist regime and played a significant part in the democratic transition in that country. Liberation theology—the commitment to 'human liberation'—was reflected in the church's role in promoting *conscientization* (critical consciousness) and participation, especially in the *comunidades eclesiales de base* (ecclesial base communities, CEB) among the rural poor. The attempt to suppress Catholic dissension pushed the CEBs to support rebellion against the Somoza regime. The Catholic Church itself was bifurcated in the process, with consequences for church-state relations. Nevertheless, the 'progressive church leaders' implemented the spirit of liberation theology in promoting both social justice and democratization in Nicaragua.

Michele Zebich-Knos places religious identity (and mobilization) within the framework of collective national identity in Chapter 2. In associating Catholicism with Spanish colonial domination, post-independence Mexico was marked by varying degrees of state-sponsored anticlericalism. However, constitutional excesses provoked armed resistance from the *Cristero* (Follower of Christ) Movement, comprised of staunchly religious Catholic peasants. And many Catholics in the poor south are believed to support armed struggle by the Zapatista Army for National Liberation. However, the dyadic relationship has become complicated with the growth in numbers of Protestant followers, who are resented by the rural Catholics.

The relationship between Christianity and politics in Haiti, notes Robert Lawless in Chapter 3, must be understood in the context of Voodoo. As Roman Catholicism became the religion of the social elites, the Catholic Church experienced a rift— particularly in the person of Jean-Bertrand Aristide—within its hierarchy. It is noteworthy that Catholicism did not supplant Voodoo practices among the poor or some of the political elites. Whereas Voodoo was a greater mobilizing force than Catholicism against the Duvalier regime, the earlier political association discredited both of these faiths in the immediate post-Duvalier period. With the growth of Protestantism, furthermore, there is a triangular struggle among the believers. Unlike Catholicism, however, Protestantism is stalwart in rejecting Voodoo practices. As both Voodoo and Protestantism are gaining popularity among the rural poor, particularly in the western part of the country, any perception of the government taking sides is likely to provoke political instability.

Unlike the previous three case studies, where Catholicism is the major religious force, in Chapter 4 Sylvia Jacobs introduces Protestantism as the predominant voice against both external domination during the colonial era and internal authoritarianism in the early postcolonial period in Malawi. While the Livingstonia Mission opposed Arab commercial intrusion in the north, the Blantyre Mission did the same for Portuguese colonial ambition in the south. The African Independent Church and Watch Tower movements in Nyasaland, furthermore, were critical of British colonialism. Whereas Charles Domingo—a graduate of the Livingstonia Mission—was deported and silenced, John Chilembwe—an ordained minister—led an armed revolt against British rule. After successfully leading Malawi to independence, however, Hastings Banda imposed a one-party rule upon the country. Despite political repression under Banda, the religious forces prevailed in ending an autocratic nightmare.

Bernard Reich and Gershon Kieval examine the synagogue-state relationship in Chapter 5 by focusing on the crucial issue of Jewish identity in Israel. In that context, the *haredim* (ultra-Orthodox Jews)—whose influence extends to observance of holy day, dietary laws, exemption from military service, and marriage license—are important players in the Israeli political scene. Reich and Kieval illustrate the political dynamics among the *haredim*, particularly through three political parties: *Agudat Yisrael* (Association of Israel), *Miflaga Datit Leumit* (National Religious Party, MAFDAL or NRP), and *Sephardi Torah Guardians* (SHAS). They note that the *Meimad* (Dimension), *Morasha* (Heritage), and *Tenuah LeMassoret Yisrael* (Movement for Jewish Tradition) are splinters from the NRP. It is interesting that SHAS itself is a bolter party from *Agudat Yisrael*. And Rabbi Eliezer Schach, who was instrumental in the formation of SHAS, subsequently established the

Degel HaTorah (Flag of the Torah) and joined the *United Torah Judaism* coalition. With the political activism of Yosef Lapid and Natan Sharansky, Reich and Kieval also draw attention to the secular end of the political spectrum. One may add that the proportional representation system in Israel enables the relatively smaller religious parties to play a disproportionate role in political maneuvering.

The relationship between the secular and political in Islam is examined in Chapter 6 by Yahia Zoubir in a case study of Algeria. With violence legitimized during the decolonization process, Egyptian expatriates promoting Islamization, and veterans of the Afghan War glorifying holy war, the socio-economic disillusion after independence provided the setting for militant expression of political Islam. Beginning with *El-Qiyam al-Islamyya* (Islamic Values) and *Jamaat al-Ulama* (Association of Religious Scholars), various Islamic groups emerged in the political landscape of the country. Lacking pluralistic democracy, the radicalized Islamic associations found voice in political violence. In a horizontal competition demonstrating commitment to Islam, albeit through violence, different groups emerged—Islamic Salvation Front, Armed Islamic Movement, and Armed Islamic Group—that confronted both the state and each other. Unless government authorities address the issue of social justice, violence is likely to continue.

Frank Trapp, in Chapter 7, observes that the *Harakat al-Muqawama al-Islamyya* (Islamic Resistance Movement, HAMAS) has the potential of introducing a religious dimension to the Israeli-Palestinian secular struggle for land. In assessing the evolving relationship with the relatively moderate Palestine Liberation Organization (PLO), he notes that Yassir Arafat has managed to marginalize the HAMAS, and that the political struggle between the moderate Gazan leaders and hardline leadership in exile did not help the HAMAS in challenging the leadership of the PLO.

The symbolism of *jihad* (holy war) and Sufi *tariqat* (path) are significant forces, as Alynna Lyon recounts in Chapter 8, in mobilizing the Muslims in Chechnya against the Russian Federation. Ironically, it was the Gorbachev-Yeltsin political maneuvering that encouraged Dzhokhar Dudayev to secede from Russia. The historical memories of Sheikh Mansur and Sheikh Shamil, as well as a clarion call by Muslim elders, hardened the resolve of the economically underprivileged Chechen Muslims against Moscow. While Dudayev was by no means a religious zealot, in Islam he found a powerful tool for mobilizing the Chechen people.

In Chapter 9, Mohammad Rashiduzzaman looks at identity politics in Bangladesh in the context of two opposing forces: religious and secular. With Sheikh Hasina and the Awami League in power, secularism has come full circle since the early years of independence. While Ziaur Rahman and the Bangladesh Nationalist Party facilitated the shift away from the secular pole, the return of Ghulam Azam and his *Jamaat-i-Islami* (Islamic Association) to politics marked an open secular-religious struggle in Bangladesh politics. However, Rashiduzzaman is careful to distinguish the Muslim majority identity in Bangladesh—and the ongoing battle over its rehabilitation—from the *Jamaat-i-Islami* goal of an Islamic state.

References

Abi-Aad, Naji and Michel Grenon (1997), *Instability and Conflict in the Middle East: People, Petroleum and Security Threats*, St. Martin's Press, New York.

Allen, Charlotte (2001), 'The Scholars and the Goddess,' *The Atlantic Monthly*, Vol. 287, No. 1, January, pp. 18–22.

Appleby, R. Scott (2000), *The Ambivalence of the Sacred: Religion, Violence, and Reconciliation*, Rowman and Littlefield Publishers: New York.

Armstrong, Karen (1993), *A History of God : The 4,000-Year Quest of Judaism, Christianity and Islam*, Ballantine Books: New York.

Baaklini, Abdo; Guilain Denoeux; and Robert Springborg (1999), *Legislative Politics in the Arab World: The Resurgence of Democratic Institutions*, Lynne Rienner Publishers: Boulder, CO.

Braibanti, Ralph (1995), *The Nature and Structure of the Islamic World*, Position Paper One, International Strategy and Policy Institute: Chicago, IL.

Braibanti, Ralph (1999), *Islam and the West: Common Cause or Clash?* The Center for Muslim-Christian Understanding, Georgetown University: Washington, DC.

Brynen, Rex; Bahgat Konary; and Paul Noble (1998), 'Conclusion: Liberalization, Democratization, and Arab Experiences,' in Konary, Bahgat; Rex Brynen; and Paul Noble (eds.), *Political Liberalization and Democratization in the Arab World*, Vol. 2: *Comparative Experiences*, Lynne Rienner Publishers: Boulder, CO, pp. 267–278.

Castelli, Elizabeth A.; Stephen D. Moore; Gary A. Phillips; and Regina M. Schwartz (eds.) (1995), *The Postmodern Bible: The Bible and the Culture Collective*, Yale University Press: New Haven, CT.

Crowther, J.G. (1995), *Six Great Scientists*, Barnes and Noble Books: New York.

Dekmejian, R. Hrair (1985), *Islam in Revolution: Fundamentalism in the Arab World*, Syracuse University Press: New York.

Eickelman, Dale F. and James Piscatori (1996), *Muslim Politics*, Princeton University Press: Princeton, NJ.

Esposito, John L. (ed.) (1990), *The Iranian Revolution: Its Global Impact*, Florida International University Press: Miami.

Esposito, John L. (1999), *The Islamic Threat: Myth or Reality?* 3rd ed., Oxford University Press: New York.

Euben, Roxanne L. (1999), *Enemy in the Mirror: Islamic Fundamentalism and the Limits of Modern Rationalism*, Princeton University Press: Princeton, NJ.

Fox, Jonathan (2000), 'Religious Causes of Discrimination against Ethno-Religious Minorities,' *International Studies Quarterly*, Vol. 44, No. 3, September, pp. 423–450.

Gerges, Fawaz A. (1999), *America and Political Islam: Clash of Cultures or Clash of Interests?* Cambridge University Press: New York.

Green, Jerrold D. (1985), 'Islam, Religionpolitics, and Social Change,' A Review Article, *Comparative Studies in Society and History*, Vol. 27, No. 2, April, pp. 312–322.

Green, John C.; Mark J. Rozell; and Clyde Wilcox (eds.) (2000), *Prayers in the Precincts: The Christian Right in the 1998 Elections*, Georgetown University Press: Washington, DC.

Gurr, Ted R. (1992), 'Third World Minorities at Risk Since 1945,' in Brown, Sheryl J. and Kimber M. Schraub (eds.), *Resolving Third Wold Conflict: Challenges for a New Era*, United States Institute for Peace Press: Washington, DC, pp. 52–88.

Gurr, Ted R. (1993), *Minorities at Risk: A Global View of Ethnopolitical Conflicts*, United States Institute for Peace Press: Washington, DC.

Gurr, Ted R. (2000), *Peoples Versus States: Minorities at Risk in the New Century*, United States Institute for Peace Press: Washington, DC.

Hadar, Leon T. (1993), 'What Green Peril?' *Foreign Affairs*, Vol. 72, No. 2, Spring, pp. 27–42.

Harrison, Lawrence E. and Samuel P. Huntington (eds.) (2000), *Culture Matters: How Values Shape Human Progress*, Basic Books: New York.

Hunter, Shireen T. (1998), *The Future of Islam and the West: Clash of Civilizations or Peaceful Coexistence?* Praeger: Westport, CT.

Huntington, Samuel P. (1993), 'The Clash of Civilizations?' *Foreign Affairs*, Vol. 72, No. 3, Summer, pp. 22–49.

Huntington, Samuel P. (1996), *The Clash of Civilizations and the Remaking of the World Order*, Simon and Schuster: New York.

Hussain, Asaf (1985), *Islamic Iran: Revolution and Counter-Revolution*, St. Martin's Press: New York.

Inglehart, Ronald (1997), *Modernization and Postmodernization: Cultural, Economic, and Political Change in 43 Societies*, Princeton University Press: Princeton, NJ.

Juergensmeyer, Mark (1994), *The New Cold War? Religious Nationalism Confronts the Secular State*, University of California Press: Berkeley.

Kedourie, Elie (1961), *Nationalism*, rev. ed., Hutchinson and Co.: London.

Krasner, Stephen D. (1999), *Sovereignty: Organized Hypocrisy*, Princeton University Press: Princeton, NJ.

Lapid, Yosef and Friedrich Kratochwil (eds.) (1996), *The Return of Culture and Identity in IR Theory*, Lynne Rienner Publishers: Boulder, CO.

Lawrence, Bruce B. (1995), *Defenders of God: The Fundamentalist Revolt Against the Modern Age*, University of South Carolina Press: Columbia.

Lawrence, Bruce B. (1998), *Shattering the Myth: Islam beyond Violence*, Princeton University Press: Princeton, NJ.

Lester, Toby (1999), 'What Is the Koran?' *The Atlantic Monthly*, Vol 283, No. 1, January, pp. 43–56.

Lewis, Bernard (1993), *Islam and the West*, Oxford University Press: New York.

Lewis, Bernard (1995), *Cultures in Conflict: Christians, Muslims, and Jews in the Age of Discovery*, Oxford University Press: New York.

Luckmann, Thomas (1991), 'The New and the Old in Religion,' in Bourdieu, Pierre and James S. Coleman (eds.), *Social Theory for a Changing Society*, Westview Press: Boulder, CO, pp. 167–182.

Marty, Martin E. and R. Scott Appleby (eds.) (1991), *Fundamentalisms Observed*, The Fundamentalism Project: Vol. 1, University of Chicago Press: Chicago, IL.

Marty, Martin E. and R. Scott Appleby (eds.) (1993a), *Fundamentalisms and Society: Reclaiming the Sciences, the Family, and Education*, The Fundamentalism Project: Vol. 2, University of Chicago Press: Chicago, IL.

Marty, Martin E. and R. Scott Appleby (eds.) (1993b), *Fundamentalisms and the State: Remaking Polities, Economies, and Militance*, The Fundamentalism Project: Vol. 3, University of Chicago Press: Chicago, IL.

Marty, Martin E. and R. Scott Appleby (eds.) (1994), *Acounting for Fundamentalisms: The Dynamic Character of Movements*, The Fundamentalism Project: Vol. 4, University of Chicago Press: Chicago, IL.

Marty, Martin E. and R. Scott Appleby (eds.) (1995), *Fundamentalisms Comprehended*, The Fundamentalism Project: Vol. 5, University of Chicago Press: Chicago, IL.

Moghissi, Haideh (1999), *Feminism and Islamic Fundamentalism: The Limits of Postmodern Analysis*, Zed Books: New York.

Moore, Barrington, Jr. (2000), *Moral Purity and Persecution in History*, Princeton University Press: Princeton, NJ.

Murphy, Cullen (1998), 'The Bible According to Eve,' *U.S. News and World Report*, August 10, pp. 46–52.

Rozell, Mark J. and Clyde Wilcox (eds.) (1995), *God at the Grass Roots: The Christian Right in the 1994 Elections*, Rowman and Littlefield Publishers: New York.

Rozell, Mark J. and Clyde Wilcox (eds.) (1997), *God at the Grass Roots, 1996: The Christian Right in the American Elections*, Rowman and Littlefield Publishers: New York.

Roy, Olivier (1994), *The Failure of Political Islam*, Translated by Carol Volk, Harvard University Press: Cambridge, MA.

Sayyid, Bobby S. (1997), *A Fundamental Fear: Eurocentrism and the Emergence of Islamism*, Zed Books: New York.

Smith, Anthony D. (1987), *The Ethnic Origins of Nations*, Basil Blackwell: New York.

Smith, Anthony D. (2000), *The Nation in History: Historiographical Debates about Ethnicity and Nationalism*, University Press of New England: Hanover, NH.

Stigler, Stephen M. (1986), *The History of Statistics: The Measurement of Uncertainty before 1900*, Belknap Press of Harvard University Press: Cambridge, MA.

Vincent-Barwood, Aileen (1998), 'Georgetown's Bridge of Faith,' *Aramco World*, Vol. 49, No. 3, May/June, pp. 12–16.

Watt, William M. (1988), *Islamic Fundamentalism and Modernity*, Routledge: New York.

Weigel, George (1992), 'Religion and Peace: An Argument Complexified,' in Brown, Sheryl J. and Kimber M. Schraub (eds.), *Resolving Third Wold Conflict: Challenges for a New Era*, United States Institute for Peace Press: Washington, DC, pp. 172–192.

1 Nicaragua: Liberation Theology as a Force for Democratic Change

DEBRA SABIA

In the last two decades Nicaragua has experienced a popular revolution, a civil war, and the international effects of an emerging new world order. Within this context, progressive Christians have played a dynamic role in working for democratic change. In the political struggle, an overwhelmingly large number of Christians found inspiration in a new form of faith: liberation theology. This chapter reviews the birth and rise of liberation theology and the role of faith in the violent interactions of both the Nicaraguan Revolution and the ensuing counter-revolutionary war. Finally, we address some of the consequences of the liberation movement in nurturing the democratic process in the contemporary Nicaraguan state.

Religion in Latin America

Religious faith plays a crucial part in promoting the values of a society and is an important component in shaping (and changing) political culture. Political culture might be understood as the basic values, ideas, and behavioral patterns governing a society (Wiarda and Kline, 1990, p. 15). Historically, the political culture of Latin America has been molded and shaped in part by the powerful influence of Roman Catholicism. This culture has been conservative, hierarchical, and authoritarian. And in Latin America, the Catholic Church had been far better at preserving antidemocratic traditions than it had been at promoting democracy.

After World War II, however, this history began to change. By the middle of the 20th century more than half of the world's Catholics were living in underdeveloped countries in conditions of crushing poverty and spiritual decay. It was a period of contradictions. In the nations of the North, economic revitalization followed the post-World War II era. In the nations of the South, however, people continued to suffer the effects of economic regression, material deprivation, and spiritual crisis. In light of these realities Pope John XXIII called the Second Ecumenical Council (1962–1965), setting the stage for remarkable change. Pope John's decision to host the historic and monumental conference reflected the fact that Catholicism has always been a religion explicitly concerned with the public order, and in many parts of the Catholic world public order appeared to be breaking down (Mainwaring and Wilde, 1989, pp. 21–29). Most troubling to the bishops in Latin America was the revolutionary triumph of Castro's Cuba. Castro's Marxist Revolution had sent a shock wave through the Catholic community. The revolution's victory had come on the heels of increasing criticism of traditional seats of power, including regional oligarchies and military dictatorships, as well as their allies, closely associated with the church. In many sectors of Latin America the triumph of Castro's Revolution appeared to have increased enthusiasm for radical solutions to the problems of the region. Much of this enthusiasm had to do with the failure of Christian democratic parties in bringing socio-political and economic change. In Latin America, Christian democratic parties (PDCs) had grown out of the postwar period in response to the problems of underdevelopment and antidemocratic regimes. Yet, the PDCs had little success in addressing the problems of their countries. In many cases, Christian party members were targeted for repression and death. In other instances, their leaders were coopted by the very regimes they hoped to challenge. In light of these concerns, Pope John called his spiritual leaders to Rome. The Vatican also invited members of the non-ecumenical community, including social scientists and non-theological scholars. In Rome, Pope John challenged his guests: how might the church understand the problems of underdevelopment? What was the responsibility of the clergy in these changing times? How might the church better understand its role in an increasingly troubled and de-Christianized world? The reevaluation of the church's role that began in Rome marked a historic turning point for Catholicism worldwide. The Council not only symbolized a rethinking of the role of the church, but also represented a major shift in Catholicism's theological formulations, liturgical practices, and understanding of its relationship with the modern world (Smith, 1991, pp. 94–98). The Vatican conference took the first important step in deviating from Catholicism's traditional view of temporal and spiritual matters. This reinterpretation revolutionized the dualistic God-centered theology of the church's past. Following Vatican II, things of the 'hereafter,' which had been the primary focus for Christians, were reoriented toward temporal matters. The church redirected its focus toward human existence on earth. At Vatican II, the bishops also accepted a new interpretation of God's historical involvement in the world. God was discerned as an active presence in the world, working for human liberation through historical change. The Council accepted the conclusion that God's active presence in temporal matters seeks social justice and the end to human suffering. God's role, understood as oriented towards man, invited the church's participation in assisting with the transformation of human life. Thus, Vatican II affirmed worldly transformation as integral to the salvation of humanity (Smith, 1991, ch. 6. Also, see Gutierrez in Cleary, 1990, pp. 9–13).

The acceptance of historical change as normal and desirable freed the church from identification with existing structures and social arrangements that degraded human worth. The Council recognized the perceived failures of Christian leadership and challenged church leaders to promote new, more active strategies in resurrecting spiritual values within the temporal structures of their states and societies (Mainwaring and Wilde, 1989, pp. 10–15). Vatican II also advocated a more participatory model in working for human rights, emphasizing the need for shared responsibility among all sectors of the Catholic community (Mainwaring and Wilde, 1989, pp. 23–29). At Vatican II, the Council challenged the faithful to work together for new sociopolitical solutions to the problems of mass poverty and deprivation (Dodson and Montgomery, 1982, p. 162). The conference's conclusions for the Catholic world (particularly for Nicaragua) were explosive. Indeed, they were revolutionary.

Shortly following the Vatican Council the Latin American bishops were called together to address how to deal theologically and pastorally with the mandates of Rome. The issues of mass deprivation and human suffering became the theme at the Latin American Bishops Conference (CELAM) that met at Medellin in Colombia in 1968 (Christian, 1986, pp. 244–247). At Medellin, the bishops addressed how the church would define its role in working for sociopolitical change. The openness of Vatican II in the use of social science made possible alternative perspectives in analyzing the socio-economic and political malaise of the Catholic world. At CELAM, a group of young, dynamic, and enthusiastic theologians provided an analysis of Latin society that was clearly socialist in orientation (Smith, 1991, ch. 7). It was this group that successfully dominated the discourse and the direction of the conference's conclusions. In analyzing the conditions of poverty many at Medellin insisted that the structure of injustice was largely imposed from the outside, from the capitalist system of dependency and exploitation. They denounced the system of dependency and the capitalist structure for establishing a class-based society rooted in exploitation, profit, and competition (Planas, 1986, pp. 82–85). Medellin's denunciations of the existing sociopolitical order had revolutionary implications for the Latin American Church. By recognizing structural inequality, the conference challenged the church to work for active transformation of the capitalist system. The Latin American Church was called upon to distance itself from the centers of established power, denounce all things opposed to social justice, and commit itself to the process of human liberation (Gutierrez, 1988, pp. 68–71). Christian liberation came to be understood as freeing people not only from individual, spiritual sin, but also from the effects of human, structural sin (ignorance, hunger, misery, and oppression) imposed by a history of exploitation (Gutierrez, 1988, pp. 22–25, 171–173). Medellin stressed the need for the clergy to participate actively in the liberation process. It called on religious leaders to become involved in the social problems of the region and to dedicate themselves to promoting change.

Despite the overwhelming enthusiasm of the majority at Medellin, there remained a division within the Bishops Conference. Not everyone embraced the conclusions of the meeting. Conservatives were opposed to the implementation of the Medellin documents and even regarded Vatican II as an excessively radical break with the church's historical past. Conservatives did not necessarily reject the need for change in the existing political and social relationships. What they questioned was the appropriate role of the church in promoting reform. Traditionally, the Catholic Church has emphasized the importance of individual morality as the proper source of change. For the conservatives, Medellin appeared to be an excessive break with that understanding (Smith, 1991, pp. 163, 189–192). Perhaps, these bishops also understood the revolutionary aspects of the conference and the threat of a liberation movement that might defy church doctrine in the name of Catholic faith.

At Medellin the church was called upon to engage the laity in a consciousness-raising evangelization. *Conscientization* (the development of a critical consciousness) and *participation* are key words that appear throughout the Medellin texts (Berryman, 1987, pp. 34–38). The goal was defined as awakening the minds of the oppressed so that by developing a critical consciousness the poor could become active agents in their struggle for liberation. Bishops at the conference recognized conscientization as the link between social and personal conversion. For that reason they recommended the promotion of these goals through a clerical identification with the poor. The challenge was to build solidarity, to promote a religious awakening that would invite participation in the process of human liberation (Gutierrez, 1988, ch. 7). The Medellin directed attention to the need for outreach programs in areas traditionally neglected by the church (Mulligan, 1991, pp. 89–98). Up until the 1960s Catholic clergy had been concentrated in colleges, schools, and wealthy parishes within the urban centers of Latin America. After Medellin that reality underwent a radical transformation. The exodus of priests and nuns to poor areas gave impetus to the establishment of thousands of small *comunidades eclesiales de base* (ecclesial base communities; hereafter 'Christian base communities' or CEBs). CEBs are small homogeneous organizations based on class, neighborhood, or village. The activity of these communities is focused on reinvigorating the Catholic faith and promoting literacy, problem-solving, Christian fellowship, and Bible study.

In the beginning there was little political content in the CEB curriculum (Sabia, 1997, pp. 29–31). As community members were taught to read the Bible from their own perspectives, however, they began to find many of their experiences reflected in the scriptures (Berryman, 1987, ch. 2). As poor people were encouraged to discuss the Bible from their own point of view, they began challenging the conventional wisdom that depicted social injustice and human exploitation as the expressed will of God. As poor people began to reinterpret their faith, they questioned the customary interpretation of Christian faith that had legitimized their suffering and oppression. This process of de-ideologizing faith eventually evolved into a highly politicized consciousness for many Catholics, especially those living and suffering in Nicaragua. In time, this gradual awakening ignited explosive interactions between the religious and political orders and served as an important source for revolutionary action.

The Church and the Nicaraguan Revolution

In Nicaragua, as elsewhere in Latin America, the environment arising from the Second Ecumenical Council and the Latin American Bishops Conference fostered a climate of change and liberation. The historical context in which the evangelization effort grew was characterized by vast poverty and human deprivation. The Nicaraguan reality was firmly rooted in the pattern of economic development of the preceding decades. It was no less a consequence of the official corruption of the Somoza dynasty that had ruled the country since the 1930s (Gilbert, 1986, pp. 88–95; Cockcroft, 1989, pp. 177–178; Booth, 1985, pp. 67–70; Christian, 1986, pp. 27–29). The Somoza dynasty had come to power with the promotion of Anastasio Somoza Garcia, a general in the newly created Nicaraguan National Guard. The infamous Guard had been created by the United States in the interest of protecting American land and business ventures in Nicaragua. The Somoza family enjoyed a positive relationship with the United States and with the Nicaraguan Church. The church's close relationship with the dictatorship reflected the general historic dependence of the Latin American Church on ruling elites (Serra, 1986, pp. 53–57). The church's historic privileges and institutional well-being were largely predicated on the generosity and approval of those in positions of political power. The same was true for Somoza, whose political well-being depended heavily on the favor of those in Washington.

The Nicaraguan bishops, it follows, were neither prepared to embrace the radical challenge that had been advocated at Medellin, nor ready to sever the church's alliance with the rich and powerful. Change, however, was inevitable and it began with the turnover of ecclesiastical leadership that occurred in Nicaragua between 1968 and 1972. In Rome, a decision had been made to replace Archbishop Alejandro Gonzalez y Robelo, a staunch supporter of the Somoza Government, with a political outsider, Monsignor Miguel Obando y Bravo. The appointment of Obando sharply altered the bishops' policy toward the Somoza regime (Booth, 1985, p. 134). That became evident when the new archbishop began issuing a series of pastoral letters that criticized the existing political order. Those letters immediately raised expectations among progressive clergy that the Nicaraguan Church would lead the struggle for political change. That was not to be the case. Despite the optimism of progressive clergy, the bishops' criticism of the dictatorship remained conservative in tone (Williams, 1989, pp. 64–102). Archbishop Obando called for political reform, but he conspicuously avoided any criticism of Nicaragua's socioeconomic structure. That position had important consequences for the nation-state. In Nicaragua, the Catholic bishops (hereafter, 'the hierarchy') would be at odds with the more radical camps developing in the country. The acrimony created schisms in the church that became explosive, fragmenting relations between the Nicaraguan hierarchy and subordinate clergy, between bishops and laity, and eventually, between the church and the state. These schisms continue to the present day.

Throughout the 1970s Christian base communities flourished in Nicaragua. As the liberation movement grew, so did political consciousness. By the 1970s the concept of human rights had begun to acquire a new and dynamic dimension, one that included the right to housing, education, social welfare, urban services, and land (Mainwaring and Wilde, 1989, pp. 1–37). Christian faith had taken on a new meaning as well: living out one's faith had come to demand a commitment to working for change in the name of greater social justice. As Catholics mobilized to demand greater rights, however, the CEBs attracted the malice of the Somoza Government. President Somoza was not patient with challenges to his authority and Christians increasingly became the target of government violence. Nicaraguans remember the terror of National Guard raids in their communities, random searches and seizures, murder of Christian leaders, and disappearances of their youth (Sabia, 1997, ch. 4).

Somoza's decision to repress Christian agitation had unintended consequences for the regime. One consequence of the terror was that many members of the base communities shifted their support from political reform to advocacy for insurrection. This advocacy attracted the attention of another group, Somoza's armed opposition: the Sandinista National Liberation Front (FSLN). The FSLN, founded in 1961, had taken its name from Nicaragua's early nationalist hero, Augusto Cesar Sandino (Christian, 1986, pp. 31–32). Sandino, a poor *campesino* (peasant farmer), had dedicated his life to expelling U.S. occupation forces from Nicaragua in the 1920s. His prolonged engagement in a guerrilla war against the U.S. Marines earned him great respect. His subsequent death at the hands of the rising National Guard general Anastasio Somoza also earned him the title of Nicaragua's greatest liberation hero. Frequent victimization by Somoza's National Guard led many progressive Christians to join the ranks of the Sandinista movement. Because the ideology of the guerrilla organization centered around the liberation of the oppressed and exploited, it resonated well with the new social Christian thinking exhibited in liberation theology (Girardi, 1989, ch. 7). The FSLN was leading a class struggle: a homegrown variety of Marxism that appeared to be in touch with the democratic, popular dimension of Marxist thought as well as the popular demands of the liberation theology movement (O'Brien, 1986, pp. 55–57; Girardi, 1989, ch. 4). *Sandinismo* (Sandinista ideology) therefore attracted the attention of many progressive clergy, particularly those working with the base communities. Priests attracted to the Sandinista struggle included Fathers Fernando Cardenal and Uriel Molina. In Nicaragua, Cardenal and Molina had founded the growing Christian student movement. In time both men became important actors in channeling youth support for the revolutionary movement (Girardi, 1989, p. 89).

It is important to recall that in the post-Vatican II climate, poverty was being acknowledged among progressive elements in the church as more than just a historical accident. Christian intellectuals were acknowledging the fact that poverty was a product of faulty societal and economic structures, and they advocated the need to replace the individualistic, selfish priorities of capitalism with the social principles of a common community ethic. Thus, many progressive elements in the church found intellectual accommodation with the Marxist thinking of the Sandinista leaders. For the Sandinistas, early contact with the liberation clergy was primarily tactical. The FSLN leadership was very conscious of the fact that they needed a strong, broad-based movement to carry out their struggle and recognized the usefulness of the Christian movement for that purpose (Randall, 1983, pp. 132–133. Also, see Girardi, 1989, ch. 2). It was obvious that the Sandinista Front could not work openly in Nicaragua. In contrast, the Christian movement had the freedom to do so. It was not lost on the Sandinista leadership that the CEB leaders could advocate the need for radical change and still be protected by the power of the Cross. The grass-roots church was also extraordinarily special because its leaders could move beyond the poor to include contact with members of the elite. For the Sandinistas, this too, would be an invaluable channel for propagating their revolutionary ideology.

Initial meetings between the Sandinistas and progressive clergy led to further and broader contact in the months to come. Some of the more radicalized clergy and laity joined the guerrilla force while others used their homes as safehouses for the rebels, or provided food, shelter, medicine, and ammunition (Sabia, 1997, ch. 4). That cooperation fostered a genuine affinity between the liberation clergy and the Sandinista leadership. That affinity had important consequences for future developments: the FSLN made the commitment to include progressive Christians in the post-revolutionary leadership. Following the insurrection, many progressives in Nicaragua hailed that decision as evidence of the Sandinistas' commitment to greater democratic plurality. In contrast, religious and political critics of the FSLN condemned the inclusion of the priests in positions of political leadership. Conservatives argued that the inclusion of clergy in the post-revolutionary government was an excessive politicization of religion. Others accused progressive Christians of being instruments of the Sandinistas (Sabia, 1997, pp. 91–95). Following the insurrection, such differences in perspectives deepened the suspicions and mistrust between supporters of the FSLN and its critics.

Of course, not all Christians, both within and outside the base communities, supported the revolutionary movement. Many Christians remained apprehensive and continued to look to the Catholic hierarchy for guidance. While some progressive priests were becoming intellectual defenders of the FSLN, members of the Nicaraguan hierarchy remained reluctant about condoning revolutionary efforts. After all, the church had little practical experience with socio-political revolution. The cases of Mexico, Cuba, and Chile seemed to suggest that revolution was inherently threatening to the institution's power. In Nicaragua, it appeared that similar fears existed—that the revolution might swallow the church's identity (Williams, 1989, pp. 65–66). While progressive priests were agitating for revolution, members of the Catholic hierarchy sought to encourage political reform. They discouraged the active involvement of priests and religious lay leaders in politicized organizations. When it was necessary, bishops defended publicly those priests accused of revolutionary activities, but at the same time, they exerted strong pressure on the clergy to abstain from such tasks. The hierarchy's opposition to revolution worked to confuse, frustrate, and alienate many Catholics (Sabia, 1997, ch. 9). It took several years to discern clearly the consequences of the hierarchy's position, but its effects eventually fractured relations among many of the faithful as well as destroyed the goodwill that had developed between the church and revolutionary leaders. The increased animosity between these factions eventually contributed to explosive interactions in the post-revolutionary state, taking the shape of a tragic civil war.

The December 1972 earthquake that devastated Managua was a pivotal moment in the deterioration of relations between the Catholic hierarchy and Somoza's regime. The dictator's hegemony over the relief effort, manipulation of reconstruction projects, and insensitivity to mass suffering intensified anti-regime feelings (Booth, 1985). As a consequence, the post-earthquake period in Nicaragua was marked by strikes, political challenge, and revolutionary violence. Opposition to the dictatorship became so acute that the Somoza Government eventually declared a state of siege that lasted thirty-three months. The tremendous violence and terror unleashed against opponents at that time accelerated the church's break with the Somoza Government. The Nicaraguan hierarchy denounced the dictator's corruption and the atrocities committed by the National Guard. The effects of the criticism weakened Somoza's international support, particularly in the United States. The thirty-three months of terror that had been imposed by the regime moved the Carter Administration to invite church leaders to Washington to testify in Congress about events in Nicaragua. The testimonials were crucial in solidifying congressional support against continued military aid to the Somoza regime. Washington's support for the dictator continued to wane and the Carter White House soon thereafter began pressuring for an interim government, one that would exclude President Somoza (Cockcroft, 1989, p. 179. Also, see Booth, 1985, p. 172).

Somoza had also lost support among the national bourgeoisie. One important opponent was Pedro Joaquin Chamorro, editor of the Conservative opposition daily, *La Prensa* (The Press) (Booth, 1985, p. 71). During the regime's thirty-three months of martial law, Chamorro had used his newspaper to report opposition activities, governmental corruption, and human rights abuses. In January 1978, Chamorro was assassinated, allegedly by members of the National Guard. His death shocked the nation and severed the last of the dictator's support (Booth, 1985, pp. 159–161. Also, see Cockcroft, 1989, pp. 178–180). Despite these events, the Catholic hierarchy and other elites were not yet ready to sanction the use of violence to overthrow the regime. Rather, both groups continued to seek alternative means for resolving the national crisis. At the base of Nicaraguan society, however, the popular mobilization began taking on a greater militancy (Booth, 1985, pp. 137–155). Chamorro's death had sparked a vast number of insurrections that occurred throughout the country. For the FSLN, the insurrections were important as they solidified popular support behind their armed movement. At the same time, the unrest in the countryside brought religious and elite groups together to search for some other viable option.

The Catholic hierarchy's decision to collaborate with the moderate opposition in Nicaragua was very much in response to the growing popularity of the Sandinistas. Many scholars have argued that the formal break with Somoza came only as the bishops realized that the church's disassociation with the dictator was necessary for preserving its own influence with the faithful (Serra, 1986, pp. 94–97; Williams, 1989, pp. 65–66, 212–213. Also, see Mulligan, ch. 7). Since the church's traditional alliance with the Somoza Government no longer seemed sustainable, the hierarchy apparently looked to moderate members of the bourgeoisie as a means of continuing its influence in society. After all, the bourgeoisie did not question the political and economic systems, but argued for reform of the system in order to avoid its radical overthrow. The church's decision to support the moderate opposition (and not the more radical camp that demanded revolution) had important implications for Christians in post-revolutionary years. The hierarchy's continued unwillingness to embrace the Sandinista alternative profoundly divided the progressive Catholic sector, a division that continued to exacerbate tensions among the faithful, and between the Catholic Church and the state. Such tensions are only now being laid to rest in Nicaragua.

In 1979, however, the two groups, the Nicaraguan bourgeoisie and Sandinista guerrillas, finally agreed to a provisional government and President Somoza was urged to resign. The dictator refused to cooperate with efforts to remove him from political office and mediation talks with Archbishop Obando broke down. As a consequence, on June 2, 1979, the bishops of the Catholic Church justified armed resistance in a pastoral letter to the people of Nicaragua. In less than six weeks the Somoza dynasty fell in a popular revolution on July 19th.

Church-State Conflict in the Post-Revolution Transition

As discussed above, an overwhelming number of progressive Christians participated in the revolution. The Nicaraguan experience is an interesting example of the explosive interaction between religion and politics, and it is the first case in history where laity and clergy took up arms against their own Christian state. Many progressive Catholics became committed to the revolution as a result of their religious faith. Motivated by the rise of liberationist Christianity, they took the call to arms as soldiers of God, working toward a more just society. During the Somoza years, Christian base communities became meeting places for revolutionary discussion and Christian organization. In time, their activities could scarcely be separated from those popular organizations that contributed to the insurrectionary struggle. Not everyone who joined the insurrection did so from a religious conviction. Some Nicaraguans became involved out of their disgust with the corruption of the Somoza Government and National Guard abuses. In the case of the Catholic hierarchy, there was the concern for institutional unity and continued influence. Still others devoted themselves to the revolution for philosophical reasons; they embraced the ideology of the Sandinista Party. Following the 1979 Sandinista triumph there appeared to be great hopes for the construction of a socialist democracy in Nicaragua. Four liberation priests accepted high positions in the executive branch of the new government and many CEB members took seats in the new representative assembly (Vanden and Prevost, 1993, ch. 3).

The political honeymoon that the Sandinistas enjoyed, however, was short-lived. The acrimony that developed reflected the fact that the coalition that had come together to oppose the Somoza dictatorship remained divergent in its vision for a new Nicaragua. Among the poor were expectations for a more equitable system of power and social justice. For the bourgeoisie there existed expectations for a new capitalist and pluralist order. Among elders of the church there existed hopes for both political and religious stability (Sabia,

1997, pp. 81–91; Vanden and Prevost, 1993, pp. 49–52). Immediately following the Sandinista victory these competing visions and hopes clashed. Dissension, rather than consensus, characterized the climate both within and outside the Nicaraguan Church. In religious circles, fundamental disagreement centered around the proper means for achieving social justice. With different and competing spiritual and political convictions, the religious community had difficulty in agreeing on the proper role of the church in this new revolutionary process. This disagreement deepened when the Sandinistas proposed an increase in the number of seats in the Council of State, giving popular organizations and base communities representation in the revolutionary government. It appeared that many elements within the bourgeoisie resisted this idea, believing that their own power and interests would be ultimately thwarted (Booth, 1985, pp. 185–186; Foroohar, 1989, p. 201. Also, see Sabia, 1997, ch. 5).

Outside the church and at the macro-level, Nicaraguans also disagreed over the proper direction of the political economy. Despite promises for respect of private property, the Sandinista Government expropriated Somoza properties and created a new agency for land reform. Banks and insurance and mining companies were nationalized; foreign trade was taken over by the state (Christian, 1986, pp. 146–147). The socialist direction of the economy was a critical and divisive issue. Bourgeois members of the first junta resigned. They included Pedro Joaquin's widow, Violeta Chamorro, and prominent business leader Alfonso Robelo. Upon their resignation, elites within the country began denouncing the revolutionary regime. Their denouncements reached Washington and the Reagan White House believed that communists had taken over in Managua. Soon thereafter, the U.S. Central Intelligence Agency (CIA) began plans for overthrowing the revolutionary government. CIA operatives assembled *Somocistas* (Somoza National Guardsmen), many of the former National Guardsmen who had fled to Miami, and began training the infamous *contra* (counter-revolutionary) forces. Some of these anti-Sandinista groups looked to the Catholic Church as their traditional ally. Many bishops and priests had personal relationships with wealthy Nicaraguan families and, apparently, they shared many of the same fears as Washington (Mulligan, 1991, ch. 9. Also, see Lernoux, 1989, p. 369). Despite the fact that the Catholic hierarchy had finally condoned the popular insurrection, support for the Sandinista revolution had never really been assured.

Much of the church-state conflict that developed in the post-insurrection years centered around the question of moral authority. The church's fear of losing its power and prestige has been among the suggested reasons for the hierarchy's conflict with the class-based project of the Sandinista Government (Mulligan, 1991, pp. 226–235. Also, see Lernoux, 1989, p. 367). The Sandinista's rise to power provoked fear that the FSLN might reduce the political, religious, ideological, and social space traditionally occupied by the church. That fear was substantiated when the Sandinista Government began assuming responsibility for such social service projects as health care, housing, and education (Mulligan, 1991, pp. 235–244). The Sandinista literacy program particularly alarmed the bishops. The Nicaraguan bishops viewed the literacy campaign as 'too secular' and 'too political' and perceived the campaign as a threat to their own historic monopolization of the educational process (Mulligan, 1991, pp. 230–235). Thus, a certain rivalry for moral leadership developed between the Sandinistas and the Nicaraguan Church.

The hierarchy's traditional fear of Marxist revolution was also exacerbated by a government position paper that was leaked during the Fall of 1979. The paper argued the need for discouraging organized religion and suggested that all religious practices should eventually be abolished. The government claimed that the position paper was simply a working document that never had the approval of the Sandinista leadership. Despite this explanation, the revolutionary government never recovered its support among the religious conservatives. The fall out between the traditional church and Sandinistas had important consequences for members of the progressive clergy. Less than a month after the resignation of Violeta Chamorro and Alfonso Robelo, the bishops unexpectedly called for the resignation of all priests holding public office (Mulligan, 1991, p. 171). On July 14, 1980, Archbishop Obando declared the leaders of the FSLN 'Marxists' and asserted that 'Christianity and Marxism could not coexist' (Foroohar, 1989, p. 202).

Despite the Archbishop's criticisms and demands, liberation clergy refused to step down from their public offices. Priests such as Ernesto Cardenal and Edgar Parrales argued that serving in the Sandinista Government was a way to live out their religious commitment (Zwerling and Martin, 1985, pp. 32–33). Indeed, they countered that their presence in organs of the state protected the integrity of the revolution in delivering on its promises of greater democratic pluralism. Clerical challenge to ecclesiastical authority heightened the will of some members of the base communities to take on greater autonomy in direct defiance of the bishops. For example, many continued to participate in Sandinista projects that had been criticized or condemned by the Catholic hierarchy (Sabia, 1997, ch. 7). Other members of the CEBs began to perceive religion as becoming 'too politicized' and eventually left the Catholic Church to join the Protestant evangelical movement. Still other Catholics left the practice of religious faith altogether, declaring themselves ardent 'Marxists.' These manifestations continue to characterize the current reality in Nicaragua's religiosity today.

There appeared to be two important dimensions to the conflict in Nicaragua. The first appeared to be secular in nature. Ideological, political, and economic differences worked to divide the Nicaraguan society and aggravated the church-state conflict. The second dimension was theological in nature and concerned such questions as the place of religion in politics, church unity, and, ultimately, the church's moral authority. Underlying the crisis were questions of doctrinal purity and concern for Catholic unity (Mulligan, 1991, ch. 10; Sigmund, 1990, ch. 6. Also, see Williams, 1989, pp. 73–77).

Intensifying these fears was a growing concern among conservative sectors of the Nicaraguan hierarchy that a separate Catholic Church was being established among the grass roots. These fears were exacerbated by the fact that shortly after the Sandinista triumph in July 1979, forty liberation theologians from eight countries had come to Managua to reflect on ways that could assist in the revolutionary process. Participants in *The Encounter of Theology* used the term *iglesia popular* (popular church) in their working papers and used the label in their speeches to describe the movement they were supporting. The conference criticized the Catholic hierarchy for hesitating to confront the bourgeoisie and failing to support the work of the revolutionary government. In its summary documents the conference members affirmed the need to push *conscientization* among the faithful and use the base communities to promote Christian participation in Sandinista activities (Christian, 1986; pp. 250–251). The theological debate, however, was not isolated to the case of Nicaragua. The growing acrimony between the progressive clergy and the Catholic hierarchy reflected a larger division within the Latin American

Church. Among conservative sectors of the region, suspicion had been mounting that a religious 'parallelism' was taking place within Latin America, a movement that ultimately threatened doctrinal purity and Catholic unity (Sigmund, 1990, ch. 6; Smith, 1991, pp. 209–221. Also, see Williams, 1992, p. 136). There was increasing fear among some bishops that the movement for social justice had become the justification for some in the church to embrace Marxism and to become directly involved in partisan politics (O'Shaughnessy, 1986, pp. 7–31). The Pope himself admonished the clergy for confusing their religious role 'with a political one' and warned against efforts encouraging the development of a parallel church (Sigmund, 1990, ch. 6. Also, see Zwerling and Martin, 1985, ch. 2).

In Nicaragua, the church-state conflict was further exacerbated by U.S. involvement in the counterrevolutionary activities of the Nicaraguan opposition. President Ronald Reagan's promise to 'roll back' communism counted on the Catholic Church as an important ally. Playing on the church's traditional fear of communism, the Reagan Administration elicited the cooperation of Archbishop Obando to legitimize efforts in arming and training counterrevolutionary forces (Crockcroft, 1997, p. 219). The alliance between the United States, the bourgeoisie, and the traditional church played badly upon the historically strong anti-imperialist sentiments in Nicaragua (Foroohar, 1989, pp. 199–211). The alliance eventually transformed the discord into a powerful class conflict. Progressive Christians found themselves once again on the side of the FSLN, justifying their support for the Sandinistas out of a Christian obligation (Sabia, 1997, ch. 8. Also, see Zwerling and Martin, 1985, ch. 2). While the United States and the bourgeoisie worked with the traditional church to undermine the unity and cohesion of the revolutionary government, many people of the lower classes and base communities threw their support behind the Sandinistas in what became the infamous Contra War. Once again, religious faith proved to be a factor in explosive interactions in the struggling nation-state.

The Contra War bitterly divided the Nicaraguan society. The costs of the war were devastating in human life, economic development, and popular support for the revolutionary government. During the civil conflict the government's national state of emergency had suspended a number of personal and political liberties. That led opposition groups within the country to challenge the Sandinistas' commitment to political pluralism and democratic values. The government was also accused of human rights abuses, including those against the Miskito Indians who had been forcibly removed from Contra War zones. The church's outspoken criticism of the regime's conscription of youth into the Sandinista Army had also led the government to censor church activities and shut down the free press. As the war dragged on Nicaragua suffered the destruction of important infrastructure and crippling effects of hyper-inflation. People waited in long lines for basic necessities and there were constant shortages of food and medicines (Sabia, 1997, p. 191). Many of the social programs that had been so popular, and had gained the government so much legitimacy, were eliminated as the war debt rose. Economic austerity measures were unpopular and led to charges that the Sandinista Revolution had ultimately failed. The civil war also cost the country the best of its youth, and in the countryside innocent people were rounded up and tortured by the Contras. Entire villages were burned to the ground. Some 50,000 Nicaraguans ultimately perished in the war (Cockcroft, 1997, pp. 222).

Despite this suffering, people's needs and demands for peace seemed to be ignored by the Sandinista leadership. Increasingly, there were charges of 'vertical authoritarianism' of Sandinista rule and the accusation that the FSLN had lost touch with the people (Sabia, 1997, p. 109). Finally, the United States gained at the ballot box what it could not achieve by means of guns: the Sandinistas were voted out of office in the national elections of 1990.

Conclusion

The growth and proliferation of the Christian base communities in Nicaragua developed alongside that of the revolution. As discussed earlier in this chapter, in Nicaragua the base community model developed as a Catholic response for pastoral care and evangelism. The liberation movement arose gradually as people reinterpreted their traditional Christian faith, discovering in that process an inspiration for sociopolitical and economic change. Liberation theology legitimized political involvement. Indeed, the movement required it as a matter of faith. The rise of a liberationist Christianity substantially changed the religious culture of significant sectors of the Catholic community in Nicaragua and led to a practical convergence with political elements seeking peaceful, democratic, and pluralist reform of the Somoza regime. In time, however, the movement became radicalized in response to events that included state terror and death of prominent citizens and community leaders. The Somoza Government's corruption and brutality fueled Christian outrage, particularly in light of the liberation movement's awakening religious and political consciousness. The dictator's implacable resistance to the Christian agitation invited revolutionary reaction. There was sympathy for the Marxist doctrine of armed opposition among many of the progressive clergy who had worked to establish many of the base communities. Many liberation theology leaders supported the idea of class struggle and opposed a number of the practices of capitalism under the Somoza regime. Yet, relatively few progressive clergy or Christians identified themselves as 'Marxists' or completely embraced Marxist ideology (Sabia, 1997, pp. 115–117). In Nicaragua, liberation clergy tended to argue for the establishment of popular democracy: a system more inclusive of and responsive to the needs of the poor majority. Many of these leaders believed that the goals of the Sandinista guerrillas were compatible with that vision. Consequently, many liberation leaders threw their support behind the armed struggle and the revolutionary process of the 1980s. While many progressive members of the Catholic community were attracted to the homegrown Marxist ideology that evolved in Nicaragua, not everyone enthusiastically embraced the stated goals of the Sandinista Party, nor did all progressive Christians support Sandinista demands for a new economic order. Some Nicaraguans supported the revolution because they grew disgusted with the terror and self-aggrandizement of the Somoza family. At the height of state terror by the dictator, many Catholics supported the guerrillas because they believed that the armed opposition was the only viable alternative to the Somoza regime.

But just as the form and substance of the liberation theology movement was conditioned by the socio-political and economic forces that helped to nurture it during the Somoza years, changes in historical conditions also worked to defuse and fragment the progressive political coalition that had evolved during the insurrectionary years. Differences in sources of inspiration for the revolution, and differing opinions in the church regarding the revolutionary experiment, led to multidimensional responses in

Nicaragua. Disagreement centered on the direction of the political economy as well as the proper role of the church in a revolutionary climate. The struggle for moral authority between the Catholic hierarchy and the Marxist state contributed to the underlying conflict and to the ultimate break between the Nicaraguan Church and the Sandinista leadership. Fears that Nicaragua had been taken over by communists helped to legitimize efforts for a new armed response by counterrevolutionary forces that were organized and funded by the United States Government. Once more, progressive Christians found their liberationist faith challenged by the turbulent political climate. Once more, many Christians heeded the call to arms, but this time their response was to defend the existing Sandinista state. For a second time in less than a decade, the Nicaraguan experience demonstrated the role that religion could play in motivating and sustaining political violence.

What have been the consequences for the contemporary Nicaraguan state? Despite the great tragedy of armed conflict, the war weariness of the Nicaraguan people helped to ripen the climate for peace. The social forces and dynamics that the liberation movement unleashed also contributed to some of the necessary features for building democracy in Nicaragua. For example, during the Sandinistas' tenure in office new political groups were allowed to participate in governmental decision-making, even those in opposition to the revolutionary project (Cockcroft, 1997, pp. 215–216). Many Christians who participated in the political process believed that their presence in the revolutionary government was an important and moderating influence (Sabia, 1997, ch. 8). When the FSLN lost in the elections of 1990, the Sandinistas also surprised the opposition by delivering on their promise to ensure a peaceful transfer of political power. Since that time, two more electoral transfers of power have been peaceful and without major incident. These are significant achievements in a country long dominated by traditions of violence and political intolerance.

The democratic impulse in the 1990s in Nicaragua must also be credited, in part, to the work of progressive church leaders. Liberation leaders created a legitimate movement for the articulation of the people's interests in Nicaragua. During the 1980s many Christians joined a variety of social movements: labor unions, political parties, neighborhood associations, and professional groups. Today, this participation continues (Sabia, 1997, ch. 10). As the protector of many of these small organizations, trade unions, and self-help groups, the progressive church helped to create a climate in which many disenfranchised people came to acquire for the very first time a sense of political efficacy. The new and growing activism of women is particularly noteworthy. Although women are still substantially under-represented in national politics, at the base of social movements their numbers and influence are strong and continue to grow. One consequence of the liberation movement in Nicaragua has been the erosion of traditional barriers between the private and public. As the barrier between the personal and political are broken down, so too are the gender roles that have defined those boundaries. Now, when women assume their roles in positions of authority they bring with them new styles of leadership that are more participatory and inclusive. In assimilating the lessons of their revolutionary experience, many Catholics have begun laying the foundation for a more democratic and pluralistic society.

The Catholic Church has not been without its tensions regarding the vision of a post-revolutionary society, however. While church leaders tended to support the notion of popular democracy, no consensus ever existed on how to achieve that ideal. Even though anti-capitalism remains an element of liberation thought, and many progressive Christians continue to identify themselves as socialists, there is less certainty that revolutionary socialism holds all the answers for Nicaraguan society (Sabia, 1997, ch. 8). International political changes, including the demise of the former Soviet Union and growing internationalization of the marketplace, have also played a significant role in these changing attitudes. According to many Nicaraguans, the church-state conflict not only exacerbated societal tensions, but also accelerated a process whereby toleration of differences and compromise could be learned (Sabia, 1997, ch 10). In the past two decades, Nicaraguans have illustrated that they have become less confrontational and more willing to acknowledge errors, think critically, and appreciate the need for negotiation (Sabia, 1997, ch. 10. Also, see Levine, 1988, pp. 241–248). These are skills that will be essential to future prospects for democracy.

Today, it appears that the liberation movement, which was once highly religious and extremely politicized, is transforming itself into a deeply spiritual and civic movement. The transformation appears more ecumenical and less rigidly ideological. Space has been opened to question all belief systems, both religious and political. In Nicaragua, there appears to be a growing maturation that recognizes the need for questioning all answers. In the context of evolving democratic change, this development is heartening. Abraham Lowenthal (1991, pp. 16–18) has argued that democracy is an internal process, rooted in a country's history, culture, and institutions. The strengthening of civil society, one that respects human rights and nurtures trade unions, professional organizations, and women's groups, among others, is important to this process. The significance and success of this process will be found not only in how readily these groups have access to the government, but also in whether the government will be able to respond to their demands. Here, too, the lessons of the revolutionary experience, and the continuing influence of religion on the political climate, will be crucial.

References

Berryman, Phillip (1984), *The Religious Roots of Rebellion: Christians in Central American Revolutions*, Orbis Books: Maryknoll, NY.

Berryman, Phillip (1987), *Liberation Theology*, Temple University Press: Philadelphia, PA.

Booth, John A. (1985), *The End and the Beginning: The Nicaraguan Revolution*, Westview Press: Boulder, CO.

Christian, Shirley (1986), *Nicaragua: Revolution in the Family*, Vintage Books: New York.

Cockcroft, James D. (1989), *Neighbors in Turmoil: Latin America*, Harper and Row: New York.

Cockcroft, James D. (1997), *Latin America: History, Politics, and U. S. Policy*, Nelson-Hall Publishers: Chicago, IL.

Dodson, Michael and Tommie Sue Montgomery (1992), 'The Churches in the Nicaraguan Revolution,' in Walker, T. W. (ed.), *Nicaragua in Revolution,* Praeger Publishers: New York, pp. 161–180.

Foroohar, Manzar (1989), *The Catholic Church and Social Change in Nicaragua*, State University of New York Press: Albany, NY.

Galielea, S. (1974), 'Liberation Theology and New Tasks Facing Christians,' in Gibellini, Rosino (ed.), *Frontiers of Theology in Latin America*, Orbis Books: Maryknoll, NY.

Gilbert, Dennis (1986), 'Nicaragua,' in Blachman, Morris J.; William M. Leogrande; and Kenneth

Sharpe (eds.), *Confronting Revolutions*, Pantheon Books: New York, pp. 88–124.

Girardi, Giulio (1989), *Faith and Revolution in Nicaragua: Convergence and Contradictions*, Orbis Books: Maryknoll, NY.

Gutierrrez, Gustavo (1988), *A Theology of Liberation*, Orbis Books: Maryknoll, NY.

Lernoux, Penny (1979), 'The Long Path to Puebla,' in Eagleson, John and Philip Scharper (eds.), *Puebla and Beyond*, Orbis Books: Maryknoll, NY, pp. 36–57.

Lernoux, Penny (1982), *Cry of the People*, Penguin Books: New York.

Lernoux, Penny (1989), *People of God: The Struggle for World Catholicism*, Viking Press: New York.

Levine, Daniel (1988), 'Assessing the Impact of Liberation Theology in Latin America,' *Review of Politics*, Vol. 50, No. 2, Spring, pp. 241–263.

Lowenthal, Abraham F. (1991), 'Can Democracy Be Exported?' *Setting the North-South Agenda*, Lynne Rienner Publishers: Boulder, CO, pp. 16–18.

Mainwaring, Scott and Alexander Wilde (eds.) (1989), *The Progressive Church in Latin America*, University of Notre Dame Press: Notre Dame, IL.

Mulligan, Joseph E. (1991), *The Nicaraguan Church and the Revolution*, Sheed and Ward Press: Kansas City, MO.

O'Brien, Conor C. (1986), 'God and Man in Nicaragua,' *Atlantic Monthly,* Vol. 258, No. 2, August, pp. 50–72.

O'Shaughnessy, Laura N. and Luis H. Serra (eds.) (1986), *The Church and Revolution in Nicaragua*, Ohio University Press: Athens, OH.

Planas, Ricardo (1986), *Liberation Theology: The Political Expression of Religion*, Sheed and Ward: Kansas City, MO.

Randall, Margaret (1983), *Christians in the Nicaraguan Revolution*, New Star Books: Vancouver (Canada).

Sabia, Debra (1997), *Contradiction and Conflict: The Popular Church in Nicaragua*, University Alabama Press: Tuscaloosa, AL.

Serra, Luis (1985), 'Ideology, Religion, and the Class Struggle in the Nicaraguan Revolution,' in Harris, Richard L. and Carlos M. Vilas (eds.), *Nicaragua: A Revolution Under Siege*, Zed Books: London, pp. 151–174.

Serra, Luis (1986), 'Religious Institutions and Bourgeois Institutions in the Nicaraguan Revolution,' in O'Shaughnessy, Laura N. and Luis Serra (eds.), *The Church and Revolution in Nicaragua*, Ohio University Press: Athens, OH, pp. 43–58.

Sigmund, Paul E. (1990), *Liberation Theology at the Crossroads*, Oxford University Press: New York.

Smith, Christian (1991), *The Emergence of Liberation Theology*, University of Chicago Press: Chicago, IL.

Vanden, Harry E. and Gary Prevost (1993), *Democracy and Socialism in Sandinista Nicaragua*, Lynne Rienner Publishers: Boulder, CO.

Wiarda, Howard J. and Harvey F. Kline (eds.) (1990), *Latin American Politics and Development*, Westview Press: Boulder, CO.

Williams, Philip J. (1989), 'The Catholic Church in the Nicaraguan Revolution: Differing Responses and New Challenges,' in Mainwaring, Scott and Alexander Wilde (eds.), *The Progressive Church in Latin America*, University of Notre Dame Press: Notre Dame, IL, pp. 64–102.

Williams, Philip J. (1992), 'The Limits of Religious Influence: The Progressive Church in Nicaragua,' in Cleary, Edward L. and Hannah Stewart-Gambino (eds.), *Conflict and Competition: The Latin American Church in a Changing Environment*, Lynne Rienner Publishers: Boulder, CO, pp. 121–144.

Zwerling, Philip and Connie Martin (1985), *Nicaragua: A New Kind of Revolution*, Lawrence Hill: New Haven, CT.

2 Mexico: Christianity and the Struggle for Collective Identity

MICHELE ZEBICH-KNOS

Mexico has for many years attempted to come to terms with the role of religion in its society. In the Spanish colonial period, the religious experience in Mexico came under the influence of the Roman Catholic Church, which was closely associated with the Spanish Crown's attempt at domination.Upon independence, the church maintained its association with conservative elements of Mexican society. As an institution, the Roman Catholic Church came to represent elite dominance and economic wealth as much as it represented spiritual nourishment of the soul. Because of its close association with conservative political and economic powers, and its religious monopoly in Mexico, the Roman Church came to be equated with religion itself. As a result, 19th century political liberals as well as 20th century revolutionaries sought to curtail the church's power and influence. Thus was born a deeply ingrained sentiment that government must control religious institutions represented by the Roman Catholic Church. It is in this historic context of religious mistrust that Mexico has struggled to create its collective identity. This quest for identity has been explosive and replete with violent tension. This chapter will examine Mexico's search for religious accommodation as its leaders strive to achieve a 21st century identity whose roots lie not only in indigenous Spanish and mestizo cultures, but also in the intersection of the traditional and modern worlds. The first part explains the conflict-ridden political history of Mexico's church-state relations; the second part discusses contemporary changes and newly emerging actors that place added strain on these relations.

In Search of a Collective Identity

The Roman Catholic Church has, since the Spanish colonial period, shaped the Mexican psyche in a love-hate relationship with its religious dominance. With the advent of the Mexican Revolution in 1910, the new political ideology actively sought to minimize the power of the economic elite *and* that of the church. To garner support for such monumental changes, revolutionary leaders built upon Mexico's indigenous heritage in order to create a new collective identity out of the ashes of armed struggle. Indigenous culture and mores became a proud reference and, soon thereafter, the revolution became associated with Mexico's indigenous heritage. This association was especially useful to the Institutional Revolutionary Party (PRI) which, since its creation under a different name in 1929, has portrayed itself as the party of all Mexicans, but especially the poor, who also tend to be from indigenous backgrounds. Jonathan Fox notes that Mexico's indigenous population comprises nearly 33 percent of those persons officially classified as living in 'extreme poverty' (Fox, 1997, p. 408). Ironically, this state-generated collective identity, with its anti-Church component, never managed to diminish the church's esteem. A 1996 survey revealed that 73 percent of Mexican respondents hold the church in high regard while only 39 percent felt political parties and the Mexican Congress deserve positive affirmation. Only 27 percent of respondents rated the Mexican police in high regard (Camp, 1999, p. 54). Past surveys revealed comparable trends and would indicate that, despite revolutionary attempts to mold and control Mexico's identity, the church is still widely respected (Camp, 1999, pp. 54–59).

Although the Catholic Church may be seen as a longstanding institution associated with its accompanying injustices, Catholicism is very much alive in Mexico today (Cleary, 1995, pp. 793–812). As such, religion must be incorporated into any formula for peaceful advancement into the modern world for Mexico's 21st century experience. The process incorporates both the traditional and modern in attaining a harmonious identity for all its citizens. Two important new actors on the Mexican religious stage include Protestant sects and the Zapatista movement, formally known as the Zapatista Army for National Liberation (EZLN). Isidro Morales Moreno (1997) theorizes that Mexican identity experienced a major shift after the signing of the North American Free Trade Agreement (NAFTA). Images and symbols of the Mexican Revolution defined the constructs that made up its 20th century identity. This identity infused 'the new with the old' and allowed the government to make policy changes as long as current leaders respected reputations of Mexico's previous post-revolutionary leaders. The sociopolitical order was stable, yet regimented. Morales Moreno implies that the implementation of NAFTA changed the traditional order because, as a condition of ratification, United States leaders sought a more transparent Mexican polity and, hence, forced Mexico to confront the shortcomings of its traditional identity (Morales Moreno, 1997, pp. 858–883). That traditional identity, heavily regimented and one in which social institutions like the church knew their roles vis-a-vis the society and government, is undergoing transformation today.

Time will tell if Mexican society and its governmental institutions will be successful in accommodating the changing face of religion and its role in that society. What is certain is that the dominant political role of one church is gradually being supplanted by some of the very societal forces responsible for ushering in the demise of the Cold War. In Mexico, these forces include greater economic openness, a shift from state economic dominance to privatization, and an increase in constitutionally-guaranteed religious freedom. Before proceeding further, let us consider Mexican society in terms of its *veneer of institutionalization* and ponder the following issues. Is the veneer deep enough to sustain Mexico's transformation to an economically-developed and politically pluralist nation-state of the 21st century? Is Mexico strong enough to accept religious pluralism as a crucial aspect of its evolving democracy? What is demanded of Mexico's political system today is the application of its legal protections for religious liberty. This requires that freedom of religion be reinforced from the *barrios* (neighborhoods) of Mexico City to the villages of Chiapas.

Catholic Dominance and State Anticlericalism

Historically, the indigenous peoples of Mexico—whether Maya, Zapotec, Olmec, or Mexica—all shared a common belief that politics was conducted according to the will of the sun god, Quetzalcoatl. Thus, political rule became intertwined with religious activity.

While armed conflict occurred frequently among the various indigenous peoples of what is now modern Mexico, conquest did not translate into radical changes for the newly-subjugated peoples. As Maria Puente notes, little social change resulted from indigenous subjugation. The imposition of new religions on the vanquished did not occur (Puente, 1992, p. 217).

But by 1519 the Spanish conquest, led by Hernan Cortes, had radically altered those conquering traditions practiced by the indigenous Mexican peoples. Instead of continuing a laissez-faire social policy, the Spanish were quick to implant their culture, language, and religion. Political structures were altered as the newly-conquered territory became known as New Spain. As Spain sought control over this acquired territory, the Roman Catholic Church (hereafter, the church) was quick to establish its own religious network in Mexico. With the blessing of the Pope, the Franciscans arrived in 1524 and were soon followed by the Dominicans (1526), Augustinians (1533) and, finally, the Jesuits (1572). The Conceptionist and Capucine orders of nuns arrived in 1565. Through this vast network of religious orders the church established a new societal position. While the church gradually dominated the social fabric of Mexico, the Spanish monarchy controlled the political system and its accompanying institutional structure. Conquest was largely completed by 1548 upon the creation of the 'Great Junta,' which officially placed the church under state control. Church appointments were decided through a system of state patronage which provided a seamless integration between church, state and the base of indigenous laborers who were expected to physically produce the Spanish Empire's economic wealth (Dussel, 1992, p. 6). Spanish Catholic domination was made evident when churches were often constructed directly over indigenous religious temples. Such was the case in Mitla, Oaxaca, and Tenochtitlan—currently Mexico City. Church construction superimposed over indigenous temples had the obvious effect of negating not only traditional religious practices, but also political ones. Both governance and the Catholic religion were inseparable in their relationship to Mexico's indigenous peoples. Octavio Paz, the world-renowned social commentator and poet, corroborates this process. Paz notes in his classic, *The Labyrinth of Solitude* (1985), that the type of Christianity brought by the church of Rome was of a syncretic nature that assimilated indigenous gods and turned them into 'saints and devils.' The process made Mexico, he further observes, a territory of 'superimposed pasts' (Paz, 1985, pp. 361–362).

As the Spanish Empire endured, the church became part of the privileged sectors within the corporatist structure formed by the Spanish monarch and the military. That colonial relationship between the church and state was never separate but was linked through the *patronato* system (royal patronage system). *Patronato* was authorized by the Vatican as a means of utilizing the Spanish bureaucracy to supervise church in administration and to collect tithes in the New World. Through *patronato* the crown acquired direct influence over ecclesiastical nominations for bishop and other Catholic prelates (Quirk, 1964, pp. 61–71). In return the church agreed to support Spanish domination as befitted the natural divine order of societal hierarchy in which one has one's own place. The church was allowed to enrich itself during this period as Spanish officials routinely ignored clerical practices of abuse. Furthermore, the church benefitted from its separate legal *persona* which implied that disputes related to the church were heard solely in religious courts. While Spain maintained political control, the church lent credibility to the conquest by providing the spiritual rationale of converting pagan souls to Christianity. With the blessing of the Pope, a symbiotic relationship existed between the Spanish government and the church. As part of that arrangement, New

World excesses by the church were frequently overlooked by the monarchy. The church thereby was ensured of acquiring economic wealth through vast landholdings as it set about tending to Mexico's Catholics.

By the early 1800s, some church representatives, such as Father Miguel Hidalgo y Costilla, attempted to push for Mexican independence. Hidalgo was not the sole religious leader to join the independence movement. J. Lloyd Mecham notes that more than 150 priests took up the cause as a means of enhancing social justice (Mecham, 1966, p.51). By 1811, however, Father Hidalgo was excommunicated and church displeasure with those who went against the Spanish political status quo became evident. Independence did arrive by 1821, and by 1824 the Mexican Constitution upheld the church's privileged status by declaring Catholicism the official state religion. Despite that gesture, meant to appease pro-church conservatives, waves of anticlericalism were spreading. What explains this growing anticlerical post-independence sentiment? The political struggle for power occurred between traditionalists, led by the Conservative Party, and their *Criollo* (Mexican born Spaniards) challengers. *Criollos* formed the bulk of Liberal Party supporters. As Mexican liberals included a significant anticlerical component, the movement forced the church to take sides. It sided with the Conservatives, who lost political control by 1833. That year, President Valentin Gomez Farias attempted to suppress religious orders and transferred the task of education from church hands to secular state run schools. Furthermore, civil enforcement of tithes—a Spanish colonial accommodation—was eliminated.

Liberal Party control of the government in 1857 marked a significant point in church-state relations. It began the very real erosion of church power and marked the entrenchment of anticlericalism in Mexican society by the government. That anticlericalism was to become a permanent fixture of Mexican Government policy until 1991. Alienation of church activities was legally manifested in the constitution of 1857. In addition, the Reform Laws (1859–1860) supported by President Benito Juarez set the stage for diminution of church powers. Separation of church and state was established, as was nationalization of church properties. Government anticlericalism was also evident in the secularization of cemeteries, recognition of civil registries for birth and marriage, and prohibition of all public religious ceremonies. While those laws pertained to all religions in Mexico, there was little doubt that the Roman Catholic Church was the main target. Protestantism—the Catholic Church's main religious rival—would not gain a foothold until the post-World War II years.

The liberal period of anticlericalism was temporarily replaced in 1876 with the dictatorship of Porfirio Diaz. He pursued a conciliatory policy toward the church and refused to enforce the Reform Laws, which had become part of the Mexican Constitution in 1873 (Mecham, 1996, pp. 375–376). Thus, the church maintained de facto power to run schools, administer religious orders, and function publicly without government interference. While pro-church, Diaz did not wish to confront the many Mexicans who viewed the church as a maligned remnant of Spanish domination. Even a Mexican dictator realized that the power of anticlerical sentiment in Mexico was a formidable force and could not easily be overcome. Puente refers to the Porfiriato period as a period of 'recuperation' for the church. New seminaries flourished, and the Pontifical University reopened its doors in 1896 (Puente, 1992, p. 223). The recuperation effort was seen by government leaders as a way to subdue political uprisings by affording the church greater control within local society. However, the politico-religious alliance evoked memories of Spanish colonialism when the church and state operated in unison for each other's benefit, to the exclusion of the Mexican masses.

Such memories were vivid among those who led the Mexican Revolution that overthrew Diaz in 1910. Influenced by the Bolshevik Revolution and European socialist movements, Mexican revolutionary leaders once again stirred Mexico's anticlerical sentiments which culminated in vigorous attempts at curtailing religion.

The Mexican Constitution of 1917 was, perhaps, one of the most anticlerical documents of its day and rivaled the Soviet Constitution in its anti-religious sentiment. This new constitution, or Magna Carta, as it is called in Mexico, invoked strong reaction from many of Mexico's Catholics. Specifically offensive to Catholics was the *Ley Reglamentaria* (Reglamentary Law), which laid the groundwork for enforcement of the constitution's anticlerical articles. In particular, Article 130 revoked the legal status, or juridical personality, of all religious organizations. The article also prohibited any public religious displays or ceremonies, recognized only civil marriages, and reserved for the government the right to determine the number of priests or ministers for each state. Furthermore, all priests or ministers had to be Mexican by birth, were denied the right to vote, and forbidden to engage in politics. Opening new churches required approval of the *Secretaria de Gobernacion* (Ministry of the Interior). In addition, Article 27 weakened religious institutions by forbidding private church ownership of property. Existing property reverted immediately to state ownership (Constitution of 1917).

The consequence of this virulent constitutional attempt by the government to crush religion was an armed rebellion by Catholic peasants whose battle cry evoked both Jesus Christ and the Virgin of Guadalupe (Puente, 1992, p. 24). By March 1926, Catholic protesters formed the League for the Defense of Religious Freedom, which came to be known as the *Cristero* (Follower of Christ) Movement. The *Cristeros* fought the Mexican Army from 1926 until 1929. With neither side able to claim victory, a peace was negotiated on June 22, 1929, between President Emilio Portes Gil and two Catholic prelates, Archbishop Leopoldo Ruiz y Flores and Bishop Pascual Diaz. Because of the high death toll from this guerrilla conflict, many Mexicans eagerly embraced political authoritarianism as a viable alternative to chaos and bloodshed (Handelman, 1997, p. 36). The *Cristeros* ceased their armed struggle and, once again, the church settled into an unwritten compromise with the government, reminiscent of what it was forced to accept during the liberal era under Benito Juarez. This compromise did not include any change in the constitution or the laws. Rather, it was an entente in which the government agreed to refrain from rigorously enforcing the laws against religious organizations for the sake of peace. A period of modus vivendi thus began and would endure from 1929 until the mid-1930s (Blancarte, 1992, p. 29). Robert Quirk refers to the modus vivendi as an 'agreement to disagree' using peaceful means (Quirk, 1964, pp. 61–71). For Pope Pius XI, acceptance of this entente was seen as a 'lesser evil'.

The Catholic Church would continue to function quietly while government officials would present a blind eye to full application of the law. This modus vivendi permitted the church's social agenda to continue unscathed and to operate within an organization called Catholic Action, which was founded in 1929. This social agenda expanded to include the creation of the Catholic Confederation of Labor, which served as a labor alternative to the Workers Mexican Regional Confederation, the government-supported labor union. Instead of promoting class struggle, the Catholic union sought to achieve harmony between worker and employer in which wage increases would be acquired through non-conflictual negotiations. Strikes would be ruled out of this model, which downplayed the status afforded the workers in the revolution (Quirk, 1964, pp. 61–71). Such a formula was bound to clash with Mexico's revolutionary government. As the church emboldened its public image, the modus vivendi gradually weakened. The December 1, 1931, celebration, marking the 400 year anniversary of the Virgin of Guadalupe, was a monumental event that was likely to upset government officials. Nearly half a million people visited the Basilica of Guadalupe in Mexico City. To no one's surprise, the government indeed reacted against the church by the end of December. A new law was promulgated which limited the number of priests in the Federal District (Mexico City) to one for every 50,000 residents. The total number of priests for Mexico City dwindled to a mere twenty-five. Eventually, as Mecham notes, the states of Chiapas and Veracruz halted religious ceremonies altogether. In a brash move by the government, Archbishop Ruiz y Flores, Mexico's representative to the Vatican and a Mexican citizen, was deported to Rome. The government reasoned that he was a 'foreigner' because of his allegiance to a foreign leader—the Pope (Mecham, 1966, p. 405).

By 1934, government control of religion increased and Article 3 of the constitution was amended to clarify the secular nature of education. Plutarco Elias Calles, a former president of Mexico, reiterated the importance of taking possession of 'young minds' in order to dislodge the conservative clerical forces which dominated the field of education. To do so, Article 3 clearly stated that only the State could impart primary, secondary, and normal education. In addition, education was to be 'socialistic' in nature. Education's anticlerical role thus became institutionalized in the constitution and its mission was now to combat 'fanaticism and prejudices' (Mecham, 1966, p. 406). Church property was seized after 1935. The justification attributed to such action was that church property was the physical site upon which religious tenets were disseminated. Despite these sustained official attempts to weaken the church's power, it managed to endure.

However, by 1937 the Pope urged Catholics to assume greater responsibility for Mexico's poor. This marked a break from past practices in that the church's social agenda would now correspond to the goals of the Mexican Revolution. The church was clearly trying to show a more attractive face to Mexico's revolutionary leaders. Consequently, in 1938, when President Lazaro Cardenas nationalized the oil industry, the church openly supported his policy. Cardenas took note of this support. Thus began a period of relative cooperation between the church and state. This church-state detente increased when President Avila Camacho publicly declared himself to be a 'believer' in 1940 (Loaeza, 1985, pp. 47–48; Reich, 1997, pp. 77–86). It appeared that church-state relations were now on a more balanced track. However, the Camacho Administration made no effort to repeal Mexico's anticlerical laws. Rather, Camacho returned to the old practice of simply not enforcing the laws. While Article 3 was amended to eliminate the term 'socialistic education,' and religious seminaries and universities were now permitted, the new education amendment continued to ban church-operated primary and secondary schools. Other anticlerical laws that remained intact, however, were not enforced. Once again, a modus vivendi between the church and state became the norm. Yet another President, Lopez Mateos, proclaimed his adherence to both Catholicism and the revolution. By the mid-1950s, it appeared that church-state relations had achieved a level of maturity and resigned tolerance for each other. By 1956, Archbishop Miguel Dario Miranda urged Catholics to be responsible citizens and support candidates who were going to do the most for both the church *and* state. Such politicization from the pulpit albeit peaceful, was generally tolerated by the dominant PRI in a gradual evolution toward improved relations between old rivals. By the same token, the anticlerical laws were overlooked during the Pope's 1979 and 1990 visits to Mexico when, as a foreign cleric, he broke them by holding public masses.

It is important to note that the quest for a mutually beneficial relationship between the church and state did not occur without some struggle. While it was true that a more peaceful coexistence resulted from the truly substantive constitutional change in 1991, that change was preceded by a tense period between 1980 and 1988. Political animosity is slow to die in Mexico and, when that animosity focuses on something as emotionally charged as the Roman Catholic Church, it follows that church-state relations would have their ups and downs.

PRI's tolerance of church politicization was tested as Mexico fought its way out of an economic slump in the mid-1980s. Mexico's oil revenues declined and its foreign debt skyrocketed to unmanageable proportions. During those trying times, when the Mexican Government was preoccupied with financial matters, the church found a window of opportunity to achieve what Roberto Blancarte calls 'recuperation of its social space' (Blancarte, 1991, p.104). It was during that period that bishops from Chihuahua proclaimed their dissatisfaction with alleged 1986 electoral fraud committed by those in power. The bishops went so far as to demand a recount of votes (Camp, 1994, p. 95). The Chihuahua election allegation provoked a strong reaction from the Mexican Congress. In 1987, the Congress enacted Article 343 of the Federal Electoral Code. The provisions called for strong penalties, including up to seven years in prison, for ministers or priests found guilty of involvement in the electoral process such as urging people to vote for certain parties or candidates, or not to vote at all. Any religious pressure on the electorate became illegal. The Chihuahua incident and Article 343 clearly illustrate the roller coaster relationship between the church and state during that period. The church pressured for greater transparency and democratization. The government, in turn, responded with Article 343—and then softened its stance on enforcement of the article. Prior to Carlos Salinas de Gortari's victory in the 1988 presidential election, conflicts took a traditional pattern of legal crackdown followed by a lack of enforcement.

Two important factors explain the major shift in the Mexican political will toward religion. The first is political freedom, also referred to as tequila *glasnost* (openness); the second is economic reform, or tortilla *perestroika* (restructuring). Both factors emerged after President Carlos Salinas took office in 1988. Unlike Soviet-style *glasnost* and *perestroika*, the Mexican versions reflected the particularities of a country sensitive to subjugation of the indigenous people by the Spanish-Roman Catholic complicity in maintaining the status quo. Salinas, a Harvard educated PRI-technocrat, quickly instituted his own plans for *glasnost* and *perestroika* much as Gorbachev was doing in the former Soviet Union at the time. Both *glasnost* and *perestroika* portended an end to the Cold War and ushered in an era of greater tolerance of different viewpoints.

For Mexico, the above global changes translated into a shift to more democratic and transparent politics, albeit for economic reasons. Mexico was slowly emerging from an insidious economic bust of the mid-1980s. Ironically, the push for recovery took place as Salinas' 1988 election victory was challenged as a fraud. Major economic reform took place as Mexico veered from *parastatals* (state-controlled and state-owned corporations) to a neo-liberal economic model in which free trade and global exports were the means for achieving higher levels of development. Many state corporations were privatized and

NAFTA became a crowning point of glory for the Salinas Administration. Simply put, it became necessary for Mexico to modify its outdated and unproductive ways, and join the shift to greater openness, transparency, tolerance and freedom. The former Soviet Union was doing it, the United States Government was encouraging it, and it became apparent to many PRI leaders that the Mexican political system needed to change if it were to weather the potentially destabilizing effect of a non-PRI win in future presidential elections. After all, the opposition National Action Party (PAN) scored a major electoral victory in 1989 when it won the governor's race for Baja California, an influential border state.[1] Increased opposition victories could threaten the stability of a system long dominated by one party. Things had to change, and that occurred 'virtually overnight,' as Jorge Vargas claims (Vargas, 1996, pp. 497–508). In addition, if NAFTA were to be accepted by the United States Congress,[2] Mexico would have to demonstrate not only greater economic freedom, but also greater political freedom. Such an atmosphere facilitated a religious change without alienating the traditional, anticlerical PRI forces. While all of Mexico focused on NAFTA, little attention was paid to religious reforms that were presented as a necessary part of tortilla *perestroika*. International shifts toward openness and political tolerance made the time ripe for Mexico's anticlerical constitution and laws to be revised.

The most profound change to Mexico's revolutionary constitution occurred at the beginning of the Salinas Administration. The anticlerical articles were amended and, for the first time since 1917, religious associations acquired legal status. No longer were churches of all faiths forced by law to operate in a clandestine manner (Vergara, 1998). They could now operate publicly and did not have to depend on any informal modus vivendi, nor be dismissed at will by the president. How could years of institutionalized religious repression suddenly change overnight? It was precisely because the church was legally restrained for so long that it no longer appeared to be a threat to Mexico's political elite. In the early 1980s, the head of the Mexican Episcopal Conference gave a prescient summation of this sentiment when he noted that clerics have for years been 'shaped' by the 'liberal mentality' and have come to accept their decreased power (Camp, 1994, pp. 69–100). Thus, change could take place in an atmosphere of self-confidence on the part of Mexico's political leaders. They were not 'giving away the store,' to use a popular phrase. Rather, they were merely acknowledging the fact that religion in Mexico could function freely, yet separately. By 1991, religion was no longer regarded as an anti-revolutionary threat. In awarding religion greater freedom of activity, political benefits for Mexico's PRI elite far exceeded any negative consequences.[3] The collective Mexican identity, which revolutionary leaders had long sought to dissociate from religion, was legitimizing what everyone knew all along: 85 percent of Mexicans were Roman Catholics while the remainder professed one of the evangelical Protestant faiths. Despite years of institutionalized anticlericalism, the affinity for religion was very much alive.

On December 10, 1991, the Salinas Government proposed changes to five articles of the constitution pertaining to religion. By December 18 those changes were approved, with only slight modification, by the Chamber of Deputies. The amendments affected sweeping changes regarding religion in Mexico. As mentioned earlier, religious organizations could now benefit from 'juridical personality,' or enjoy legal status in their dealings with the state. When officially recognized by the state, churches were free to organize and run their own internal operations. Religious groups could conduct ceremonies, crusades, or rallies in public facilities (Reich, 1997, pp. 77–86). The January 1999 public mass officiated by the Pope, for example, was legal—unlike the activities of his previous visits to Mexico. The clergy were also given greater freedom. While they were still required to register with the *Secretaria de Gobernacion* (Ministry of the Interior), the clergy could now vote, hold office and occupy appointed positions provided they relinquished their religious positions. In addition, churches and religious groups could now own property (Constitution of 1917, 1991 amended version). What remains unclear is the extent to which religious groups can voice opinions on sensitive political or social issues. This aspect of church-state relations will be examined in greater detail later in the chapter.

Protestantism and the Triangular Conflict

Historic patterns of religious conflict focused on the Roman Catholic Church, but that gradually shifted to include a growing number of Mexican Protestants. Catholic-Protestant tensions in the 1980s marked a new phase in Mexico's struggle toward defining its identity. The Roman Catholic Church no longer has a monopoly on religious belief in Mexico. Matthew Marostica explains this surge in Protestant 'religious innovation' as a logical result of the country's increase in civil liberties during the 1980s (Marostica, 1998, pp. 45–51). That tidal wave rapidly gained strength during the tequila *glasnost*. According to the 1990 Mexican census, roughly five to seven percent of the people identify themselves as Protestant. The rate of growth has been the most in the southern states of Campeche, Chiapas, Morelos, Oaxaca, Tabasco, Veracruz, and Yucatan where the church had traditionally been less entrenched (Reich, 1995, p. 76).

Mexico's Protestants[4] are referred to as Evangelicals[5] because of the popularity of evangelical sects such as the church of God, Seventh Day Adventist, Pentecostals, and Jehovah's Witness. They represent a new cross-cutting cleavage in the Roman Catholic Church's well established, albeit conflicting, relationship with the state. Roman Catholic leaders know how to maneuver amidst the barrage of laws, anticlerical constitutions, and government constraints. Likewise, the Mexican Government was accustomed to dealing with the Roman Catholic Church. However, neither was ready for the new spiritual affront posed by the Evangelicals. Both parties knew that the rules of the church-state engagement developed over a long period of Mexico's tormented history. Neither the church nor the state knew how to face the rising tide of Evangelicals. After all, the Catholic culture had for so long been the dominant religious force in Mexico. In the past, political activities had been directed at the Catholic Church. Now, the Mexican Government is forced to contend with both the Catholics and Evangelicals and their differing demands on the administration.

Protestants come largely from the lower socioeconomic classes and conversion rates are proportionately greater in poor states like Chiapas or Oaxaca. Evangelical converts are drawn to the decentralized church structure that emphasizes family, community, and a strong aversion to alcohol consumption. This latter point has developed beyond social confines and is a source of violent tension within communities. Roderic Camp believes that the level of tension between Catholics and Evangelicals is higher in the late 1990s than it was in the previous thirty years (Camp, 1994, p. 69-100). Mexico's recent religious tension is complicated by the belief of some Catholic leaders and government officials that

Protestant infiltration into Mexico is the result of excessive foreign proselytizing that includes the complicity of U.S. intelligence agencies (Camp, 1997, p.95). David Stoll points out that U.S.Congressional hearings in 1975 revealed an information-sharing relationship between the U.S. Central Intelligence Agency and various missionary groups throughout the world. Adding fuel to the Catholic-Protestant fire was the 1980s decision by the Protestant Wycliffe Bible Translations to operate in Mexico under the name Summer Institute of Linguistics. Cloaked in the guise of language research, the group was able to overcome Mexico's pre-1991 religious ban on foreign church organizations until its true mission was eventually discovered (Stoll, 1990, pp.17–18). The Protestant stress on religious autonomy and self-directed moral character, rather than obedience, most worries traditionalists in the Mexican Government. Catholics, once coopted by the ruling PRI, are more likely to follow Church pronouncements to support the government than are independently-minded Evangelicals. The latter stress honesty, moral character, and egalitarianism over obedience to a religious hierarchy. Examination of Mexico's Evangelicals should, thus, be undertaken from both a religious and political standpoint.

Paul Bonicelli's study points to the April 1987 kidnaping in Oaxaca of three Evangelicals and their families by villagers angered about the preaching of 'individual liberty and salvation.' Such religious teachings were regarded as a threat to the 'established order,' and the Evangelicals were herded to the Santiago Atitlan Jail and charged with disorderly conduct. The incident turned violent when, instead of releasing them, angry villagers shot the three detainees. Family members in custody were told to leave town and not return. Illustrative of Protestant-Catholic tensions, a municipal official explained the events as one in which villagers would not tolerate those in their midst who reject Catholicism. He reiterated that the natural sequence is expulsion from the community (Bonicelli, 1997, pp. 107–130). Protestantism will continue to grow in Mexico, however, for two reasons. First, as long as Mexico's least fortunate believe they are being ignored by Mexico's economic, political, and Roman Catholic institutions, they will increasingly look for alternative solutions to their problems. One option is to turn to churches that offer a safety net for turbulent times while attending to spiritual needs. Second, as many of Mexico's poorest families continue to endure hardships associated with high rates of alcohol abuse among males, interpersonal relationships will continue to be strained. The spiritual comfort, solidarity, and hope offered by Protestant sects are now considered viable alternatives. Changing denominations in Mexico provokes a real shift in that country's national identity because it negates religious history, albeit flawed with injustice. Maria Casas Perez alludes to this rough transition: as a country modernizes in the Western tradition, it is obliged to become more transparent, participatory, and democratic. Yet, the very essence of modern democracy, with its tolerance for a variety of religious groups, goes against the grain of Mexico's authoritarian political and social structures devoid of pluralism (Casa Perez, 1996, pp. 71–84).

Nowhere in Mexico are battle lines more sharply drawn than in the southernmost state of Chiapas. It is Mexico's poorest state and heavily populated by a variety of Mayan indigenous peoples. It is estimated that 32 percent of the population within the state speak indigenous languages most of the time and have only a limited command of Spanish. The state is unique in having the highest number of Protestants (16 percent) in the country (Camp, 1998). Presbyterians comprise the largest group in Chiapas, totaling about 117,000; Seventh Day Adventists and Pentecostals make up the second largest group

(Woehr, 1995, pp. 46–47). Mayan religious rites also abound and are often found blended into Catholic tradition. It is within this mixture of poverty, indigenous peoples, and a growing Evangelical component that Chiapas finds itself trying to manage a murky triangular religio-political conflict. Most outsiders associate the Chiapas conflict with the Zapatista Army for National Liberation and its armed rebellion against the government. In fact, the state of Chiapas is actually engaged in a two pronged conflict: the Zapatistas-government struggle and the Catholic-Protestant cleavage. According to one estimate, some 300 persons were killed since the initial uprising in 1994 and another 4,000 are thought to have been displaced from their homes (*Economist*, 1998, p. 37). The following pages will examine the Catholic-Protestant dimension in greater details.

Samuel Ruiz Garcia, Chiapas' Catholic Bishop, is said to preach a modern version of liberation theology, and he has often been accused by the government of being too soft on the Zapatistas. As a result, many of Chiapas' Catholics have experienced harsh reprisals from the Mexican Army that often associates peasant Catholics with the Zapatistas. To complicate matters, conservative Catholics side with the government while Protestants avoid taking sides, but more often than not, take the government's side. The pro-government stance of the Evangelicals, however, has provoked a backlash from Catholics who feel that their state government is not responding to their needs. Traditional conflict in Chiapas remains rooted in the insignificant voice afforded to the indigenous population. Marginalized by governmental structures, indigenous voices went unheard in Chiapas until the world took notice of the startling Zapatista attack on January 1, 1994, and the short-lived takeover of a main urban center, San Cristobal de las Casas (Whitmeyer and Hopcroft, 1996, pp. 517–538). Of principle concern was the issue of land tenure and how to seek an equitable solution to the dispute over land. Even though many Mexicans support the Zapatista goals of expanded democracy and a more just distribution of Mexico's income, they have come to dislike the accompanying violence. This holds especially true within the state of Chiapas, which remains at the heart of the armed conflict. It comes as no surprise that religious organizations have sought to fill the void as an alternative spokesperson for the state's disaffected citizens, known as *Chiapanecos*. Interestingly, while the Zapatista armed rebellion has largely subsided, Catholic-Protestant violence continues unabated.

It is important to understand that the Catholic-Protestant conflict is more complex than a simple denominational struggle. The Catholics in Chiapas can be divided into 'modern' and 'traditional'. Modern Catholics include those led by Bishop Samuel Ruiz who aspire to Pope John Paul II's goals of ministering to the poor. These Catholics are largely tolerant of their Evangelical neighbors. However, traditional Catholics are indigenous peasants who incorporate Mayan religious practices under a veneer of Spanish imposed Catholicism. These traditionals often hail from rural areas of Chiapas where both priests and formal church structures are absent. Within these villages, *caciques* (local political leaders), who also happen to be Catholics, are wont to protect traditional Mayan religious customs that include the sacrificial offering of alcohol, candles, and other materials to ward off evil spirits. The sale of these materials, especially the lucrative sale of alcohol, is controlled by local *caciques*. Evangelicals do not use such materials in their rituals and, hence, pose a threat to the continued economic well being of local *caciques*. As Evangelicals generally abstain from alcohol, they also contribute to the overall decline in social consumption of alcohol. Under the banner of 'cultural protection', traditional Catholic Mayan villagers have engaged in protecting their village from encroaching Protestant influences. This mind-set is manifested by mass expulsion of local Evangelical converts. It is estimated that 35,000 persons have been expelled from Chiapas' villages since the 1960s, mainly around the municipality of San Juan Chamula (Riley, 1998, p. A15). In response to the religious tensions, a Reconciliation Commission was established for the town of Chamula. However, Juan Roque Flores, its president, notes that there still exists a clear violation of the constitutional guarantee of freedom of religious expression (Ruiz, 1998). That was illustrated by Florencio Collazo Gomez, Chamula's mayor, vowing to prevent external ideas from infiltrating the Mayan community. In one instance, Protestant school children were banned from the town's public schools in an attempt to stop 'bad ideas' (Riley, 1998, p. A15). Chris Woehr reports that in 1994 six hundred exiles chose to return to Chamula and requested police protection during their reintegration into the community. No protection was forthcoming; two exiled spokespersons and the wife of one spokesperson were murdered. Evangelical advocate Abdias Tovilla Jaime noted that no suspects were arrested and, instead, the state Congress urged Protestants to continue their support of the government.

Ironically, such violence has yet to drive the Evangelicals into the Zapatista camp. Their aversion to political struggle, which is tinged with leftist liberation theology, has prevented the politically conservative Evangelicals from abandoning the political system. Yet, as more Evangelical government representatives get elected, the spotlight will increasingly be placed on the lack of due process. Protestants point to the election of Chiapas' state Senator Pablo Salazar Mendicuchia, himself a Protestant, as a positive force who will keep the issue alive (Woehr, 1995, pp. 46–47). It is noteworthy that supporters of Bishop Ruiz have also encountered violence, perpetrated by paramilitary forces. This violence is typified by the December 1997 massacre of forty-five unarmed Mayans of Tzotzil origin in the community of Acteal. In his analysis of the Acteal massacre, Richard Stahler-Sholk writes of paramilitaries opening fire on escaping villagers and of gruesome mutilation by machetes. The sympathies of state authorities appeared to rest with the paramilitaries. That was evidenced by the non-intervention of security forces during the massacre (Stahler-Sholk, 1998, p. 11). Such sympathies came to light only after Father Gonzalo Ituarte, a member of the National Mediation Commission (CONAI), exposed the government attempt to declare the massacre a result of family feud. Media coverage was so intense that Mexican authorities removed the governor of Chiapas and the state chief of police. The mayor of the Chenalho municipality, in which Acteal was located, was subsequently arrested. The Tzotzils were members of the Civil Society of the Bees. They had set up a refugee camp along the road to Acteal, approximately twenty miles from San Cristobal. The Civil Society of the Bees sold honey and was supported by the Diocese of San Cristobal. Bishop Ruiz maintained that the society was a peaceful group engaged in commerce rather than politics, but he admitted that some members were Zapatista sympathizers.

Chiapas remains the most volatile state in Mexico, a state wrought with complicated religious and political tensions. The state's main religious actor, Bishop Ruiz, is also a political actor. Until January 1998 he served as chief mediator for CONAI, which was charged with finding a solution to the Zapatista conflict. Separating religious violence from political violence cannot and, perhaps, should not be attempted. This is because the religious and political violence in Chiapas is, indeed, intertwined. It will take many years for religious harmony ever to become a reality.

Conclusion

After examining the role of religion in Mexico's collective identity, one can conclude that Mexico is in the throes of, what might be called, an 'accommodation shift'. That is, while religious freedom was constitutionally forthcoming at the national level by 1991, there was a dearth of religious tolerance at the grassroots level. One can postulate from this that Mexico's rural villages, especially in the impoverished south, are potential powder kegs of religious violence awaiting a spark. This spark may take the form of increased Catholic-Protestant 'turf-wars' within villages. Another catalyst may be expansion of politically motivated guerrilla groups seeking sympathies from activist Catholics concerned with poverty and institutional injustice. While the Zapatistas have gathered most of the world's attention, one should be reminded that the People's Revolutionary Army (ERP) of Guerrero state also harbors the potential for linking religion to its political cause. The outcome would undoubtedly expand the violence to a state that is home to the well-known resort, Acapulco.

Salinas' opening of greater religious freedom translated not only in the ability for Protestant sects to proliferate, but also in increased power for the Roman Catholic Church. Cooptation has long been used by the PRI to bring errant groups back under its control and influence. In one sense, increased religious liberty for the Roman Catholic Church provided the basis for cooptation. The church would theoretically be indebted to governmental *glasnost*. Indeed, it has demonstrated overall support for governmental actions. This, however, has not always been the case in recent years and Chiapas' Bishop Ruiz serves as a visible reminder that the Mexican Church has not been totally coopted as one might assume. A testimonial to change, Pope John Paul II's visit in January 1999 set the tone for what he regarded as Mexico's 21st century problem areas. First, the Pope indirectly criticized the Mexican Government's record in handling the country's social ills. Second, he warned of the fallacies of other religious ideologies. That, of course, was a direct reference to the rising tide of Protestant conversions in Mexico. Along that line, he drew attention to poverty, poor health care, low wages, and ill effects of corruption. Those points were not new revelations; they had been discussed by religious leaders since the 1968 Second Latin American Episcopal Conference (CELAM II) in Puebla, Mexico. At that meeting, issues of poverty, justice, and the evolving state of religion were discussed within the context of modern Latin American society and political institutions (Pomerlau, 1981, pp. 540–549). The one obvious difference between the Pope's 1999 speeches and those of CELAM II is the fact that the latter broadly focused on Latin America and did not single out Mexico.

In a move that illustrated a newfound religious confidence, Mexican Cardinal Norberto Rivera Carrera also addressed the crowds during the Pope's 1999 visit. He expressed the belief that many Mexicans lead desperate lives and continue to be 'manipulated' by Mexico's political and economic elite (Stanley, 1999, p. 9). While both the Pope and Cardinal avoided direct reference to the government or Chiapas conflict, they did stress the need for Mexico's political leaders to improve the socio-economic conditions in that impoverished state. Even though indirect, the words uttered by Mexican Church leaders during the Pope's visit illustrate the imperative of addressing the church's two most pressing challenges: poverty and the rising tide of Protestant converts. A closure to these problems must be achieved before realizing a modern collective identity for Mexico.

Notes

1   Roderic Camp's research notes that PAN always had a close affiliation with the Catholic Church, and Salinas' religious reforms were an attempt to coopt the church as well as PAN supporters. Consequently, it comes as no surprise that the 1988–1994 PAN platform called for constitutional revisions of the articles pertaining to religion (Camp, 1994, pp. 69–100).

2   In the United States, the political arena was in the midst of accommodating the rising influence of the Christian Right. Mexico's anti-religious constitution and laws did little to hearten anti-NAFTA forces in the United States and, in fact, could be used to provide fuel for its defeat.

3   Luis Scott, Mexican religious scholar, offered a different interpretation. Scott asserted that Salinas might have actually lost the 1988 election and, as a result, reached out to the church for support. In exchange for the church's affirmation of his 'win,' Salinas sought to change the anticlerical constitution (Bonicelli, 1997, pp. 107–130).

4   The mainstream denominations are Methodist, Presbyterian, and Lutheran.

5   In this essay, 'Protestants' and 'Evangelicals' will be used interchangeably.

References

Blancarte, Roberto (1991), *Poder Salinismo e Iglesia Catolica: Una Nueva Convivencia?* (Salinas' Power and the Catholic Church: A New Beginning?) Editorial Grijalbo: Mexico City (Mexico).

Blancarte, Roberto (1992), *Historia de la Iglesia Catolica en Mexico 1929–1982*, (History of the Catholic Church in Mexico 1929–1982), Fondo de Cultura Economica: Mexico City (Mexico).

Bonicelli, Paul (1997), 'Testing the waters or ópening the floodgates? Evangelicals, politics, and the "new" Mexico,' *Journal of Church and State*, Vol. 39, No. 1, Winter, pp. 107–130.

Camp, Roderic A. (1994), 'The Cross in the Polling Booth: Religion, Politics, and the Laity in Mexico,' *Latin American Research Review*, Vol. 29, No. 3, pp. 69–100.

Camp, Roderic A. (1998), 'Testimony, Committee on International Relations, Subcommittee on the Western Hemisphere,' *Federal Document Clearinghouse Congressional Testimony*, July 29, Lexis/Nexis.

Casas Perez, Maria de la Luz (1996), 'Democratizacion y cultura en Mexico: Modernizacion, identidad nacional y resistencia cultural' (Democratization and Culture in Mexico: Modernization, National Identity and Cultural Resistance), *Revista Mexicana de Ciencias Politicas y Sociales* (Mexican Political and Social Science Review), Vol. 41, October-December, pp. 71–84.

Cleary, Edward L. (1995), 'Human rights organizations in Mexico: growth in turbulence,' *Journal of Church and State*, Vol. 37, Autumn, pp. 793–812.

Constitution of Mexico (1917, with 1991 amendments), Political Database of the Americas, http://www.georgetown.edu/LatAmerPolitical/Constitutions/Mexico/mexico1917.html.

Fox, Jonathan (1997), 'The Difficult Transition from Clientelism to Citizenship: Lessons from Mexico,' in Chalmers, Douglas A.; Carlos M. Vilas; Katherine Hite; Scott B. Martin; Kerianne Piester; and Monique Segarra (eds.), *The New Politics of Inequality in Latin America*, Oxford University Press: New York.

Handelman, Howard (1997), *Mexican Politics: The Dynamics of Change*, St. Martin's Press: New York.

Loaeza, Soledad (1985), 'Notas Para El Estudio De La Iglesia En El Mexico Contemporaneo' (Notes for a Study on the Church in Contemporary Mexico), in De la Rosa, Martin and Charles Reilly (eds.), *Religion y Politica en Mexico* (Religion and Politics in Mexico), Siglo Veintiuno Editores: Mexico City (Mexico).

Marostica, Matthew (1998), 'Religion and global affairs: religious activation and democracy in Latin America, *SAIS Review*, Vol. 18, No. 2, Summer/Fall, pp. 45–51.

'Massacre in Mexico' (1998), *The Economist*, Vol. 346, No. 8049, p. 37.

Mecham, J. Lloyd (1966), *Church and State in Latin America*, University of North Carolina Press: Chapel Hill.

Morales Moreno, Isidro (1997), 'Mexico's National Identity After NAFTA,' *American Behavioral Scientist*, Vol. 40, No. 7, June, pp. 858–883.

Paz, Octavio (1985), *The Labyrinth of Solitude*, Grove Press: New York.

Pomerlau, Claude (1981), 'The Changing Church in Mexico and Its Challenge to the State,' *Review of Politics*, Vol. 43, No. 4, October, pp. 540–549.

Puente, Maria Alicia (1992), 'The Church in Mexico,' in Dussel, Enrique (ed.), *The Church in Latin America: 1492–1992*, Orbis Books: Maryknoll, N.Y.

Quirk, Robert E. (1964), 'Religion and the Mexican Social Revolution,' in D'Antonio, William V. and Frederick B. Pike (eds.), *Religion, Revolution, And Reform: New Forces for Change in Latin America*, Frederick A. Praeger: New York.

Reich, Peter L. (1995), *Mexico's Hidden Revolution*, University of Notre Dame Press: Notre Dame, IN.

Reich, Peter L. (1997), 'The Mexican Catholic Church and constitutional change since 1929,' *The Historian*, Vol. 60, No. 1, pp. 77–86.

Riley, Michael (1998), 'Mexico's 3-sided religious war,' *Washington Times*, March 31, p. A15.

Ruiz, Rafael Victorio (1998), 'Solicitan la Intervencion de la Segob Para Resolver el Conflicto Religioso en Chiapas,' (Interior Ministry Intervention Sought to Resolve the Religious Conflict in Chiapas), *El Excelsior* (The Excelsior), August 20.

Stahler-Sholk, Richard (1998), 'The Lessons of Acteal,' *NACLA: Report on the Americas*, Vol. 31, No. 5, pp. 11–14.

Stanley, Alessandra (1999), 'John Paul Tells Mexicans That Faith Must Overcome Corruption,' *New York Times*, January 26, p. A9.

Stoll, David (1990), *Is Latin America Turning Protestant? The Politics of Evangelical Growth*, University of California Press: Berkeley.

Vargas, Jorge A. (1996), 'Mexico's Legal Revolution: An Appraisal of Its Recent Constitutional Changes, 1988–1995,' *Georgia Journal of International and Comparative Law*, Vol. 25, No. 3, Summer, pp. 497–508.

Vergara, Jesus Aceves (1998), 'La Iglesia Catolica en el Presente de Mexico' (The Catholic Church in Today's Mexico), *Este Pais* (This Country), March 1.

Whitmeyer, Joseph M. and Rosemary Hopcroft (1996), 'Community, Capitalism, and Rebellion in Chiapas,' *Sociological Perspectives*, Vol. 39, No. 4, Winter, pp. 517–538.

Woehr, Chris (1995), 'Chiapas evangelicals have little faith in new government,' *Christianity Today*, Vol. 39, No. 2, pp. 46–47.

3 Haiti: Voodoo, Christianity, and Politics

ROBERT LAWLESS

One major problem in investigating the interrelations of religion and politics in Haiti has been the difficulty faced in evaluating the function of Voodoo in the politics of the nation. In 1970, one investigator wrote about the impossibility of accurately gauging Voodoo's role in Haitian politics (Byers, 1970, p. 308). And in 1976, another investigator added that measuring Voodoo's impact on the politics of Haiti is an 'abstruse and doubtful' project (Rotberg, 1976, p. 342). More than two decades later, and after a serious socio-political upheaval in which various religious groups played important roles, the question of the role of Voodoo is still unanswered. The role of the other religions is somewhat clearer. David Nicholls (1970, pp. 407–414) summarizes the relationship between Francois Duvalier and the Roman Catholic Church as one of tension and distance. Leslie Desmangles (1992) and Anne Greene (1993) bring us up-to-date concerning the Catholic Church: Desmangles by showing that Roman Catholicism in Haiti can be understood only within the context of Voodoo, and Greene by documenting the role of the church in the decline of the Duvalier dynasty. Indeed, there is evidence of the dynamics between Protestantism and politics (Lawless, 1992, pp. 110–125). The measure of Voodoo is still problematic, however. Little seems to have been learned since the seminal article on the topic by Remy Bastien was published in 1966.

Voodoo and Christianity

Part of the problem is assessing the influence of Voodoo on politics lies in the widespread misunderstanding of Voodoo. Popular writings equate it with African sorcery and witchcraft. Alfred Métraux (1959, p. 15), writing the first full-length anthropological study of Voodoo, states that Voodoo responds, as does every religion, to the needs of humanity. In other words, Voodoo provides remedies for ills, the satisfaction of needs and desires, and gives hope for survival. No contemporary scholar argues anything but that Voodoo is a legitimate religion. While it is certainly the major religion of Haiti, it is difficult to determine with any precision the number of Voodooists. Most Haitians are aware of its bad press, and many deny to outsiders that they are Voodooists. Also, Voodoo has a strong admixture of Catholicism. Because it is necessary to be baptized as a Roman Catholic to be a Voodooist, it is not entirely clear what Haitians mean when they may reply to a question about their religion by saying that they are 'Catholics'. Combining the estimates of two North American anthropologists with many years of experience in Haiti, Gerald F. Murray and Glenn R. Smucker, with those of the Haitian anthropologist Max Paul, former Director of the Haitian Bureau d'Ethnologie—estimates given to this author in private conversation in 1991—one can gauge that between 50 and 75 percent of the population of rural Haiti actively practices Voodoo. And up to 90 percent passively believes in

Voodoo. What is clear is that Voodoo is the indigenous creation of Haiti and comes far closer than anything else to being the national religion of Haiti.

Why, then, is it so difficult to gauge the impact of Voodoo on politics? Voodoo is essentially a family religion practiced within the household and consists largely of healing rituals and ancestor worship. Glenn Smucker, an anthropologist with a long-term and intimate knowledge of Voodoo, states that Voodoo is based on spiritual inheritance and kinship ties with the deceased and other spirits as 'quintessentially local spirits' that are individually inherited though they reflect recognizable archetypes. There are, however, local spirits whose names are known only within a particular community or household (Smucker 1984, p. 41). Voodoo legitimizes a web of relationships with relatives, the land, and experiences of growing up, becoming ill, getting cured, and dying. Ideologically, there is little connection between Voodoo and national politics. Also, Voodoo is a diffused and unorganized religion. No region-wide or nation-wide organizations of Voodoo priests exist, and Voodoo theology is not widely disseminated. Certainly there are no theological schools, and there is no Voodoo bible. The astute anthropologist Melville J. Herskovits (1937, p. 153) has observed the 'extreme degree' of informality of Voodoo. Having said all this, however, what we are left with is the fact that Voodoo may actually be somewhat of a substitute for formal government institutions, which are traditionally scarce in rural Haiti and urban slums. In terms of the polity of the community Voodoo reinforces group solidarity, reduces anxiety in the face of uncertainty, presents entertainment and recreation, and furnishes Haitians with a coherent worldview (Lawless, 1992, p. 156). Indeed, the Voodoo temple itself has been described variously as a clubhouse, courthouse, dance hall, hospital, pharmacy, sanctuary, and theater all rolled into one edifice (Jahn, 1961, p. 54). Although Voodoo beliefs cross class boundaries, it is, in common practice, largely a folk religion of the peasantry and urban poor. When middle- and upper-class families participate, it is rarely in public settings. The traditional upper classes and upwardly mobile families often strongly identify with the French-Haitian cultural heritage and evade public affiliation with the practice of Voodoo—if not the beliefs—to avoid the social stigma of identification with Afro-Haitian cultural traits and the lower classes (Smucker, 1984, p. 37). Certainly the ruling elite has found the egalitarian and democratic character of Voodoo quite threatening; Voodoo is, after all, the religion of the masses, slave revolution, and peasant uprising and labor unrest.

The relationship of the state to Voodoo has, then, been an uneasy one. For the most part, members of the ruling elite have ignored Voodoo though some of them, indeed, have privately practiced it. Occasionally, the government has become involved in attempts to suppress Voodoo, most notably during the notorious 'anti-superstition' campaign of the early 1940s. Among the very few presidents who seemed to favor Voodoo was Dumarsais Estime, whose administration lasted from 1946 to 1950. Certainly Francois Duvalier, whose regime lasted from 1957 to 1971, gave the impression of having a close alliance with Voodoo, especially early in his administration. Duvalier practiced his own brand of black populism, which included the cooperation (or cooptation) of such amorphous groups as taxi drivers and black power intellectuals. An integral part of Duvalier's appeal to the masses included his seeming reliance on the advice of Voodoo priests.

In 1971, Duvalier the elder was succeeded by his son Jean-Claude. The United States Government supported him and set up a new economic program featuring private investments from the United States that would be drawn to Haiti by such incentives as no custom taxes, a minimum wage kept very low, the suppression of labor unions, and the right of U.S. companies to repatriate their profits. The U.S. Government also began an aid program to build a supportive infrastructure, but most of the projects were never completed and most of the funds found their way into the pockets of Jean-Claude Duvalier and his cohorts. Jean-Claude showed little interest in Voodoo, and, in fact, presented himself as adhering to the beliefs of the Roman Catholic Church. For this and other reasons few Haitians displayed any real affection for him, as they had for his father. Voodooists, while not suppressed, remained in the background—smoldering. Jean-Claude Duvalier had little real political support beyond the self-serving *mulatto* (people of African and European mixed ancestry) business community and the fickle young elite technocrats. And his elaborate wedding in 1980 to Michele Bennett, the daughter of a mulatto business family, alienated many Voodoo-aligned followers of his father. The second Duvalier regime rarely met any of its economic promises. With little good will for Duvalier the junior, Haitians began public protests against the government in late November 1985. The Roman Catholic Church certainly played a role in these protests, as illustrated in the next section. A little over a year later a U.S. aircraft transported Jean-Claude Duvalier into exile. That day Voodooists were seen in the streets of Port-au-Prince holding tree branches and symbolically sweeping away the evil spirits of the Duvaliers.

In the campaigns leading to the first two post-Duvalier presidential elections in November 1987 and January 1988, Voodoo priests and others sympathetic with Voodoo increasingly played a role in representing the people as the Roman Catholic Church began to fade into its own hierarchical labyrinth. There was, however, a backlash against Voodoo priests, occasioned, at least in part, by the identification of some of these leaders with the Duvalier regime. Members of the Francophile elite and various foreign missionaries were also involved in this attempt at another 'anti-superstition' campaign. A letter calling for the provisional government's support for the destruction of Voodoo temples was published in the February 17, 1986, issue of the newspaper *Le Nouvelliste* (The Newsmonger) (Benjamin, 1986, p. 5). A Roman Catholic radio station, a Protestant one, and two independent stations supported the call. Several Voodoo priests were killed over the next few days. Some probably were killed as part of a larger public protest against the continued presence of Duvalier's henchmen. The government, however, did little to stop the killings until foreign publicity (Cooper, 1986, p. 43) forced it to request the radio stations to cease their inflammatory broadcasts.

Roman Catholicism

Although Roman Catholicism has long been the official religion of Haiti, sometimes in law and sometimes in practice, Article 30 of the 1987 Constitution (which is the one currently in effect) clearly forbids the establishment of any official religion and declares all religions and cults to be 'at liberty' (Asanble, 1987, p. 4, my translation). The article also secures the right of anyone to hold any religious beliefs as long as they are not contrary to public peace and order (Asanble, 1987, p. 4). As have many other scholars before him, Desmangles demonstrated that Voodoo is an integral part of Haitian culture. He concluded his recent study by pointing out that Voodoo 'works' because it is such an integral part of Haitian life and that its accord with Haitian culture far exceeds that of the Roman Catholic Church (Desmangles, 1992, p. 180). Roman Catholicism has, however, played a role on the national political scene in the absence of a national Voodoo Church and organization. Haiti, in fact, has always had a curious relationship with Roman Catholicism, which was, after all, historically the religion of the slave owners. Before independence everyone was officially a Roman Catholic; the French baptized all slaves when they arrived in the New World. Although the constitution established by Governor-General Toussaint Louverture in 1801 declared Catholicism the official religion, Jean-Jacques Dessalines in 1804 stated that independent Haiti would have no official religion, and for the next half century Haiti was isolated from the Roman Catholic Church. In 1860, the government of Haiti and the Vatican signed a Concordat that reestablished Catholicism as the state religion to be run primarily by priests from France. Few Haitians, however, are practicing Catholics. Most have little to do with the church after baptism, and there are few priests at the parish level. Various authorities have told this author that probably fewer than five percent of the Haitians attend mass more than once a year—and most of these are in Port-au-Prince.

Generally the Catholic Church has collaborated with the ruling elites and urban-based governments. During 1941–1942, under President Elie Lescot, the government engaged in the notorious 'anti-superstition' campaign that was supposed to rid the nation of Voodoo forever, and the Catholic Church enthusiastically supported the campaign. Duvalier's nationalist policies, however, eventually clashed with the Catholic Church, and Duvalier was excommunicated. In 1966, the president and the Vatican agreed on a compromise in the appointment of Haitian bishops, and thereafter Duvalier did not fight the Catholic Church. By the 1980s, in an ironic turnabout, the Haitian Catholic Church itself had become nationalist. Then, on March 9, 1983, Pope John Paul II made a speech at the airport in Port-au-Prince attacking injustice, inequality, and oppression, and declaring, in an often quoted phrase, that 'something must change' in this country. The government did not expect such a homily, and although the Haitian press censored the Pope's comments, the Roman Catholic radio station broadcast the words. Greene (1993, p. 148) believes that the church station played a significant role leading to the overthrow of the Duvalier regime; it broadcast in Creole and had a catchy theme song that became a symbol of the efforts to oust Duvalier. The broadcasts of the station and the words of the Pope created shock waves throughout the country. By the next month 860 priests and others had signed a statement calling for social change. The local Catholic organizations, known in Creole as *Ti Legliz* (Little Church), became a focus of government oppression. The Roman Catholic radio station was destroyed on July 21, 1985, the day before Duvalier's sham referendum on his dictatorship. After that, the Catholic Church became quite public and instrumental in the people's movement to expel Duvalier.

The flash point of the revulsion against Duvalier was reached on November 28, 1985, when militiamen fired on student protesters and killed three students at the College of the Immaculate Conception. Inspired by liberation theology, the protest movement spread throughout Catholic schools (Chardy, 1986a, 1986b). Despite her sympathy for the role of the Catholic Church in the downfall of Jean-Claude Duvalier, Greene (1993, p. 73) also recognizes that the history of the church is 'unheroic' and that the church was largely irrelevant to Haitians until the 1970s. The church mission changed as a consequence of Vatican II, indigenization of the Haitian hierarchy in 1966, and regional conferences of

Medellin, Colombia, in 1968 and Puebla, Mexico, in 1979. According to Greene (1993, p. 132), evangelism in the church shifted from spiritual concerns and a focus on educating the urban elite to the collective well-being of the nation, especially its poor. And since 1966, the church has increasingly used Creole, incorporated Haitian culture into its rituals, and taken its evangelical message and development expertise into rural areas (Greene, 1993, pp. 132–133). The Roman Catholic Church has few structures through which it can formally participate in politics. After helping to organize the initial protests against the Duvalier dynasty, the church has become largely irrelevant (Lawless, 1992, p. 104).

Greene (1993, p. 253) agrees that whatever may have been the significance of the Catholic Church in the departure of Duvalier, the church has reverted to the past and has remained silent despite the military coup, political repression, and economic misery. The hierarchy of the Catholic Church rarely supported any progressive change, and currently only a few in the Catholic Church offer leadership for the oppressed in Haiti. The opposition of the Roman Catholic Church to the reform-minded former priest and democratically elected President Jean-Bertrand Aristide attests to the socially and politically conservative stance of the church. Indeed, the Vatican was the only state to recognize the repressive miliary regime that overthrew the democratically elected Aristide Government. For many years Aristide has been at odds with the Roman Catholic Church and especially with the Haitian mirror of the church hierarchy, which tried to silence him many times, including expelling him from his order. In 1988, paramilitary gangs destroyed his church. He obviously despises the doctrinaire Pope John Paul II and the reactionary hierarchy of the church, asserting that the people no longer buy the 'package' that the Vatican is trying to sell (Aristide, 1990, p. 21). In his first book Aristide clearly illustrated that he has a close identification with the suffering in Haiti. And he also identified the struggle of the people in Haiti with the struggles of the powerless everywhere, especially in Latin America, observing that Haitians consider an attack against Latin America as an attack on Haiti (Aristide, 1990, p. 47).

In an often quoted metaphor Aristide wrote that the rich of Haiti sit at a huge table overflowing with good food while the rest of the population starves huddling under the table in the dirt. He went on to predict that one day the people under that table will rise up, knock over the table, and take what is rightfully theirs (Aristide, 1990, p. 9). Active in human rights movements for many years before he became president, Aristide has an obvious—and perhaps volatile—appeal to many segments of the Haitian population, especially the peasantry and urban poor. After a series of military coups following the ouster of Jean-Claude Duvalier, Jean-Bertrand Aristide won the presidency in a landslide of 67 percent of the estimated 75 percent of the two million registered voters who cast ballots in the December 1990 elections. The Haitian Army ousted Aristide in an extremely bloody coup just 236 days after his February 7, 1991, inauguration. The Organization of American States declared the new regime to be illegitimate and, in November 1991, the United States imposed an embargo on Haiti demanding that the army allow the democratically elected government to be reinstated. On October 15, 1994, Aristide returned (under the watchful eye of the U.S. military) to an extraordinarily jubilant welcome from the Haitian masses as their rightful president.

Aristide was succeeded by his protege Rene Preval, who was prime minister during the first months of Aristide's administration in 1991. Having been endorsed by Aristide and receiving 87.9 percent of the nearly 931,000 valid votes cast, Preval was inaugurated in February 1996. The following April, the 19-month U.S. military intervention ended. The Roman Catholic Church seemed to have played no role in those events.

Protestantism

In 1970, Nicholls (1970, p. 400) observed that Protestant groups only peripherally impact politics in Haiti. Such irrelevance is probably no longer quite the case, but, nevertheless, nobody seems to have a clear idea of just what the Protestant Churches are doing in Haiti and what their impact might be on the politics of the country. They have been having considerable success in at least superficial conversions. The Haitian perception of these conversions is, however, considerably different from those of the missionaries (Lawless, 1992, p. 110). As do all people, Haitians fit alien religious beliefs and practices into their own indigenous cognition system. And unlike the Roman Catholic Church, which makes some (admittedly superficial) compromises with Voodoo, Protestant missionaries in Haiti generally regard Voodoo and Protestantism as mutually exclusive. Protestantism emphasizes that converts must totally renounce Voodoo in order to become true Christians. For many Haitians, then, conversion to Protestant Christianity is really conversion *from* Vodun (Johnson, 1970, p. 19). My own work in the Cap-Haitien area suggests that most converts to Protestantism are trying to escape community obligations that they would have under Voodoo rather than simply escaping from Voodoo beliefs and practices. Indeed, the conversion experience is often interpreted within the context of their Voodoo worldview as a ritual for dealing with some extreme disease, discomfort, or malaise that has not been amenable to Voodoo cures (Bourguignon, 1951, p. 180).

Although there were Protestant missionaries in Haiti earlier, the beginning of sustained, semi-official missionary work was marked by the invitation in 1817 from President Alexandre Petion to John Brown and others (Pressoir, 1945, p. 83). The earliest permanent Protestant Church in Haiti was the Methodist Church, which focused its proselytizing on the Catholicized urban elite and gained converts among some segments of these elites. For example, the head of the Methodist Church in Haiti was the treasurer and apparent spokesperson for the 1987 Provisional Electoral Commission. Estimates of the number of Haitian Protestants range from ten percent (Weinstein and Segal, 1984, p. 73) to 25 percent (Smucker, 1984, p. 36). The significant growth in converts has come in the poorer rural areas since World War II. The American Baptist Convention has almost 80 percent of its membership in rural areas. Other Baptist Churches have supplied some of the recent leaders in Haitian politics. It is noteworthy that a Baptist minister, Sylvio Claude, was a leading presidential candidate in the November 1987 elections.

Even though one might find Protestant missionaries with an understanding of Haiti, most of them exhibit the bigotry well illustrated in the words of one who wrote that Haitians struggle between being a born-again Christian and a fear-ridden Voodooist (Burdick, 1970, n.a.). And missionaries usually refer to Voodoo as a superstition (Anderson, 1979, pp. 11–12). Several missionaries told this author that they thought there was a definite connection between Voodoo and poverty in Haiti, on the one hand, and Christianity and wealth in the United States, on the other (Conway, 1980, pp. 24–25). At least one missionary lamented that Haitians usually want to work a little on their own land, their own project, only for themselves, just enough to get along and then spend it all. They do not really understand the social power and dignity of work and cooperation. He added that part of the Christian message is to teach the dignity of working for others, the power of saving money, investing in one's family needs, and not complaining all the time and fighting the government in trying to change things. When things get really bad, he concluded, they will get the point. The work of the Protestant missionaries does, indeed, revolve around their notion of Voodoo as, at best, a collection of African superstitions and, at worst, the devil's religion. The goal of most such missionaries is to 'free' Haitians from the chains of Voodoo. Such a perspective is illustrated by a song that this author once heard a group of Haitian evangelical Protestants sing while they were standing outside a house where some Voodooists were conducting a curing ceremony on a seriously ill person. In their song, the Protestants chastised the practice of Voodoo as 'evil'.

The origin of the 13-year Haitian Revolution is traced to a Voodoo ceremony held in August 1791 and presided over by a slave and Voodoo priest named Boukman. In August 1998, a band of evangelical Protestants launched a crusade to posthumously convert Boukman to Christianity. Three Haitian Protestant missionaries, one of them a former police attache, threatened to hold a service to 'exorcize' the spirit of Boukman at Bois Caiman, a site near Cap-Haitien that is sacred to Haitians. Their crusade failed to gain much popular support and, in fact, was opposed by the Ministry of Culture. Furthermore, more than a dozen grassroots organizations charged that the Protestants' project would be a 'desecration' of Bois Caiman and the memory of Boukman. There had been previous attempts by Protestant missionaries to overrun the site, which met with strong local resistence. Protestant missionaries, however, have typically been allowed to go their way in Haiti because they generally avoid questions of exploitation and tend to teach that their converts must obey the wishes of the state. Unlike many in the Roman Catholic Church, most of the Protestant leaders in Haiti—with few exceptions—have studiously avoided politics. And because Protestants were not prominently involved in the ouster of Duvalier, they have been considered by some as part of the Duvalier regime. Several Haitian Protestants did, indeed, hold high positions under the Duvaliers.

The Explosive Potential of Religion and Politics

In times of crises, Haitians—even those who are members of the elite—often turn to Voodoo. In February 1986, Haiti was awash with rumors of Voodoo rituals and sacrifices in the National Palace as Jean-Claude and Michele Duvalier prepared for the exile. The 80-year-old Emile Jonassaint, who functioned as provisional president for a few months before the U.S. takeover of Haiti in September 1994, summoned Voodoo spirits to deal with the invasion (Shacochis, 1999, pp. 51–53. Also, see Ballard, 1998). The potential for explosive interactions between religion and politics is most likely between those sympathetic to Roman Catholicism or Protestantism that attempt to suppress Voodoo and those sympathetic to Voodoo who try to hold in check the more aggressive Protestant evangelical missions. The years 1941–1942 saw the best example of a government sympathetic to Roman Catholicism attempting to suppress Voodoo as President Lescot carried out the so-called 'anti-superstition' campaign. An insider's account by a Roman Catholic priest clearly documents the collaboration of the church (Riou, 1975). A tremendous amount of property was destroyed. Ironically, in a country suffering from deforestation, the government felled hundreds of trees that were regarded as sacred to Voodoo. Fear of instability has increased every month since January 1999 when President Preval's sister was wounded and her driver killed in Port-au-Prince as her car was sprayed with bullets in a daylight attack. The government seems immobilized and unable to adjust to democratic procedures (Dupuy, 1997). Preval is only the second democratically elected president of Haiti, which is trying to recover from decades of dictatorship and whose seven million people wrestle with crushing levels of illiteracy and unemployment. The people also have been brutalized by the former military regime, which was characterized by the extreme violence practiced by paramilitary gangs and regular army units largely against the peasantry and urban slum dwellers (Stotzky, 1997).

Random violence and interpersonal crimes such as muggings and rapes have traditionally been rare in Haiti. Such crimes have been reported on a large scale only beginning in the late 1980s after the army took control with the fall of the Duvalier dynasty. Consistent state-supported violence probably began on a significant scale in the early 1960s in the Francois Duvalier regime. Almost three decades of violence—seemingly increasing with each decade as the country devolved into chaos—has resulted in an apparent desensitization to savagery. As is historically common, large numbers of Haitians are turning to Voodoo for solace. At the same time, the efforts of aggressive evangelical Protestant missions are increasing—particularly in the poorer rural areas, such as the northwest and the southeast. The potential for an explosive confrontation increases whenever the government intervenes on behalf of either side. So far, government agencies have generally sided with the Voodooists, such as in the Boukman controversy, but the general weaknesses of these agencies make them susceptible to the will of whomever may be able to pay their bills. The government, then, may become a pawn in the hands of religious zealots, while members of the elites, who have traditionally keep passions under control, abandon the government (and perhaps the country) as unmanageable.

Conclusion

Haiti may be best understood as a predatory state run by an elite class that makes its living by exploiting the masses. Government institutions do not operate for the benefit of the larger society; the government largely serves the needs of the elite. Directly and indirectly, then, members of the elite depend on the government for their income. To maintain and increase their income, various segments of the elite feel it is imperative to control the government. All members of the elite, however, cannot be in control at the same time, and so individuals, families, and groups must make alliances with those who are managing the agencies of government at any given time (Lawless, 1997, p. 145). The political difficulties seen in the succession of coups, aborted and fraudulent elections, incompetent governance, and gross violations of human rights reflect the efforts of these competing groups of the elite to sustain themselves economically. Loss of power by any subgroup would result not only in its loss of control and prestige, but also in the loss of its livelihood. The long, 30-year reign of the Duvalier family undermined the traditional balance among the competing groups of the elite. After the downfall of Jean-Claude Duvalier in February 1986, the government, which was largely a machine for political repression, devolved into chaos. Democratic traditions are still too weak and too shallow to offer a workable alternative.

While the elite has always made its living through control of the state apparatus, which one contemporary Haitian scholar called 'state fetishism' (Trouillot, 1990, p. 9), religious groups have maintained their claim to power and influence through connections with the ruling elite as well as with the major patron of Haiti, the United States. When regimes paid attention to Voodoo, as did Estime and Francois Duvalier, Voodooist leaders had some influence. Only Protestant groups maintain any contact with U.S. government agencies dealing with Haiti, and their influence on U.S. policy makers remains relatively low. And after their initial role in ousting Duvalier, the Roman Catholic Church has withdrawn from Haitian politics. The inability of the government to assert itself, that has largely characterized Haiti throughout 1999, appears to depend little on any input from any religious groups. In January 1999, President Rene Preval announced his decision to bypass a hostile parliament and rule by decree. Preval installed Jacques Edouard Alexis as the prime minister without the parliament's approval. The opposition immediately accused Preval of conspiring with his mentor, former president Aristide, to establish a dictatorship. Parliamentary elections, invalidated by fraud allegations in 1997, have not yet been rescheduled. Haiti has not had a published budget in two years and millions of dollars in foreign aid are on indefinite hold. Preval has been plagued by an opposition-dominated parliament that has refused to act on his nominees for prime minister. No legitimate church group has seriously commented on these events.

One expectation was that the so-called new black middle class would play a political role in the nascent democratic government. Largely a product of Francois Duvalier's efforts in countering the old, *mulatto* elite, this class makes its living from mercantile, capitalist, and service enterprises. As a class, it supports whatever political apparatus offers the most socio-political stability. For the most part, this middle class has been politically neutral and socially silent throughout the recent upheavals (Lawless, 1997, p. 164). The religious affiliation of this class seems as vague as its political tendencies: the adults believe in Voodoo but rarely practice it, children attend Roman Catholic schools, and the large numbers of migrants that this class sends to the United States generally profess Protestantism. The socio-political repression that has been such a major part of the political scene for so long, and that is keeping the democratic institutions from developing, operates to keep the poor from claiming their share of Haiti's meager resources. What divides the elite into seemingly arbitrary, and often competing, segments is their non-cooperative efforts to gain individual and familial power. At this point in the struggle religion can only play a very minor role. In the very near future, however, religion, in the form of competing Voodooists, Roman Catholics, and Protestants, will struggle for control of the government—and then there will be an explosive violence that will become legendary.

References

Anderson, Mildred (1979), *Beyond all This: Thirty Years with the Mountain Peasants of Haiti*, Baptist Haiti Mission: Grand Rapids, MI.

Aristide, Jean-Bertrand (1990), *In the Parish of the Poor: Writings from Haiti*, Orbis: Maryknoll, NY.

Asanble, Konstitiyant la (1987), *Konstitisyon Repiblik Ayiti* (*Constitution of the Republic of Haiti*), Ministè Enfòmasyon ak Kowòdinasyon: Port-au-Prince (Haiti).

Ballard, John R. (1998), *Upholding Democracy: The United States Military Campaign in Haiti, 1994–1997*, Praeger: Westport, CT.

Bastien, Remy (1966), 'Vodoun and Politics in Haiti,' in Courlander, Harold and Remy Bastien (eds.), *Religion and Politics in Haiti*, Institute for Cross-Cultural Research: Washington, DC.

Benjamin, Marcel (1986), 'Une lettre au conseil nationale de gouvernement' (A Letter to the National Council of Government), *Le Nouvelliste* (The Newsmonger), Port-au-Prince (Haiti), February 17, p. 5.

Bourguignon, Erika Eichhorn (1951), *Syncretism and Ambivalence in Haiti: An Ethnohistorical Study*, Ph.D. dissertation, Northwestern University: Evanston, IL.

Burdick, Sandra L. (1970), 'Preface,' in Burdick, Sandra L. (comp.), *God Is No Stranger*, Baker: Grand Rapids, MI.

Byers, James F. (1970), 'Voodoo: Tropical Pharmacology or Psychosomatic Psychology?' *New York Folklore Quarterly*, Vol. 26, No. 3, Summer, pp. 305–312.

Chardy, Alfonso (1986a), 'The Church Tests Its Power,' *Miami Herald*, February 17, pp. 1A, 6A.

Chardy, Alfonso (1986b), 'Youths: We Were Seed of Haitian Revolt,' *Miami Herald*, February 15, pp. 1A, 13A.

Conway, Frederick J. (1980), 'Pentecostalism in Haiti: Healing and Hierarchy,' in Glazier, Stephen D. (ed.), *Perspectives on Pentecostalism: Case Studies from the Caribbean and Latin America*, University Press of America: Washington, DC.

Cooper, Nancy (1986), 'Haiti's Voodoo Witch Hunt,' *Newsweek*, May 26, p. 43.

Desmangles, Leslie G. (1992), *The Faces of the Gods: Vodou and Roman Catholicism in Haiti*, University of North Carolina Press: Chapel Hill.

Dupuy, Alex (1997), *Haiti in the New World Order: The Limits of the Democratic Revolution*, Westview: Boulder, CO.

Greene, Anne (1993), *The Catholic Church in Haiti: Political and Social Change*, Michigan State University Press: East Lansing.

Herskovits, Melville J. (1937), *Life in a Haitian Valley*, Knopf: New York.

Jahn, Janheinz (1961), *Muntu: An Outline of the New African Culture*, Grove: New York.

Johnson, Harmon A. (1970), *The Growing Church in Haiti*, West Indies Mission: Coral Gables, FL.

Lawless, Robert (1992), *Haiti's Bad Press: Origins, Development, and Consequences*, Schenkman: Rochester, VT.

Lawless, Robert (1997), 'Haitians: From Political Repression to Chaos,' in Ember, Melvin; Carol R. Ember; and David Levinson (eds.), *Portraits of Culture: Ethnographic Originals*, Vol. 2: *South and Middle America*, Prentice-Hall: Englewood Cliffs, NJ.

Metraux, Alfred (1959), *Voodoo in Haiti*, Oxford University Press: New York.

Nicholls, David (1970), 'Politics and Religion in Haiti,' *Canadian Journal of Political Science*, Vol. 3, No. 4, Fall, pp. 400–414.

Pressoir, Charles Fernand (1945), *Le Protestantisme haitien* (*Haitian Protestantism*), Societe Biblique et des Livre Religieux d'Haiti: Port-au-Prince (Haiti).

Riou, Roger (1975), *The Island of My Life: From Petty Crime to Priestly Mission*, Delacorte: New York.

Rotberg, Robert I. (1976), 'Vodun and the Politics of Haiti,' in Kilson, Martin L. and Robert I. Rotberg (eds.), *The African Diaspora: Interpretive Essays*, Harvard University Press: Cambridge, MA.

Shacochis, Bob (1999), *The Immaculate Invasion*, Viking: New York.

Smucker, Glenn R. (1984), 'The Social Character of Religion in Rural Haiti,' in Foster, Charles R. and Albert Valdman (eds.), *Haiti—Today and Tomorrow: An Interdisciplinary Study*, University Press of America: Lanham, MD.

Stotzky, Irwin P. (1997), *Silencing the Guns in Haiti: The Promise of Deliberative Democracy*, University of Chicago Press: Chicago.

Trouillot, Michael-Rolph (1990), *Haiti: State Against Nation: The Origins and Legacy of Duvalierism*, Monthly Review Press: New York.

Weinstein, Brian and Aaron Segal (1984), *Haiti: Political Failures, Cultural Successes*, Praeger: New York.

4 Malawi: A Historical Study of Religion, Political Leadership, and State Power

SYLVIA M. JACOBS

On July 6, 1964, Nyasaland gained independence from Britain as Malawi. Unlike other colonies in Africa, where there were many ethnic or religious groups vying for political power, Malawi, a predominately Christian colony with less than a dozen ethnic groups, made a peaceful and nonviolent transition to independence. Predominately Bantu-speaking, the Chewa, accounting for 90 percent of the population, is the largest ethnic group.[1] With 20 percent Muslims, and another 5 percent practicing indigenous traditions, 75 percent of the people are Christians. Protestants, however, outnumber Roman Catholics by a ratio of about three to one. Hastings Kamuzu Banda was elected president at independence, and he became president-for-life in 1971. He established a dictatorship that lasted until 1994. Earlier, in November 1993, Banda was stripped of his title of president-for-life because of poor health. That year, a successful referendum abolished the one-party system and paved the way for free elections. The May 1994 elections resulted in the ratification of a provisional constitution that facilitated a multiparty democracy with nine political parties, including the ruling party, the United Democratic Front.

Malawi has had a long and continuous history that included conflict and compromise among different groups. That history has revolved around religion, political leadership, and state power. Like many precolonial states on the continent, chieftaincy or kingship in Central Africa was closely linked with religious power. Before the introduction of foreign religions and limited political parameters for Africans, spiritual and political power in traditional African societies were intertwined. In fact, there was very little distinction between secular and religious power (Ambert, 1977, pp. 46–47). Chiefs and kings legitimized their rules in their role as mediators in traditional religion or having ancestral links with the spirit world. They were guardians of the 'spirits of the land' (Shillington, 1995, pp. 139–140). In precolonial Africa, political leaders often gained control because of their religious affiliation or through religious wars. While religious and political leadership are generally distinct in postcolonial Africa, in the past the two spheres often intertwined, sometimes resulting in explosive interactions.

Religion in Historical Perspective

In central and southern Malawi, the idea of chieftaincy came from the religious cults that were guardians of the 'spirits of the land.' Around 1400, by marrying into a local group, the Phiri people gained control over the chiefs living south of Lake Malawi. The Phiri took the royal title of Kalonga, which also became the name of their dynasty. Like many of their contemporaries, the Phiri believed in religious kingship; it linked religion with political leadership and state power (Shillington, 1995, p. 145). During the 16th century, several states of modern-day southern Malawi broke off from the Kalonga dynasty, including the Lundu Kingdom among the Manganja of the Shire valley and the Undi Kingdom among the Chewa who lived between the Shire valley and the Zambezi River. Subsequently, the chiefdoms in that region were organized under those three principal ruling dynasties. Fire played an important role in the religious rituals of the Phiri people. Thus, it was not a surprise that the inhabitants of the Kalonga, Lundu, and Undi Kingdoms were collectively known as the *Maravi* (Peoples of the Fire) (Shillington, 1995, p. 145; Williams, 1978, pp. 17, 24–26). Here, it is noteworthy that Malawi derives its name from these *Maravi* people.

In the early 1600s, Kalonga Masula reasserted authority over the Lundu and Undi Kingdoms. During his reign, from about 1600 to 1650, he built a powerful *Maravi* Empire, largely through military conquest. By 1635 Masula's empire stretched from the Zambezi River in the west to Mozambique in the east (Kalinga, 1998, p. 539). However, after Masula's death in 1650, the *Maravi* Empire declined (July, 1998, p. 278; Shillington, 1995, pp. 203–204). The lack of a powerful and central *Maravian* authority left the way open for penetration of violent slave caravans and slave raids of the early 19th century (Shillington, 1995, pp. 203–204). Although a small scale slave trade from the East African coast to Central Africa had existed for many centuries, in the second half of the 18th and early 19th centuries the trade moved from the coast into the interior (Williams, 1978, pp. 30–32). Slave traders not only exported slaves, but also brought Islam to the region (Shillington, 1995, pp. 253–254). After its introduction, however, Islam spread very slowly among the *Maravi* people. Today, Islam continues to be a minority religion in Malawi. Interestingly enough, however, the current president of the country, Bakili Muluzi, is a Muslim. Projecting a separation of religion and political leadership, however, the current decoupling is explained by the people's obsession with ending Hastings Banda's autocracy in the postcolonial period.

David Livingstone, the Scottish missionary and explorer, first traveled to Africa in 1841 and hoped to convert Africans to Christianity (Wills, 1973, p. 83). In exploring unknown regions of Africa, he was appalled by the effect of the slave trade on the continent. He believed that the slave trade in Central Africa could be replaced by legitimate indigenous trade. In particular, he hoped that others would join him in building Central Africa into 'a highway' for religion and trade (Williams, 1978, pp. 38–44). Inspired by Livingstone, British Christian missionaries were attracted to Central Africa. Two years after Livingstone's death in 1873, both the Church of Scotland and the Free Church of Scotland sent missionary groups to Nyasaland. The Free Church of Scotland organized an expedition in 1875 from South Africa that reached the mouth of the Zambezi in July. Its station, Livingstonia Mission, was first established at Cape Maclear. Because of an unfavorable climate, however, the station was moved to Bandawe. Also, the same year, the Church of Scotland founded its headquarters at Blantyre, named after Livingstone's birthplace (Williams, 1978, pp. 45, 108–111; Wills, 1973, pp. 108–111). The Blantyre Mission resisted the Portuguese in the south; the Livingstonia Mission fought the Arab slave traders in the north (Wills, 1973, p. 111).

Attempts by missionary societies to establish Christianity as an alternative to the slave trade were aided by the African Lakes Company, a British trading company with strong links to the Scottish Evangelical movement (Afigbo, et. al., 1986, p. 235; Shillington, 1995, pp. 251–152). In 1878, the British-sponsored African Lakes Company began building trading posts in Nyasaland. In 1884, Cecil Rhodes' British South Africa Company received a charter to develop the country. Rhodes was a British administrator and businessman who helped to extend British control over Southern and Central Africa. In expanding to Central Africa in the 1880s, Rhodes' company came into conflict with Arab slave traders in the area (Williams, 1978, pp. 49–53). Pressure from British missionaries and trading interests in Malawi led to the 1889 British Government's declaration of a protectorate over the Shire highlands. During 1890–1891, agreements between the Portuguese and German Governments, on the one hand, and the British South Africa Company, on the other, set the boundaries of the British Central Africa Protectorate. The United Kingdom established the British Protectorate of Nyasaland in 1891. However, Rhodes' South Africa Company continued to finance peacekeeping functions there. In 1893, the British Protectorate of Nyasaland became the British Central Africa Protectorate. In deference to missionary distrust of the motives of Rhodes' South Africa Company, in 1895 all administrative functions in the protectorate were taken over completely by the British Government. In 1904, the colony was renamed the Nyasaland Protectorate (Kalinga, 1998, pp. 534, 539; Williams, 1978, p. 52).

Church and Political Leadership

Beginning in the 1870s, isolated groups of Africans in South Africa reacted to color prejudice in religious observances and the growing racism among whites in the two Boer Republics by forming their own religious communities. In 1884, Nehemiah Tile, a Methodist minister, broke from the Wesleyan Mission and founded a separate church, the Tembu Church (Afigbo, et. al., 1986, pp. 183–184). In protest against discrimination and white domination, Mangena M. Mokone, another Methodist minister, founded the Ethiopian Church in November 1892 near Johannesburg. It was from Mokone's church that the Ethiopian movement,[2] or African Independent Church movement,[3] took its name. The Ethiopian movement, primarily a religious movement, also had a political element (Afigbo, et. al., 1986, p. 184; Geiss, 1974, pp. 141–142). One of the ways that Africans felt safe in criticizing European colonial rule without retribution was through religious expression. By rejecting European churches, and through the Independent Church movement, Africans carved out a religious space of their own making. At the beginning of the 20th century, the Ethiopian movement spread throughout Africa. Stimulated by fundamentalist missionary activity at that time, a number of African revivalist churches appeared in Nyasaland. Some educated Africans left established churches for independent churches that gave them some religious autonomy. Those independent churches, controlled and led by Africans, were also an outlet for political frustration. Independent churches provided an institutional base for venting African political and social grievances (Williams, 1978, p. 98).

In 1906, Elliot Kamwana became a protege of Joseph Booth, a freelance missionary who had come to Nyasaland in the late 1890s. Kamwana, formerly a Livingstonia student who had been a medical aide in a Rhodesian hospital, set up a branch of the Watch Tower movement   in Nyasaland (McCracken, 1998, p. 243; Wills, 1973, pp. 232–233). Established by Jehovah's Witnesses, the Watch Tower movement was a mixture of fundamentalist religious beliefs and a radical attitude towards government. Members believed that the government did not understand the Kingdom of God in either the secular or spiritual sense. Not surprisingly, African followers interpreted these religious beliefs quite differently from whites (Williams, 1978, pp. 99–100). From an African perspective, their ancestral political leaders understood the relationship of religion and the state. Their traditional chiefs were the depositors of religion, and it was through them that religion was interpreted for the people. Thus, they believed that African history had already shown that a government can find a balance between religion, leadership, and state power. According to these African disciples, not all governments were corrupt, only white ones. To the African followers, that meant it was inevitable that they would replace Europeans as leaders in their countries (Williams, 1978, pp. 99–100). Watch Tower literature encouraged the idea of Judgment Day, and Africans interpreted that as the day when the righteous (Africans) would take the seats of the mighty (Europeans). Although the authors of those Watch Tower tracts were only concentrating on their religious meaning, African adherents saw political implications for them as well. Africans proclaimed that those religious pamphlets predicted the collapse of white rule (Williams, 1978, pp. 99–100). The Watch Tower movement attracted many recruits and Kamwana is said to have baptized as many as ten thousand people. Kamwana talked about the Second Coming of Christ, which he predicted would happen in 1914. He believed that the Second Coming would usher in the end of colonial rule. Concerned about Kamwana's influence among Africans in Nyasaland, colonial authorities deported him in 1909. The Watch Tower movement in Nyasaland was not strong enough to survive without its leader; the movement ceased for some time (Williams, 1978, pp. 99–100). After Malawi gained its independence, the Jehovah's Witnesses regained followers and converts among Africans. Unfortunately, however, the Banda Administration surreptitiously condoned violence against Jehovah's Witness members and eventually banned the church.

Another religious leader in the development of the Independent Church movement in Nyasaland in the early 20th century, and who was probably viewed by Europeans as a political threat, was Charles Domingo. Born in Mozambique, in 1881, he was taken to British Central Africa as a young boy by William Koyi, an African preacher transferred to the Livingstonia Mission from Lovedale, South Africa. Domingo was educated, and in 1897 he became the first African to complete Livingstonia's teacher training course. Three years later, he completed theological training; in 1902 he received a license to preach. In 1907, he was appointed to the Loudon congregation, but was informed by church leaders that he would continue to be under the supervision of European missionaries in the district. Few African graduates of Livingstonia were assigned to senior positions at the mission, and even fewer became members of the Livingstonia staff (Williams, 1978, pp. 97, 100–102). Domingo broke away from the Livingstonia Mission in 1908 and set himself up as a Seventh Day Baptist preacher. He was very bitter about the racial attitudes of Europeans toward Africans. He resented European racial arrogance and domination. For a short time in 1916, Domingo was deported. Before his return to the protectorate, the American Seventh Day Baptists withdrew their support from the mission. After that, Domingo apparently no longer took part in religious or political activity (Williams, 1978, pp. 101–102).

More than other missions in the region, the Scottish Mission Church at Livingstonia tried to identify and educate talented young Africans in the surrounding villages. In fact, because of the Mission Church's rigorous curriculum, its graduates were well respected in Central Africa. Of course, there were substantial benefits for educated Africans throughout the continent. Thus, many Africans joined churches because they believed that church membership was a prerequisite for access to mission schools (Williams, 1978, pp. 97–98).

Two American churches initiated missionary work in Nyasaland after 1900: the National Baptist Convention, U.S.A., Inc., a black church, and the Seventh-day Adventists, a white one. The missionaries of the National Baptist Convention were Landon Cheek and Emma DeLany. From 1901 to 1906 Reverend Cheek and DeLany worked in the Chiradzulu district in the southern province of Nyasaland. During that time, in 1904, the mission station where they worked was named the Providence Industrial Mission (Adams and Talley, 1944, p. 23; Jordan, 1901, p. 132; Phiri, 1982, p. 255). From 1902 until 1907 the Seventh-day Adventists were represented by Thomas Branch. In the southern region of the colony Branch opened the initial mission of the Seventh-day Adventist Church in Nyasaland, the Plainfield Mission Station, named in honor of their headquarters in New Jersey (Neufeld, 1966, p. 151; Shepperson and Price, 1958, p. 135). In the early 20th century Europeans throughout Africa came to perceive the presence of African American[4] missionaries, who had worked on the continent for over eighty years, as a threat to the colonial system. Black American missionaries were accused of encouraging political revolts. Colonial governments, suspicious of them, discouraged their entry into Africa. Cheek left Nyasaland permanently in 1906; DeLany took a furlough in the United States that same year. When Delany attempted to return to the country, she was denied permission by British authorities (Shepperson and Price, 1958, p. 135). Because the Seventh-day Adventist Church wanted its mission to be viewed in a more positive light by the British Government, and hoped to remove all doubts of the church's loyalty to the colonialists, the General Conference decided in 1907 to send a white man to the Plainfield Mission Station to take charge. Within four months Branch permanently left the country (Neufeld, 1966, p. 151; Roome, 1926, p. 46). Although Cheek and Branch were located over thirty miles from one another, with little if any contact, both were later accused by the British Government of having conspired to incite disorder in Nyasaland.

Probably one of the most notable examples of what Europeans feared could happen when Africans were exposed to foreign religious and political ideologies took place in Nyasaland in 1915. In January of that year, John Chilembwe, an American-educated missionary, hoping to strike a final and permanent blow against British colonialism, led an uprising of indigenous Africans in Nyasaland (Rotberg, 1967, pp. 23–24; Shepperson and Price, 1958, p. 135). Chilembwe's career may be regarded as a classical example of Ethiopianism,[5] illustrating the way in which Christian missions in Africa unwittingly facilitated the development of nationalism and the desire for political leadership among Africans (Geiss, 1974, p. 145). Like Kamwana, Chilembwe was a protege of Joseph Booth, the British Evangelist in Nyasaland. As a boy Chilembwe had worked for Booth, a radical and outspoken missionary. Booth, with his 'Africa for the Africans' slogan, had a major impact on Chilembwe's thinking (Geiss, 1974, p. 210; Williams, 1978, p. 45). After Booth took him to the United States, Chilembwe studied for three years at the African American National Baptist Convention school, Virginia Theological Seminary and College in Lynchburg. He was the first in his village to become an ordained minister (Weisbord, 1973, pp. 39–40; Williams, 1978, pp. 108–109). After returning to Nyasaland in 1900, Chilembwe parted company with Booth. Chilembwe was certain that he had been sent to America as an instrument of Divine Will. He felt that it was his destiny to guide his people to a promised land free of European colonialists. For the next ten years after his return to Nyasaland, Chilembwe focused his attention and efforts on building a church in the Chiradzulu district, gathering a congregation, and teaching school (McCracken, 1998, p. 243; Williams, 1978, pp. 108–111; Wills, 1973, pp. 230–232). Chilembwe became increasingly virulent in his denunciation of Europeans. His preaching became more radical and apocalyptic. His dissatisfaction with British rule finally led him to orchestrate an uprising on January 15, 1915. Chilembwe and a few of his followers were killed; the government crushed the uprising eleven days later (Rotberg, 1967, pp. 29–52; Williams, 1978, pp. 110–114).

European administrators in Nyasaland believed that foreign missionaries in the country had promoted a spirit of independence, insubordination, and discontent amongst Africans which resulted in a protest movement as illustrated in the Chilembwe uprising. They held that the protectorate had been free of such subversive elements until the foreigners entered the country. The foreign missionaries were accused of teaching revolution rather than religion. The six-member Nyasaland Native Rising Commission— appointed by George Smith, governor of the colony—in investigating the Chilembwe uprising, mentioned 'European and American Missions' as one of the contributory elements of the Chilembwe disturbance. Furthermore, the commission insisted that those small, insufficiently financed missions, conducted by unsuitable persons, and under no proper control, had sown the seeds of revolt. The missionaries were described as persons of narrow views who encouraged dissent among Africans (Du Plessis, 1917, p. 346; Phiri, 1982, p. 256). The commission recommended that only 'properly accredited missions' without a political agenda be allowed to operate in the protectorate (Du Plessis, 1917, p. 346; Phiri, 1982, p. 256). Ironically, the Christian colonial officials were alleging that the Biblical and other religious teachings of American and European Christian missionaries in Nyasaland had encouraged rebellion among their African converts.

The allegation that Africans in Nyasaland were not unhappy with European colonial rule before the introduction of American or European missionaries is ludicrous. All along, Africans understood the inequality and racism of colonial rule. Nevertheless, acting on this mistaken belief, from 1915 to 1925 British colonialists closed Nyasaland to all foreign missionaries (Shepperson and Price, 1958, p. 391). The real significance of Chilembwe's uprising was not so much how it affected events at that time, but rather how it impacted on the subsequent political and religious history of the colony. Chilembwe had died a martyr, but he had not died in vain. He envisioned an independent future for his country, but he was ahead of his time. In fact, Governor George Smith acknowledged that Chilembwe's uprising had initiated a new and very different period in the history of Nyasaland (Williams, 1978, p. 114). After 1915 'the Shadow of Chilembwe' could be seen throughout the colony: on the European estates, in the mission stations, chambers of the legislative council, and relations between whites and blacks. The year 1915 signaled the end of an era, and the beginning of another one, that would culminate in independence in 1964. Chilembwe's rebellion was an instrument of change, even if it was fifty years ahead of its time (Williams, 1978, p. 114). Here again, another movement in Nyasaland had both religious and political overtones. Chilembwe had a religious education and background, but the colonial experience of Africans in Nyasaland led him to stage his ill-fated political uprising. Perhaps, that was his way of making both a religious and a political statement. It was through theological and spiritual activities that Africans sought to find some political expression. Chilembwe indeed became a martyr and the father of nationalism in his country (Geiss, 1974, pp.209–210). For Africans in Nyasaland, his uprising gave them hope for a better future. Today, January 15 is a national holiday in Malawi; it is John Chilembwe Day!

Secular Challenge for Leadership

Chilembwe's uprising had shown the possible explosive consequences of combining religion and politics. After the rebellion, British colonialists in Nyasaland not only refused to admit foreign missionaries, but also were suspicious of the African Independent Church movement. Africans in Nyasaland were still wary of European religious institutions, but fearful of possible repercussions if they joined African ones. As independent churches or religious communities faced repression and censure, Africans in the country channeled their energies in another direction. During the 1920s and 1930s religion played a secondary role in the move for political leadership; the principal political voice of educated Africans in Nyasaland at that time was the so-called 'native associations.' Although the associations were initially organized as a political forum for the educated elite, they did accept some educated traditional rulers. These groups were not simply vehicles for political protest, but were concerned with marriage, housing, public works, labor, and trade. They gave Africans a voice in colonial affairs and the British Government used their concerns as a way of gauging public opinion (Williams, 1978, pp. 117–118).

As early as 1912, the North Nyasa Native Association was founded. Two years later, the West Nyasa Native Association was established (Williams, 1978, p. 105). In 1925, Levi Mumba, a founding member of the North Nyasa Native Association, suggested the formation of a national or regional organization, one made up of the various associations in central Nyasaland. However, at that time there was no support for his idea (Williams, 1978, pp. 119–120). Just as Mumba saw the need for the establishment of a united group in promoting the interests of Africans, Europeans in Nyasaland came to believe that there were advantages for them in a Central African union. At the end of World War I, when German East Africa (later British Tanganyika) was occupied by British forces, Nyasaland colonialists contemplated an East African union (Hargreaves, 1996, p. 145). Nyasaland, after all, was landlocked, remote, and, unlike some of its neighbors, lacked any significant mineral resources (Mkandawire, 1972, pp. 172–173; Williams, 1978, pp. 129–130). The Hilton Young Commission of 1927 looked into the idea of a Central or East African union. At a 1935 conference, Central African governors agreed that each could benefit from a closer union among their colonies (Hargreaves, 1996, p. 146). The next year, at the Victoria Falls Conference, Europeans in Nyasaland joined European representatives from Southern Rhodesia in a motion for amalgamation. Although there was no united African voice on union during the 1920s, by the early 1930s the possibility of merger among Central African colonies brought about increased political activity and a revival of their associations among Africans in Nyasaland, which resulted in less religious activity (Williams, 1978, pp. 130–131).

In two measures introduced in Nyasaland in 1933, the government gave a greater voice to traditional leaders. That was a blow to the associations, which, even though generally comprised of the educated elite, still believed that they spoke for the majority of the people. The 1933 Native Authority Ordinance recognized and gave some limited powers to traditional rulers, who as the local African authorities, could appoint subordinates and levy taxes and dues. The same year, Native Courts Ordinance established courts which would be convened by the chiefs. They were empowered to apply traditional law to Africans violating a range of non-capital offenses (Kalinga, 1998, p. 532). Government officials in Nyasaland decided to give more authority to African traditional leaders because the officials believed that the associations were gaining too much influence, status, and power. The associations that were most adversely affected by the 1933 ordinances were those in the central and northern provinces where there were more paramount chiefs than in other provinces. In the other provinces, where most of the existing associations were already weak, there was less constraint on their development. European landowners in those areas preferred the less powerful associations to the strong traditional chiefs (Williams, 1978, pp. 123–127).

With the loss of their position and recognition by colonial officials, the associations lost much of their support in the early to mid-1930s. Having languished for over a decade, the Independent Church movement was revived at that juncture. For a while, the associations were overshadowed by the surge of independent churches such as Chief Mwasi's Blackman's Church of God, Reverend Charles Chinula's *Eklesia Lanangwa* (The Christianity of Freedom), and Y.M. Mkandawire's African Reformed Presbyterian Church. Some of the men who gained prominence in these churches had previously been active in the associations. These men believed that once the associations were revived, they would return to them (Williams, 1978, p. 124). Africans in Nyasaland, as throughout the continent, experimented with participation in religious and political groups to see if membership in one or the other would give them a better chance of wresting political control from the Europeans. For them, religion was a means to an end; their ultimate goal was political independence. In any event, the associations got a boost when Africans in Nyasaland learned of the renewed interest of European administrators in a possible merger with the Rhodesias. In 1935, the Blantyre Native Association was headed by Levi Mumba, one of the first graduates of the Livingstonia Mission. He organized other associations and representatives in the southern province to write a petition, which was sent to the Colonial Office, expressing total opposition to any alliance with other British colonies. Members of the Blantyre Association circulated its minutes to other southern associations, debated regulations concerning crops and labor, petitioned for schools, and urged African political representation in the legislative council. Those activities inspired political participation among some Africans in Nyasaland (Williams, 1978, pp. 123–127). In 1938, the move for national coordination of associations was further promoted when James Frederick Sangala moved to Blantyre. Sangala agreed with Mumba's idea of consolidating the regional associations into a national organization. He became Assistant Secretary of the Blantyre Native Association and demanded educational opportunities for Africans in Nyasaland. Along with political protest, Africans saw education as another avenue for change (Williams, 1978, pp. 123–127).

A commission headed by Lord Bledisloe was set up in 1938 to investigate, again, the possibility of union in Central Africa. The Bledisloe Commission recommended that Nyasaland and Northern Rhodesia be united, and encouraged inter-territorial cooperation with Southern Rhodesia. Acknowledging that Africans in Nyasaland and Northern Rhodesia were opposed to any Central African union, the commission cautioned that

African opposition should not be taken lightly (McMaster, 1974, pp. 13–14). Many Africans in Nyasaland and Northern Rhodesia had worked in the mines and on the farms in Southern Rhodesia and South Africa. Well aware of race relations and the racial policies of ruling white settlers in both countries, the Africans had no interest in union with either one (Hargreaves, 1996, pp. 149–150; Kalinga, 1998, pp. 539–540; Mkandawire, 1992, pp. 175–178). However, the outbreak of World War II, for a time, ended the discussion of amalgamation among Europeans regarding Central Africa.

James Sangala, a Blantyre-educated government clerk, circulated a letter in October 1943, addressed to 'All Africans' living in the Nyasaland Protectorate, where he discussed the formation of an association representing Africans in Nyasaland. The Nyasaland African Association (later renamed the Nyasaland African Congress) was formed a year later and held its first meeting in Blantyre the same month. Levi Mumba, head of the Blantyre Native Association, was elected president-general of the Nyasaland African Association. Mumba, a senior government clerk, linked his political philosophy to the Christian values that he had learned at Livingstonia (Williams, 1978, pp. 126–127). So, again, there is a relationship between a leader's religious training and his political style. But what was most pronounced during that period was the fact that religion was increasingly decoupled from politics. Although Sangala was not able to attend the meeting, he was made a member of a committee. Charles Matinga,[6] Charles Wesley Mlanga, and Isaac Macdonald Lawrence, well-known   leaders in Nyasaland, were elected officers of the Nyasaland African Association (McCracken, 1998, pp. 233–234; Williams, 1978, pp. 126–127). Hastings Banda, then practicing medicine in Great Britain for almost two decades, became a life member of the association. Until his return to Nyasaland, Banda contributed financial support and advice to the group. Members of the Nyasaland African Association hoped to unite Africans in the country to fight for their progress, education, and eventual freedom. By 1953, the organization had 5,000 paid members, mostly educated men and a few women (McCracken, 1998, p. 234). In December 1944, the colonial government formally recognized that the new organization represented all of the African associations in the country. Unfortunately, within a few years of its formation the Nyasaland African Association was divided and on the verge of bankruptcy. Rivalries and antagonisms among its members had splintered the group. In addition, as the threat of a Central African union gained momentum, Africans throughout Nyasaland saw the association as impotent in stopping the union and it began to lose members (Williams, 1978, pp. 127–128).

World War II slowed the movement among Europeans for a union of British Central African colonies. Nonetheless, in the late 1940s, white settlers of the Rhodesias and Nyasaland renewed their proposal that the three territories be joined in a federation. Fearful that continuing activity by Africans in the form of political agitation could be disastrous for the white settlers, the amalgamation was an attempt to preempt the emergence of an African independence movement. Godfrey Huggins of Southern Rhodesia and Roy Welensky of Northern Rhodesia, the leading proponents of union, publicly declared that white domination would have to characterize any federation (Hargreaves, 1996, pp. 146–149; July, 1978, pp. 464–469). White settlers held a conference in 1949 at Victoria Falls to renew pressure on the British Government to seriously consider a closer association for the three aforementioned African colonies. Officials from the Central African territories and British Colonial Office met twice in 1951 to discuss the shape of the proposed union. Although those gatherings were intended to be exploratory, delegates reached a unanimous conclusion that closer association in Central Africa was imperative for continued white control. A final conference was called in London in early 1953. At that meeting the British Government expressed its concern over the possibility of a Central African union similar to the then racist Union of South Africa and accepted the idea of a federation instead (Afigbo, et. al., 1986, pp. 262–263). In September of that year, the British Parliament approved the federation. The following month the colonies of Northern Rhodesia, Southern Rhodesia, and Nyasaland were combined to form the Federation of Rhodesia and Nyasaland (Central African Federation) (Davidson, 1989, pp. 150, 156–157; Hargreaves, 1996, pp. 148–149; July, 1998, pp. 464–467; Wills, 1973, pp. 313–320). Thus, despite vigorous African opposition to federation, it was pushed through by the British Government and the white settlers.

The failure of the Nyasaland African Congress to have a real impact on federation, along with disputes over the strategy that was needed to protest the federation, resulted in a loss of support for the organization throughout the country. When the white settler-controlled Central African Federation was formed in 1953, the Nyasaland African Congress had three hundred branches. The following year the number dwindled to fifteen, with only one that remained active. Bitter disputes among its leaders and the elitist nature of its membership resulted in a sharp decline in participation in the group (Williams, 1978, pp. 161–167). In a 1957 agreement with the white federation leaders, the British Government stipulated that it was moving toward granting dominion status, and, subsequently, independence to the federation. Such a transition would strengthen white domination of these governments in Central Africa. It was not surprising that the agreement revived African political protest in Nyasaland. The Nyasaland African Congress joined the Northern Rhodesian African National Congress (founded in 1948) in staging a series of boycotts, strikes, and demonstrations. Demands by Africans in Nyasaland for greater participation in their government gained momentum after 1957. The colonial government reacted by suppressing protests, banning political parties, and imprisoning African leaders. Ironically, in spite of the threat of dominion status for the federation, the Nyasaland African Congress continued to have little mass support.

It was not until Hastings Banda returned home in 1958 and took over leadership of the organization that it gained support from the masses of Africans in Nyasaland (McMaster, 1974, pp. 20–21; Williams, 1978, pp. 175–177). Although Banda practiced medicine in Britain and, later, in Ghana for over two decades, he nonetheless kept in close touch with political developments in Nyasaland. He was convinced that any extension of power of the white settlers would have disastrous consequences for Africans (Williams, 1978, pp. 140–141). After returning to Nyasaland in 1958, Banda organized a campaign of protest which included demonstrations, strikes, and riots. After months of unrest, colonial authorities declared a State of Emergency on March 3, 1959. Banda and 208 of his supporters were arrested and detained (McMaster, 1974, p. 23). The following September the banned Nyasaland African Congress was reorganized as the Malawi Congress Party, with the jailed Banda as its leader. The name Malawi, which commemorated the 17th century *Maravi* Empire, was substituted for Nyasaland (Kalinga, 1998, p. 539). Membership in the Malawi Congress Party numbered in the thousands within two weeks of its formation (McMaster, 1974, pp. 22–23). By the time Banda was released in April 1960, a well organized mass movement had been created (Afigbo, et. al., 1986, p. 263; Kalinga, 1998, pp. 538–539; McCracken, 1998, pp. 237–238). The British

Government finally came to realize that it was futile to continue to support white minority rule over the African majority in the Central African Federation. Militant African groups were hostile to federation because they believed that the ultra-conservative white minority settlers in Southern Rhodesia had too much influence on the governments of the other two colonies in the federation. The Africans protested and finally brought down the federation (Hargreaves, 1996, pp. 215–219). As each colony in the federation came under the control of groups hostile to it, the federation lost support. Finally, it ceased to exist after December 31, 1963 (Afigbo, 1986, pp. 266–267; Shillington, 1995, pp. 393–397; McMaster, 1974, p. 30).

Religious Resistance to State Power

Following Banda's release, the British Government undertook a series of constitutional negotiations between 1960 and 1962 with African politicians in Nyasaland and Northern Rhodesia. Elections followed and the Malawi Congress Party, led by Banda, won easily. In February 1963, Nyasaland became a dominion and Banda was named prime minister. On July 6, 1964, the territory gained independence from Britain as Malawi, and Banda was elected president (July, 1998, p. 508). Two years later, the Malawi Congress Party was officially recognized as the only political party in the country. In 1971, Banda was named president-for-life (Shillington, 1995, p. 409). He instituted a dictatorship that lasted until 1994 when he lost his bid for reelection as president (Kalinga, 1998, pp. 538–539). During the Banda Administration the one-party system led to an abuse of state power, including suppression of any criticism of the government. On June 9, 1978, the country held its first parliamentary elections after independence. However, Banda required all prospective voters to take an English examination, thereby disqualifying 90 percent of the population from voting. Thus, Banda took control of parliament, and anyone who criticized him was imprisoned or expelled from the country. He crafted a one-party state system based on what he called 'law and order' and 'peace and calm', which demanded complete loyalty and obedience to him. His enemies were hunted, detained, imprisoned, exiled, and killed (Kalinga, 1998, p. 541; McCracken, 1998, 239–241).

Throughout his thirty years rule, one religious group or another faced harsh treatment by the Banda regime. Missing in his administration was the intertwining of the traditional values of morality in politics. Even on the eve of independence there were attacks on members of different religious groups in many parts of Malawi, and repression continued throughout Banda's reign. In January 1964, as Malawian citizens were registering for a referendum on independence, there were 600 reported cases of attacks on religious members. The following month that number doubled. Generally at that time the violence was confined to burning houses or crops. However, there were also instances of beating men and women (McCracken, 1998, p. 244).

Beginning in the 1960s, Banda seemed to direct his brutality to one religious group in particular: the Jehovah's Witnesses. They faced systematic and sustained violence against them that appeared to have been actively encouraged by the country's top political leadership. In accordance with their religious doctrine, Jehovah's Witnesses kept themselves detached from politics, refused to register to vote, and did not purchase party cards. Banda claimed that the church encouraged its members and other citizens in Malawi to stop paying their taxes. He accused the church of urging its members not to renew their Malawi Congress Party cards (McCracken, 1998, pp. 243–244; Williams, 1978, pp. 248–249). Banda convinced his followers that the Jehovah's Witnesses were traitors. In retaliation, Jehovah's Witnesses were assaulted by members of Banda's Malawi Congress Party, the Malawi Youth League, and the Malawi Young Pioneers. He denied to the press any association between the assaults and the refusal by Jehovah's Witnesses members to buy party cards. On the contrary, he insisted that church members were a part of 'a vicious propaganda' campaign against both himself and his government. Yet, Banda constantly ridiculed the Jehovah's Witnesses, and he eventually banned them from the country (Williams, 1978, pp. 248–249). At least eight Jehovah's Witnesses and one member of the Providence Industrial Mission (founded in 1904 by John Chilembwe) were killed in 1964. In another incident, Malawi Youth League vigilantes attacked a Providence Industrial Mission Church during a religious service, killed one member of the congregation, and severely beat several others. In two other separate cases in the Lilongwe area, five Jehovah's Witnesses were murdered by youths who appeared to have been affiliated with the Malawi Congress Party. In 1967, persecution of Jehovah's Witnesses again resumed on a large scale: they were subjected to a premeditated campaign of arson, rape, and assault (McCracken, 1998, p. 244). Considering the radical attitude that Jehovah's Witnesses had toward government, it was not surprising that Banda despised them, particularly because the group dared to speak out against him. After 1972, thousands of Jehovah's Witnesses fled Malawi when the government refused to protect them from continued attacks. Banda insisted that he had not ordered attacks against the Jehovah's Witnesses. Instead, he claimed that the Jehovah's Witnesses were the target of violence because they provoked others to break the law (Williams, 1978, pp. 248–249).

Banda continued to act as if he did not have to answer to anyone for his vicious directives. One author observed that Banda was able to benefit from his projected 'face of moderation' in directing others to carry out his repressive measures (McCracken, 1998, p. 242). Religious leaders and mission stations continued to be attacked and in some instances citizens were murdered. In 1983, at Mwanza, three ministers and a Member of Parliament were murdered. As time passed religious dissent was silenced as political opposition went underground. During his administration about 250,000 people were detained in Malawi. Amnesty International reported that more than 10,000 Malawians were tortured, killed, or vanished during Banda's rule. His human rights record was horrendous and abuses touched every family, village, district, and region in the country (Williams, 1978, pp. 248–249; Lwanda, et. al., 1998, p. 1; Meldrum, 1995, p. 57; Munthali, 1999, pp. 2–3).

Aside from the transfer of power to majority rule in South Africa, the collapse of Banda's regime was probably one of the more dramatic events in Southern Africa over the last decade. Pressure for change intensified in the late 1980s and early 1990s. Again, the protests came from religious-cum-political groups. In response, Western donors supported the protests by suspending non-humanitarian aid to Malawi in May 1992 (McCracken, 1998, pp. 231–232). The reformers joined to form a Public Affairs Committee, an umbrella of religious and political groups calling for change in Malawi. The Alliance for Democracy, chaired by Chakufwa Chihana, and the United Democratic Front, chaired by Bakili Muluzi, were formed in September 1992. Those two groups joined with the Public Affairs Committee in denouncing Banda's abuses (Munthali, 1999, p. 2).

In 1993, Banda was stripped of his title of president-for-life, ostensibly for poor health. His government finally agreed to hold an internationally supervised national referendum on the one-party system (Meldrum, 1995, p. 57). In a referendum the same year over 78 percent of the adult population voted, with 63 percent supporting a multiparty system. The referendum effectively abolished the one-party system in Malawi and paved the way for free elections. Subsequently, elections were held in May 1994 (McCracken, 1998, p. 231).

The elections of 1994 also resulted in a provisional constitution. Under the new constitution the president of the country served as the head of both the state and government; he did not control parliament, the courts, and other branches of government, as had Banda during his rule. Bakili Muluzi was elected president. He won the election with about one-third more votes than his nearest rival, Hastings Banda. Muluzi's ruling United Democratic Front formed a coalition government with nine large and small registered political parties (Meldrum, 1995, pp. 57–59). The revised constitution was finalized in May 1995 and it provided for a multiparty democracy. It curtailed the absolute powers of the president. Henceforth, the president would be elected every five years by direct universal suffrage.

In January 1999, Nevers Mumba, a Zambian Evangelist, politician, and presidential hopeful, argued that Christianity had a place in politics. Preaching at a conference in Blantyre, he asked Christians to educate their children so that politicians could not take advantage of them. He urged churches to become involved in politics because he believed that many African political leaders lacked morality. He cautioned that participation in politics had to be paramount to all African Christians. Politics, he insisted, was the future (Vokhiwa, 1999, p. 1). In contrast, meanwhile, Aleke Banda, first vice president of Malawi's ruling United Democratic Front, argued that mixing religion with politics was dangerous and only caused conflicts. Addressing delegates at the same conference, Aleke Banda cautioned that events from all over the world had demonstrated that it was dangerous to mix politics and religion, particularly in a country with many different faiths. Aleke Banda complained that some newspapers in the country were campaigning against President Muluzi, a Muslim, in the forthcoming election, and were stirring up a hate campaign against Muslims in the country. Aleke Banda rejected allegations that Muluzi was trying to Islamize Malawi. He contended that there had not been a single case of religious persecution under Muluzi's rule (Vokhiwa, 1999, pp. 1–2). As noted above for the 1999 presidential debate, the issue of the relationship between religion and political leadership continues to be debated by Southern Africans.

Conclusion

In precolonial Malawi, there was harmony between religion and politics. After all, the statesmen, chiefs and kings, were also the religious mediators and guardians of the 'spirits of the land.' Traditionally, religion and politics had played a major role in the lives of the people of Malawi; the very nature of the society linked the religious and secular worlds. Often religion was used as the justification for conflict and violent interaction between political groups. Religious loyalty and ethnic or political allegiance were inseparable; they had a collective identity. During both the precolonial and colonial periods in Nyasaland, African political and religious leaders and their institutions, along with Europeans, were in the forefront of the movement for the abolition of the slave trade, spread of Christianity, protest against the exploitation of indigenous people, and resistance to the abuse of state power. Religion played a major role in the ideology of these African political leaders because most of them had been educated in mission schools. As this case study has shown, religion could be an explosive force in relation to political leadership and state power. Furthermore, even today, the relationship between religion and politics remains unsettled in Malawi; the controversy is likely to continue in the foreseeable future.

Notes

1   The minority Europeans and Asians make up 10 percent of the population.
2   It was from Mokone's Ethiopian Church that the so-called Ethiopian movement took its name. Like the African American independent churches, first formed in the late 18th century, the African Ethiopian movement was directed against white domination. The term was really a catch-all for the rise of independent African churches that developed after 1892.
3   The African Independent Church movement was actually a number of movements which resulted in Africans forming their own churches separate from white churches. These independent churches were usually affiliated with a white denomination.
4   The phrase 'African American' is used as a synonym for 'black American' and not hyphenated throughout this essay.
5   Ethiopia held an important position amongst Africans and African Americans. First, the greatness of ancient Ethiopia was a source of pride. Second, in early classical literature Ethiopia was used synonymously with the continent of Africa. Third, Ethiopia's defeat of the Italians at the Battle of Adowa in 1896, which prevented Italy from gaining Ethiopia as a colony during the European partition of Africa, was further proof to Africans and African Americans of Africa's potential strength. Finally, the symbolic ideological and religious meaning of Ethiopia was significant. For Africans and African Americans, the Biblical quote from Psalm 68: XXXII ('Ethiopia shall soon stretch forth her hand unto God') prophesied a bright future for Africa. The interpretation of Christian Africans and African Americans of this Biblical verse reflected the role of Christian missionaries and churches in their lives. Although the successful achievements of ancient and modern-day Ethiopia was the basis of the term Ethiopianism, it did not originate in, was not associated with, and did not develop in that country. Ethiopianism was the philosophy behind the African Independent Church movement.
6   Matinga became president-general after the sudden death of Mumba in January 1945.

References

Adams, C. C. and Marshall A. Talley (1944*), Negro Baptists and Foreign Mission*, Foreign Mission Board of the National Baptist Convention: Philadelphia, PA.
Afigbo, A. E.; E. A. Ayandele; R. J. Gavin; J. D. Omer-Cooper; and R. Palmer (1986)*, The Making of Modern Africa*, Vol. 2, Longman: New York.
Ambert Cecile (1997), 'Development, the State and its Leadership in Malawi and Madagascar,' *Africa Insight*, Vol. 27, No. 1, Winter, pp. 44–53.
Davidson, Basil (1989), *Modern Africa: A Social and Political History*, 2nd ed., Longman: New York.

Du Plessis, Johannes (1917), *Thrice Through the Dark Continent: A Record of Journeyings Across Africa During the Years 1913–1916*, Longmans, Green and Co.: London.

Geiss, Imanuel (1974), *The Pan-African Movement: A History of Pan-Africanism in America, Europe and Africa*, Africana Publishing: New York.

Hargreaves, John D. (1996), *Decolonization in Africa*, 2nd ed., Longman: New York.

Jordan, Lewis Garnett (1901), *Up the Ladder in Foreign Missions*, National Baptist Publishing Board: Nashville, TN.

July, Robert (1998), *A History of the African People*, 5th ed., Waveland Press: Project Heights, IL.

Kalinga, Owen J. M. (1998), 'The Production of History in Malawi in the 1960s: The Legacy of Sir Harry Johnson, the Influence of the Society of Malawi and the Role of Dr. Kamuzu Banda and his Malawi Congress Party,' *African Affairs*, Vol. 97, No. 389, October, pp. 523–549.

Lwanda, John; Grace Phiri; and Winston Chakudika Msowoya (1998), 'Three Views of Banda,' *New African*, March 1998,
http://www.africalynx.com/icpubs/na/mar98/nacm0301.htm.

McCracken, John (1998), 'Democracy and Nationalism in Historical Perspective: The Case of Malawi,' *African Affairs*, Vol. 97, No. 387, April, pp. 231–249.

McMaster, Carolyn (1974), *Malawi: Foreign Policy and Development*, St. Martin's Press: New York.

Meldrum, Andrew (1995), 'Legacy of a Dictator,' *Africa Report*, March-April, pp. 57–59.

Mkandawire, Richard M. (1992), 'The Land Question and Agrarian Change in Malawi,' in Mbone, Guy C. Z. (ed.), *Malawi at the Crossroads: The Post-Colonial Political Economy*, SAPES Books: Harare (Zimbabwe), pp. 171–204.

Munthali, Makhumbira (1999), 'Malawi's Human Rights Record,' http://www.math.unh.edu/~llk/hmnrts.html.

Neufeld, Don F. (1966), *Seventh-Day Adventist Encyclopedia*, Herald Publishing Association: Washington, D.C.

Phiri, Kings M. (1982), 'Afro-American Influence in Colonial Malawi, 1895–1945: A Case Study Of the Interaction Between Africa and Africans of the Diaspora,' in Harris, Joseph E. (ed.), *Global Dimensions of the African Diaspora*, Howard University Press: Washington, D.C., pp. 250–267.

Roome, William J. W. (1926), *A Great Emancipation: A Missionary Survey of Nyasaland, Central Africa*, World Dominion Press: London.

Rotberg, Robert I. (ed.) (1967), *Strike a Blow and Die: A Narrative of Race Relations in Colonial Africa by George Simeon Mwase*, Harvard University Press: Cambridge, MA.

Shepperson, George and Thomas Price (1958), *Independent African: John Chilembwe and the Origins, Setting and Significance of the Nyasaland Native Rising in 1915*, University Press: Edinburgh (United Kingdom).

Shillington, Kevin (1995), *History of Africa*, rev. ed, St. Martin's Press: New York.

Vokhiwa, Hamilton (1999), 'Malawi Offers Two Faces of Christianity and Politics,' *Africa News Online*, January 11,
http://www.org/south/malawi/stories/19990111_feat1.html.

Weisbord, Robert G. (1973), *Ebony Kinship: Africa, Africans and the Afro-American*, Greenwood Press: Westport, CT.

Williams, T. David (1978), *Malawi, the Politics of Despair*, Cornell University Press: Ithaca, NY.

Wills, A. J. (1973), *An Introduction to the History of Central Africa*, 3rd ed., Oxford University Press: London.

5 Israel: Synagogue, the State, and Politics

BERNARD REICH and GERSHON R. KIEVAL

The crux of the synagogue-state relationship, or religion and politics, in modern day Israel—indeed throughout the state's history—is the relationship between the religious (or Orthodox) and secular segments of the population. This relationship manifests itself in numerous ways today that range from closing a street in a religious neighborhood on the *Sabbath* (Jewish holy day) to military deferments for *yeshiva* (religious seminary) students. In Israel, these and a host of other issues have divided the population between secular and religious Jews. These issues have generated riots and demonstrations, political voting patterns, differences over legislation in parliament, and violence. In the final analysis, it is a question of interpreting the meaning of the concept 'Jewish' in the Jewish state and defining 'who is a Jew.' Thus, the controversy concerns the role of religious forces and movements within the state.

Despite perceptions to the contrary, Israel's Jewish population is only simplistically divided into Orthodox and secular Jews. And for most analyses of Israel this almost suffices. In fact, Israel's Jews comprise four categories. In addition to *hiloniim* (secular Jews), the non-secular Jews divide into three subgroups: *haredim* (ultra-Orthodox); *datiim* (religious Zionists); and *masortiim* (traditional Jews). Based on various studies and analyses, it is generally estimated that the secular-religious divide is about 80 percent to 20 percent. However, if one focuses on the further division within the non-secular group, the proportions vary most interestingly. Some eight percent are *haredim*, 17 percent *datiim*, and 55 percent are *masortiim* (Reich and Kieval, 1993, p. 10). The Jewish population is composed of immigrants from numerous countries and reflects a variety of ethnic and linguistic groups, religious preferences, and cultural, historical, and political backgrounds. The dispersion of the Jews had led to the creation of numerous communities located throughout the Diaspora,[1] each of which was influenced by those local customs integrated into its religious rituals and practice. Each community developed diverse institutions, customs, languages, physical traits, and traditions. These were transferred to Israel with their communities when they emigrated.

The Debate

The debate between secular and religious perspectives has been a continuing characteristic of Israel. It has, in fact, been played continuously in the political process, the creation of political parties, and competition for cabinet posts and influence on government policy. The debate was foreshadowed in the drafting of the Declaration of Independence, which not only recalled the religious and spiritual connection of the Jewish people to the land of Israel, but also guaranteed Israel's citizens 'freedom of religion and conscience.' Also, the conflict was the cause of substantial debate during consideration of the proposed constitution. One faction insisted on the primacy and enshrinement of Jewish religious values while the other sought to focus on more secular themes, thus limiting the role of religion in the state (Reich and Kieval, 1993, p. 20). The religious issue has its origins in the Zionist political goal of establishing a Jewish state. The Jewish return to the Holy Land was seen by religious Zionists as a divine pledge, but the ultra-Orthodox opposed the notion of a Jewish state established by people and wanted to await the coming of the messiah. At the same time, there were other anti-Zionists, including some Reform[2] Jews who did not wish Judaism to be bound up with Jewish nationalism. Opposition to the creation of a Jewish state became academic after Israel's independence but continued to be expressed by small—but vocal—fringe groups at both ends of the religious spectrum. Reform opposition all but disappeared, with some exception.[3] Although concerned about the power and role of the Orthodox leadership in religious affairs within Israel, the Reform movement has been increasingly identified with the strongest Jewish supporters of Israel. Opposition within the ranks of the Orthodox dwindled, and the remaining high-profile group, consisting of several hundred families, is the *Neturei Karta* (Guardians of the City) located in Jerusalem and in Brooklyn, New York. That group challenges the legitimacy of the state, expresses support for the Palestine Liberation Organization, and continues in its refusal to recognize the authority of the state or deal with it in any meaningful way.

The role of religion in Israel and the relationship between religious institutions and the state continues to be an intensely emotional issue that deeply divides the population and affects many and diverse aspects of Israeli life. Whereas there are polarized extreme positions, including advocacy of total links as well as total separation between religion and the state, most Israeli Jews are prepared to accept some linkage between synagogue and the state if only because of a perceived necessity to do so. The various views are strongly held, but all parties have accepted a working arrangement that has prevented major clashes and reflects the reality of the situation as it developed in the period prior to independence. This arrangement has its basis in the so-called status quo agreement worked out by David Ben-Gurion, leader of the Jewish community in Palestine and the first prime minister of Israel, on the eve of Israel's independence. It retained the situation as it had existed upon independence: individuals would be free to pursue their religious practices in private as they saw fit, but public matters would be frozen with what prevailed before statehood. According to this agreement, the *Sabbath* and *kashrut* (Jewish dietary laws) were to be officially observed in the state, religious authorities would oversee marriage and divorce, and the ultra-Orthodox would maintain an independent educational system. Ben-Gurion later agreed that students in *yeshivot* (religious seminaries) would be exempt from military service. There were only a few hundred such students when the agreement was made; today there are around 30,000. Ben-Gurion's rationale for the religious compromise that was agreed to was the need for widespread Jewish support for the government to carry out the daunting tasks ahead facing the new and beleaguered Jewish state. To obtain the broadest political support for the essential policies and programs to establish and advance the Jewish state, he was prepared to make concessions on issues that he considered to be of a minor or subsidiary nature (Ben-Gurion, 1970, p. 218). Thus, in Ben-Gurion's view, and as adopted in Israeli practice, *kosher* (ritually killed and prepared) food might be a secondary matter for the secular Jew, but it was of paramount importance to the religious Jew. The Jewish state could not force an Orthodox segment (however small) of the population to concede on a matter of central concern, but the secular majority could concede on these issues of lesser importance to them.

This arrangement continued during the millet system used by the Turks when the Ottoman Empire controlled Palestine. Under this plan, the various non-Muslim religious communities were allowed substantial autonomy to govern themselves through their own communal council, in accordance with their own canon law, and under the jurisdiction and control of their ecclesiastical authorities. The system was retained, with alterations, during the British Mandate of Palestine. At that time, the several non-Muslim religious communities organized their affairs under the leadership of their chosen religious functionaries. Thus, the Jewish community remains organized today with two chief rabbis (one *Sephardi*, Oriental Jew, and one *Ashkenazi*, European Jew), rabbinical courts, and related institutions. Similarly, Jewish religious courts were granted jurisdiction over matters of personal status (marriage, divorce, and alimony). Today, these courts and other religious institutions of the state recognize only the Orthodox Jewish approach and interpretation of *halachah* (Jewish law). Although there are non-Orthodox congregations, institutions, and rabbis in Israel, Conservative and Reform rabbis and organizations have been denied any real role in the religious system. Israel utilizes a similar procedure for its non-Jewish religious communities. The religious authorities of each non-Jewish community (Christian, Druze,[4] and Muslim) exercise jurisdiction in litigation involving personal status and family law (marriage, divorce, alimony, and inheritance) and apply religious codes and principles in their own judicial institutions. Various matters that are secular concerns in other states are within the purview of religious authorities in Israel. Even though there is no established religion, all religious institutions have a special status and authority granted by the state and, to a substantial degree, are supported by state funds. The secular government takes into account the requisites of the segment of the population that observes religious tradition. Religious institutions receive government funding, and the public school system includes religious schools receiving state support. Laws pertaining to the *Sabbath* and Jewish dietary requirements are part of the state's legal system.

The ministry of religious affairs has primary responsibility for meeting Jewish religious requirements, such as the supply of *kosher* meat, for rabbinical courts and *yeshivot* as well as for the autonomous religious needs of the non-Jewish communities. These functions are noncontroversial; few dispute the duty to meet the religious requirements of the people. Nevertheless, a subject of sharp and recurrent dispute is the extent to which religious observance or restriction is directly or indirectly imposed on the entire population. The observant community, which faithfully follows the laws and rules of the Orthodox Jewish tradition, through its political movements and parties as well as membership in government coalitions, has been able to achieve government agreement for the establishment of separate school systems, exemption of observant girls from military service upon application, curtailing of business and public activity on the *Sabbath* (subject to limited local exception), and limitations of the role of non-Orthodox Judaism in Israel. Those who are less observant of traditional Judaism often argue that they do not have full religious freedom and are subject to religious coercion because of governmental acquiescence to the demands of the observant Jewish groups. Historically, the religious parties have been able to secure concessions because the need for coalition governments has given them a larger voice in politics than is dictated by their strict numerical strength. This reality has necessitated inclusion of the political parties of the religious community as coalition partners in virtually all cabinets. Generally they have had control of the ministry of religious affairs and the ministry of the interior. This has given the religious parties substantial political power and, thus, an ability to enforce many of their demands and perspectives concerning the role of religion in the Jewish state.

Despite religious party participation in the parliament and cabinet, there have been government crises over religious questions, most notably, the question of 'who is a Jew?' Jews have special positions under the 1950 Law of Return[5] and 1952 Nationality Law, but the term was not defined in either piece of legislation. During the country's early years, when there was a special effort to encourage immigration, David Ben-Gurion, who was then the prime minister, encouraged a broad and liberal interpretation of who is a Jew, essentially permitting each individual to decide. The Orthodox leadership, on the other hand, sought to restrict Jewish identification and ensure its conformity with Orthodox doctrine as determined by traditional Orthodox authorities. Thus, the only person who could be Jewish, according to that perspective, was one who met the requirements of Jewish law, which stipulated that an individual was a Jew only if born to a Jewish mother or converted to Judaism by an accepted Orthodox authority. Over time, a number of celebrated instances have arisen relating to the question of who is a Jew. In 1958, the issue became one of considerable significance and generated a major controversy when the National Religious Party withdrew from the coalition government because it opposed the cabinet's definition of 'Jew' in connection with the issuance of new identity cards for Israeli citizens. The *Knesset* (Israeli parliament) debated the matter, but later it was postponed. Other prominent cases have included the *Brother Daniel case* (1962); the status of the Falashas of Ethiopia; the status of the Bene Israel of India; and the *Shalit case* (1970). On those and other instances the focus has been on a particular aspect of the broader problem, but the issue has not been resolved. Those episodes have strained relations not only between the various factions within Israel, but also between Israel and some of its Jewish supporters abroad. There has been discord over other religious questions such as the religious education of children in immigration camps, compulsory military service for women, and the question of uniform national education. More recently, the issues have involved the matter of conversion, introduction of daylight saving time, permissible activities on the *Sabbath*, and draft deferments for *yeshiva* students.

After Israel took control of East Jerusalem in 1967, a controversy developed with regard to the status of the Western (Wailing) Wall and the nearby areas where the Temple of Solomon once stood. Although there was agreement that the locality was among the holiest of Jewish sites, there were differing perspectives concerning its treatment. In 1976, it was a religious issue—a no-confidence motion in the *Knesset* based on the charge that a government-organized ceremony precipitated violation of the *Sabbath* since those attending would be forced to travel on the *Sabbath*—that ultimately led to the resignation of the Rabin Government, call for new elections, and succession of the Likud party under the leadership of Menachem Begin.

The Religious Right

The religious-secular debate has increasingly been played out in the political process and expressed in the formation and dissolution of political parties. Only in 1999 was there a secular party that specifically targeted only the secular factor in the debate. In contrast, parties with a religious orientation have played a major role in the debate and, hence, in Israel's political life. These religious political parties are a direct response to the emergence of political Zionism at the end of the 19th century, and a point of difference among them has been their perspectives on Zionism. In the ultra-Orthodox camp were those who denied the basic validity of the Zionist idea on the grounds that it contradicted the traditional conception of divine redemption of the Jewish people. Nevertheless, some who opposed Zionism as a secular nationalism encouraged Jews to settle in Israel as a means of fulfilling a religious obligation. As historical developments[6] made the idea of a Jewish state more logical, many of the ultra-Orthodox who continued to oppose Zionism began to recognize the importance of both Jewish settlement in Israel and of the state of Israel itself to the survival of the Jewish people. The religious Zionists took an alternative approach. Although there were (and are) exceptions, they tended to see Zionism as a solution to the problems faced by Jews in the Diaspora and the first stage in the messianic process. Thus, Israel's independence was, in their view, the beginning of redemption, and the process became religiously significant.

The above approach was reinforced by Israel's victories in the 1967 Six Day War and spawned movements such as *Gush Emunim* (Bloc of the Faithful), which linked Israel's accomplishments with both religious concepts and Zionist ideals. During the first four decades of Israel's statehood, *Miflaga Datit Leumit* (National Religious Party, MAFDAL or NRP) and *Agudat Yisrael* (or *Agudat Israel*, Association of Israel) were at the core. Their centrality has been overtaken in recent years by the relative political newcomer, *Sephardi Torah Guardians* (SHAS). Like *Agudat Israel*, SHAS is an ultra-Orthodox party. Only in the First *Knesset*, however, did the religious parties run as a single bloc—the United Religious Front—which gained 16 seats.

In contrast to *Agudat Israel*, the NRP has participated within the mainstream of Jewish life and the activities of the state since Israel's independence. Consequently, it has wielded substantial political power. It has been a member of every Israeli Government except that of Prime Minister Yitzhak Rabin in 1974 and, during his second term as premier, in 1992. The NRP was founded in 1956 by *Mizrahi* (Spiritual Center) and *Hapoel Hamizrahi* (Workers of the Spiritual Center) as a religious party seeking to combine religious concerns and a moderate socialist orientation in economic matters within a Zionist framework. The NRP's origins lie in the prestate period. Although its central concept can be identified as early as the 1880s, *Mizrachi* came into being in 1902. The founders of the movement did not see a contradiction between Judaism and Zionism. After independence, the NRP became a significant partner in Israel's governments, securing concessions on religious matters in exchange for support on matters of greater importance to the prime minister, such as foreign and defense issues.

Agudat Israel (henceforth, *Aguda*) focuses its attention on the religious nature of the state and seeks to have Israel function in accordance with the principal of the Torah. It is a religiously oriented political party representing the interests of a section of Orthodox Jewry living both within and outside the Jewish state. The *Aguda* was formally established, and its policies and programs were delineated, in 1912 in *Kattowitz* (Katowice), Poland, during a conference of the major East European, German, and Austro-Hungarian Orthodox rabbis. The *Aguda* was to be a Torah movement directed by *Moetzet Gedolei Hatorah* (Council of Torah Sages), which was to be the supreme authority in all matters. The Council, instituted in the 1920s, is a group of rabbinical scholars who represent the various factions of the *Aguda* movement and are chosen for their scholarly merit and prestige in the realm of Orthodox Jewry. *Moetzet Gedolei Hatorah* continues to be the supreme decision-making body for *Aguda* adherents and its decisions are sovereign in all questions affecting the membership, including religious and political matters such as joining or remaining in a government coalition. This authority is derived from the personal standing and reputation of the members of the Council, who have been viewed with high esteem by members of *Aguda*. Even though the *Aguda* initially opposed Zionism as religiously unacceptable (a position similar to that of *Neturei Karta* today), in the 1930s and 1940s *Aguda* cooperated with the Jewish Agency and other bodies of the *yishuv* in several clearly and specifically defined areas. That stemmed from purely pragmatic considerations based on the reality of the prevailing situation, particularly the rise of Nazi Germany, widespread European anti-Semitism, and the understanding that the Holocaust required some mechanism to save the persecuted and threatened Jews of Europe. Ultimately, *Aguda* gave partial backing to the Zionist endeavor when it supported the establishment of Israel and participated in the institutions of the new state. It joined the provisional Council of State and was represented in Israel's first cabinet. The decision to move into the mainstream of Israeli politics led to a split within the *Aguda*, with its more conservative elements rallying around Satmar Rebbe who opposed Zionism and formed the *Neturei Karta*.

Aguda did not participate in any government from 1952, when it resigned from the Labor-led coalition, to 1977, when it joined the government formed by Menachem Begin. During that period it neither displayed hostility to Israel nor consistently opposed the state's actions, though it generally did not concur with the government. There were elements within the *Aguda* whose attitudes were similar to those of the *Neturei Karta* and who refused to cooperate in any way or engage in dialogue with other groups in Israeli society. The *Aguda* still does not belong to the Zionist organization, but this is primarily a voice against that organization's secular bias, not opposition to Israel. The *Aguda* supports the state and participates in its institutions without necessarily accepting all of its policies or particular ideologies. It does not link Israel with the Biblical promise of redemption. Rather, it supports Israel because of a pragmatic perspective that sees the state as vitally important to the survival of the Jewish people because of worldwide conditions. Opposition to and complaints about the secular nature of Israel's political and social system remain a very significant part of the *Aguda* approach even while it supports the state as a necessity. At the same time, *aliyah* (immigration) must be encouraged for religious and practical reasons though no 'holy' role is assigned to the state. Throughout its political involvement, the *Aguda* has been motivated by its desire to ensure that no legislation would harm Orthodox interests and its religious and educational institutions would receive maximum support from the government. The *Aguda* has sought to secure expansion of Torah institutions and Jewish law within the political system. It has focused it attention on such issues as financial support for various religious institutions, education, and schools. Also, it worked on extending the religious perspective into essentially secular realms such as military service for females and the question of 'who is a Jew,' which gets to the core of the Orthodox viewpoint and perspective. To achieve its goals, the *Aguda* was prepared to support governing coalitions despite often times uneasy alliances. Finally, in 1977, with the coming to power of Likud, it found a less uneasy partner and was able to gain more from the Begin Administration than under the previous Labor governments.

There are two major differences between the *Aguda* and the NRP. Many observers stress that NRP members tend to be more modern than *Aguda* members. That distinction, which others question, is overshadowed by the differences in perspective concerning the relationship between Zionism and a secular society. The *Aguda* focuses more on the rejection of modern secular culture or its acceptance only within the closed framework of Jewish life and society. In contrast, the NRP adherents accept modernization and participation in broader aspects of Jewish society and culture. Division within the ranks of the religious movements have become more pronounced in recent years, eclipsing the NRP-*Aguda* split. Numerous factions, each with its own leadership and agenda, compete to secure loyalty, votes, programs, and political patronage.

In the 1981 election, the issue of ethnic representation led to the creation of *Tenuah LeMassoret Yisrael* (Movement for Jewish Tradition, TAMI), an offshoot of the NRP, formed as a North African-oriented religious party. The new list won three *Knesset* seats in that election, drawing support from the Oriental community. The TAMI seats appeared to have a major impact on the NRP, which saw its *Knesset* strength cut in half from twelve to six seats. TAMI's political fortunes, however, declined steadily thereafter. In the 1984 election, TAMI won only one seat. In 1988, the party's leader was coopted into Likud, ending TAMI's independent existence. The NRP further splintered in 1984, when the party's right-wing *Matzad* faction broke away and joined with two independent right-wing *Knesset* members to form the *Morasha* (Heritage) party. *Morasha* won two seats in the 1984 election; the NRP again lost ground, falling to four *Knesset* seats. *Morasha*, however, collapsed in 1988 when *Matzad* left to rejoin the NRP. The reintegration of the right-wing *Matzad* faction strengthened the nationalist tendencies within the NRP, and changes within the party leadership also contributed to the NRP's rightward shift. The NRP's new leadership was committed to retaining the occupied territories and took a less conciliatory position on domestic religious issues, particularly the question of changing the Law of Return to recognize only Orthodox conversions. Even though the NRP suffered a small additional percentage loss in the popular vote in the 1988 election, it managed to secure five parliamentary mandates. In the June 1992 election, the NRP won six seats, a slight increase from its previous standing. The party's campaign strongly identified with the political right wing—and implicitly with Likud—which virtually ruled out any chance that NRP leaders would be able to maneuver after the election to join the new Labor coalition under Prime Minister Yitzhak Rabin. The NRP fared significantly better in the 1996 election, winning nine seats. The party's platform called for applying Israeli sovereignty over greater Jerusalem, including the *Gush Etzion* settlement bloc and the settlements of *Ma'ale Adumim* and *Givat Ze'ev*. Furthermore, it favored strengthening Jewish settlements throughout the West Bank, including Hebron, and retaining all of the Golan Heights.

In response to the NRP's rightward trend, party doves left in 1988 and formed the *Meimad* (Dimension, the religious-center camp) party under the leadership of the head of the *Hesder yeshivot*, which combines religious and military training. *Meimad* fell about 7,000 votes short of the one percent threshold for attaining a seat in the 1988 election. Although *Meimad* did not compete in subsequent elections, it remained a political movement. In 1999, it joined with Labor and the centrist *Gesher* party to form the One Israel electoral alliance under the leadership of Ehud Barak.

The ultra-Orthodox *Aguda* also underwent some splintering. In 1984, the former *Sephardi* Chief Rabbi Ovadia Yosef and other *Sephardi* rabbis decided to leave the *Ashkenazi*-dominated *Aguda* and set up SHAS after *Aguda* leaders refused to place enough *Sephardi* candidates on the party's list for the 1984 election. Eliezer Schach, a Lithuanian-born (and *Ashkenazi*) rabbi and leader of *misnagdim* (non-Hasidic elements) within *Aguda*, helped to engineer the creation of SHAS. Schach was troubled by the influence of *Aguda's Hasidic* trends over its *Sephardi* followers and thought the formation of a separate *Sephardi* ultra-Orthodox party would force *Aguda's Hasidic* leadership to pay more attention to the party's non-*Hasidic* members. SHAS won four *Knesset* seats in 1984; *Aguda* won only two (a loss of two seats from the 1981 election). SHAS's strength increased to six *Knesset* seats in the 1988 election. The party's success was largely the result of its participation in the previous national unity government. SHAS controlled the interior ministry—traditionally the bastion of the NRP—which enabled it to channel funds through local governments in providing services to its constituency of *haredi Sephardi* Jews, whose share of the population was growing rapidly. Also, SHAS exploited the *Sephardi-Ashkenazi* split, stressing in its platform the restoration of Oriental culture to a position of prominence in Israeli society. Furthermore, the party benefitted from having as its spiritual mentor former *Sephardi* Chief Rabbi Ovadia Yosef, who was popular even among non-Orthodox Orientals. SHAS's success among non-Orthodox Orientals in the 1988 election was underscored in survey results that indicated that the party was favored to win as much as 16 percent of the votes in *Sephardi*-dominated towns, which had previously voted overwhelmingly for Likud.

The *Aguda* was again split in 1988. This time, Rabbi Eliezer Schach, who had helped to engineer the creation of SHAS four years earlier, left *Aguda* with his followers over what he saw was the growing influence within the party of the Lubavitch *Hasidic* sect and its leader, Brooklyn-based Rabbi Menachem M. Schneerson. So, on the eve of the 1988 election, Schach formed the rival ultra-Orthodox party *Degel HaTorah* (Flag of the Torah). This development led Schneerson to mobilize his followers to vote for *Aguda*, and his efforts were largely responsible for *Aguda's* success at the polls. It secured nearly three times the number of votes it had in 1984 and increased its *Knesset* seats from two to five. *Degel HaTorah* won two seats. *Degel HaTorah* was all but negotiated out of existence prior to the June 1992 election when Rabbi Schach agreed that the party join *Aguda* in a unified election list called United Torah Judaism. Also joining the bloc was a small break-away party from SHAS, the *Moriah* party. Schach accepted the fifth and seventh spots on the joint list for his *Degel HaTorah* representatives. Compared to the seven seats that the three constituent groups had held in the outgoing *Knesset*, the new electoral alliance won only four seats in the election. The *Moriah* party representative, who had the number-two slot on the party list, was forced by a preelection promise to resign his seat in order to allow *Degel HaTorah* to take up the party's fourth and final seat in the new *Knesset*. United Torah Judaism retained its four *Knesset* seats in the 1996 election, but it was the only religious party that failed to increase is representation in parliament. The party solidly supported Likud leader Benjamin Netanyahu in his bid to become prime minister, heeding the injunction of *Aguda's Moetzet Gedolei Hatorah* to vote for the candidate who would be more likely to adhere to the spirit and tradition of Judaism. Clearly that was an anti-Peres message.

In contrast to United Torah Judaism's poor showing in the 1992 election, SHAS gained votes. However, SHAS did not manage to increase its *Knesset* representation beyond the six seats it already held. During the election campaign, the party's advertisements and statements by its leaders strongly suggested that SHAS intended to throw its lot only with a Likud-led government. When it became clear, however, that Labor had emerged as the leading vote getter in the election and would be in a position to block a Likud-led coalition, SHAS leaders reconsidered their options and eventually decided to join the new government headed by Yitzhak Rabin. SHAS made significant gains in the 1996 election, increasing its seats in the *Knesset* to nine and confounding the pre-election predictions of pollsters. The party continued to stress to its constituents a combination of ethnic pride and traditional values to compensate for the sense of cultural alienation felt by many of them. Also, SHAS exploited the strong mystical tendencies among potential SHAS voters, distributing 150,000 amulets blessed by the elderly mystic Rabbi Yitzhak Kadourie. In addition, it continued to benefit from having as its spiritual mentor the former *Sephardi* Chief Rabbi Ovadia Yosef, who remained popular among non-Orthodox Orientals. In the prime minister's race, the party's leaders refused to back either Likud leader Benjamin Netanyahu or Labor counterpart Shimon Peres and allowed their followers to vote for either candidate. That way, Yosef left all options open for joining either a Likud- or Labor-led coalition afterwards.

Despite their areas of discord, the religious parties have a major common denominator: the effort to represent the interests of Israel's Orthodox community. They share a loyalty to traditional religious Judaism and realize the need to organize and mobilize the religious community to prevent secular intrusion in the religious domain. Also, they are determined to ensure the perpetuation of religious values and lifestyles in Israel. Partly because of these concerns, the parties have created communal and educational frameworks to draw together those Jews who are faithful to the Orthodox perspective. They may differ in their approaches to secular society and views of Zionism, but they agree that there must be no contradiction of *halachah* and Orthodox religious interests must be preserved and enhanced.

The 1999 Elections

The depth of the religious-secular schism in Israeli society and politics was vividly displayed in the issues and events surrounding the May 1999 elections and in the results of the ballots. Secular and ultra-Orthodox Israelis alike approached the vote with a strong sense of dissatisfaction with the 'status quo' on religious issues; all segments of the population felt that they were losing ground. On the one hand, the non-religious feared that the growing power of the ultra-Orthodox was eroding the democratic and pluralistic foundations of the state. On the other hand, the ultra-Orthodox believed that the secular culture in Israel was morally corrupt and threatened to displace the state's Jewish character. At the extreme margins in each camp there was a strong feeling that it was either 'them or us,' and there was no real discussion of trying to forge a new consensus on the key issues of conversion ('Who is a Jew?'), marriage, the military draft, observance of the *Sabbath*, and state funding for education.

Several recent decisions of Israeli courts set the tone for the religious-secular debate in the campaign. In December 1998, The High Court of Justice (Israel's highest judicial body), in an expanded bench of 11 justices, rejected the then current situation whereby policy on deferments from military service for *yeshiva* students is set by the minister of defense. It ruled that the *Knesset* must regularize the situation within one year. If the *Knesset* failed to act within a year, however, *yeshiva* students would be subject to conscription. The High Court argued that it is a major social issue as it often leads to an entire sector of the population being dependent on state funding and private charity because they cannot work in order to obtain a deferment. Shortly after the High Court's decision on military deferments for *yeshiva* students, the Chief Judge of the Jerusalem District Court ordered the Israeli Government to accept and register as Jews individuals who had been converted to Judaism by Reform or Conservative rabbis. Then in March 1999, Aryeh Deri—the leader of SHAS—was convicted in the Jerusalem District Court on charges of bribery, fraud, and breach of trust when he was a government minister in the late 1980s. As a result of these decisions, the *haredi* community engaged in a battle against the High Court and issued vitriolic attacks against High Court judges. The decisions were labeled 'anti-Semitic' and the Chief Justice was called an enemy of the Jews. SHAS's Rabbi Ovadia Yosef called the judges various names utilizing Jewish epithets for non-observant Jews. Menachem Porush, the leader of the rival United Torah Judaism party, threatened rebellion if the Court did not refrain from interfering in matters of religion. To the Orthodox Jews, it was a campaign against Judaism and the Jewish heritage. Orthodox Jews and their leaders believe the courts are interfering in religious affairs by ruling on matters that the Orthodox believe should be determined by Jewish law. In February 1999, the rhetoric sparked an estimated quarter of a million ultra-Orthodox individuals to attend a prayer vigil and protest rally in Jerusalem against the High Court's involvement in religious issues. At the same time, tens of thousands of secular Israelis gathered in another part of the city in support of the High Court.

Although SHAS had no official election platform in 1999, the party's leaders stressed throughout the campaign that they opposed both religious and secular coercion. Nevertheless, they insisted that Israel's Jewish character be preserved, businesses not be permitted to operate on the *Sabbath*, and *yeshiva* students be encouraged to continue to study rather than serve in the army (http://www.jpost.co.il/Info/Elections99/Platform /platform.html, 29 May 1999). SHAS also championed the cause of its embattled leader, Aryeh Deri, exacerbating deep feelings of resentment among *Sephardim*, stemming from perceived mistreatment by the secular *Ashkenazim* during Israel's early years. It distributed a video claiming that Deri was framed. Also, it created campaign commercials that celebrated *Sephardic* culture and accused Israel's Russian immigrants of harboring prostitutes and thieves. The NRP said it wanted to see the role of the chief rabbinate strengthened as the supreme authority on *halachah.* Furthermore, it advocated the passage of new laws to encourage the observance of *kashrut* and prevent the sale of non-*kosher* food. The party urged that the Law of Return be amended to define a Jew as one born to a Jewish mother or converted according to *halachah*. In addition, it maintained that army service is a *halachic* obligation for all Israelis (http://www.jpost. co.il/Info/Elections99/Platform/ platform. html, 29 May 1999). United Torah Judaism campaigned on the pledge to oppose both army service for students in *yeshivot* and the issuance of work permits for the *Sabbath* and festivals. It also said that it opposed recognition of and activities by the Reform and Conservative movements in Israel. In addition, it promised to push for amending the Law of Return to limit the definition of who is a Jew to *halachah* (http://www.jpost.co.il/Info/Elections99/Platform/platform. html, 29 May 1999).

On the other side of the political spectrum, Meretz and *Shinui* (Change) took up the banner for a secular Israel. Yosef (Tommy) Lapid, the leader of *Shinui*, in particular conducted a no-holds barred campaign against the ultra-Orthodox. He accused the *haredim* of being 'wheeler-dealers' who use political manipulations to try and split the people of Israel in opening the door to 'Khomeinism' and loss of liberty. Lapid pledged that, if elected to the *Knesset*, he would not join a government that included SHAS (http://shinui.org.il/matza-eng.html, 29 May 1999). Meretz's position on religious-secular issues was slightly less extreme that *Shinui's*. Meretz leaders said that they would work to ensure that religion and politics would remain separate as would religious and state institutions. Citizenship, under the Law of Return, would be granted to anyone declaring in good faith that they are Jewish. Conservative and Reform conversions would be recognized, and civil marriages and divorces would be permitted. The party also advocated that public services, including transportation, would operate on the *Sabbath*. Furthermore, it said that *yeshiva* students should be drafted while taking into consideration their conditions of study and needs of the Israeli Defense Force (http://www.jpost.co.il/Info/Elections99/Platform/ platform.html, 29 May 1999).

The religious parties together fared better than Meretz and *Shinui* in the May 1999 elections, largely due to the success of SHAS. The religious parties won 27 seats, an increase of five over their total in the Fourteenth *Knesset*. SHAS alone gained 17 seats (an increase of seven) and, in the process, was transformed from a medium-sized party to the third largest in the *Knesset*.[7] United Torah Judaism won five seats (an increase of one), but the NRP lost four seats, winning only five in the Fifteenth *Knesset*. Meretz held its own in the ballots, increasing its *Knesset* representation from nine to ten seats. The results for *Shinui* represented a major victory for a party that was on the verge of extinction until Lapid agreed to take the helm and lead it into the election. The party's success in the election could be attributed to a backlash against SHAS and the resentment many secular Israeli Jews felt towards the massive government funding of SHAS's and the other ultra-Orthodox welfare programs.

SHAS's success at the polls complicated Ehud Barak's prospects for forming a governing coalition. Upon his victory Prime Minister-Elect Barak declared that he wanted to form a broad-based coalition, presumably including Likud and SHAS. That would give him a sufficiently large base in parliament to pursue peace negotiations with the Palestinians and Syria. And such a coalition would not allow any single faction to threaten to bring down the government. Likud had little leverage to bargain with Barak other than to try to exploit that desire for a broad-based government. SHAS, in contrast, was in a slightly stronger position owing to its new-found position as the third largest group in the new parliament and as the dominant religious party. However, it first had to resolve the issue of Aryeh Deri's status as party leader since Barak insisted that Deri resign as a condition for including SHAS in his government. Deri quit as the leader of SHAS one month after the election, thereby clearing one hurdle for the inclusion of SHAS in the new coalition. But there were still significant policy differences between SHAS and Barak's One Israel that had to be overcome, including the question of military deferments for *yeshiva* students and funding for SHAS's educational network and welfare projects. In addition, there was the matter of the allocation of ministerial portfolios. SHAS demanded four cabinet posts, including that of the minister of interior, but that position had already been promised by Barak to Natan Sharansky, leader of the Russian immigrant party

Yisrael Ba'aliyah[8] (Israel for Immigration). SHAS held that portfolio in the outgoing government of Prime Minister Benjamin Netanyahu and was accused by Sharansky and other Russian immigrant leaders of using the post to slow down the immigration of people from the former Soviet Union, whose Jewishness was questioned by SHAS leaders.

Barak required almost the entire 45-day period allotted by law to form his governing coalition. In the end, he managed to construct a broad coalition of 75 deputies in which there was considerable representation for the ultra-Orthodox and religious segment of the population. The new government included SHAS—but not Likud—as well as the other two religious parties, the NRP and United Torah Judaism. SHAS received four portfolios as it had demanded, but not the ministry of interior. That went to Sharansky. Nor did any of the religious parties receive the ministry of education. That position went to Meretz and its head, Yossi Sarid. The February 2001 elections turned yet another leaf in Israeli politics. As the new Prime Minister-Elect Ariel Sharon forms his coalition government, it remains to be seen how he handles the religious-secular dynamics in Israeli society.

Conclusion

Ehud Barak's decision not to give the education and interior ministries to the religious parties underscored his determination to create a new balance in the government between religious and secular interests. The policy guidelines of the new government papered over the fundamental differences between the secular and religious sectors that dominated much of the election campaign. They called for the need to design an 'appropriate' solution for the relationship between religion and the state through dialogue, grounded in consensus and mutual tolerance (http://www.israel-mfa.gov.il, 7 July 1999). Also, they affirmed the validity of the Supreme Court rulings on the matter of military deferments for *yeshiva* students and call for the passage of *Knesset* legislation in accordance with those rulings.[9] The religious parties, by accepting secular control of the education and interior ministries and recognizing that Aryeh Deri could not remain as the party leader, appear to have accommodated to the new political dynamics in the wake of the May 1999 elections. Special allocations to the ultra-Orthodox sector would not end completely, but their political leverage was circumscribed. And if they needed to be reminded of this, *Shinui's* Tommy Lapid—who remained true to his campaign pledge not to sit in a government alongside SHAS—promised to remain focused on stopping the ultra-Orthodox encroachment on Israeli society. He pledged to introduce in the *Knesset* at least 30 bills aimed at limiting Orthodox control, including allowing civil marriage and divorce, regulating government monies to ultra-Orthodox institutions, and ending draft deferments for *yeshiva* students.

Ultimately, the 1999 elections did not result in a clear mandate for the government and the parliament to deal with the question of religious politics in the Jewish state. It established some new parameters and added new elements to the question, but did not identify clear answers to the central questions of who is a Jew and what is a Jewish state. While the dust has yet to settle from the 2001 elections, there is yet no indication that the above two issues are likely to find definitive answers during the term of the incoming administration.

Notes

1   The dispersion of the Jews outside of Palestine after the Babylonian captivity and the Jews or Jewish communities outside of Palestine or Israel.
2   The following terms are often used in the literature to identify subgroups among Jews both within and outside Israel: Orthodox, Conservative, and Reform.
3   The exception included the American Council for Judaism and offshoots such as American Jewish Alternatives to Zionism.
4   Although a splinter group from the Ismailis, who are themselves a sect of the Shi'ite minority among the Muslims, the Druzes are considered a distinct identity group in the Middle East (Abi-Aad and Grenon, 1997, pp. 69–70).
5   The Law of Return, adopted by the Knesset on July 5, 1950, has provided the formal basis for the substantial immigration to Israel that has taken place since independence in 1948.
6   The Balfour Declaration, the Holocaust, growing anti-Semitism, and Jewish assimilation that threatened many of the great centers and institutions for the study of the Torah.
7   In the May 1999 elections SHAS had only two seats fewer that the former ruling Likud party and nine fewer than the Labor-dominated One Israel bloc.
8   *Yisrael Ba'aliyah* also means Israel on the Rise.
9   However, it was not specified what the new laws would entail for relationship between religion and the state.

References

Abi-Aad, Naji and Michel Grenon (1997), *Instability and Conflict in the Middle East: People, Petroleum and Security Threats*, St. Martin's Press: New York.

Ben-Gurion, David (1970), *Ben Gurion Looks Back In Talks With Moshe Pearlman*, Schocken: New York.

http://shinui.org.il/matza-eng.html, 29 May 1999.

http://www.israel-mfa.gov.il, 7 July 1999.

http://www.jpost.co.il/Info/Elections99/Platform/platform.html, 29 May 1999.

Reich, Bernard and Gershon R. Kieval (1993), *Israel: Land of Tradition and Conflict*, 2nd ed., Westview Press: Boulder, CO.

6 Algeria: Islamic Secularism and Political Islam

YAHIA H. ZOUBIR

The Algerian decade-long multifaceted crisis (1988–1999) has claimed 100,000 lives, mostly innocent civilians. Many observes were puzzled by the level of brutality with which security forces and armed Islamist groups have fought one another in the cities and countryside. Although many of its underlying aspects will remain difficult to elucidate, other elements of that savage war can be explained through an examination of Algeria's history, especially colonial, and the relationship that characterized Islam and politics. Anthropologists, sociologists, and political scientists alike have been bewildered by the degree of violence and sheer barbarity that the protagonists used in that fratricide. Even though this chapter does not purport to explain the roots of the violence, it posits at the outset, however, that roots of the violent behavior can be traced to the lack of democratic political culture and the elite's simplistic version of the war of liberation (1954–1962). Indeed, post-independence rulers have propagated the view, with a degree of success, that Algeria owed its victory to armed struggle alone. While armed struggle is only a moment, albeit inevitable, in the march toward national independence and nation- and state-building, Algeria's rulers glorified violence against the enemy at the expense of politics. Combined with the absence of democratic channels and the suppression of an autonomous civil society after independence, that vision helped create belief in violence as the ultimate alternative to resolve conflict. While the responsibility of successive regimes is indisputable, that of the Islamists (even those who did not necessarily believe in violence) is also irrefutable. Indeed, the responsibility of the Islamists consisted of falsifying history and the claim that the Algerian war of liberation was a *jihad* (holy war) against the enemy to reestablish Islam in the country. It is therefore no wonder, whatever the absurdity of their claim, that the armed Islamist factions fought for the overthrow of the infidel state and for the establishment of an Islamic state. Thus, killing, even of innocent civilians, was justified since the struggle was conducted in the name of *Allah* (God) for the establishment of an Islamic state and society. The redemption of society required all means, including the most atrocious that any nation has witnessed in this century. An examination of the place of Islam in contemporary Algerian society will shed some light on recent events.

Islam in Historical Context

Politics and religion in Algeria have always been intertwined. The Islamic religion and traditions have permeated both civil society and the state. Yet, Islam cannot be seen merely as the populations's dominant religion. In fact, Islam in Algeria—more than in any other Middle Eastern society—has come to constitute the basis of identity and culture. The Islamic beliefs regulate social behavior and, to a large extent, also govern social relations. Like other states in the Middle East and North Africa, the Algerian state has, since independence in 1962, despite its secularist inclinations, always resorted to Islamic symbols to establish and reiterate its legitimacy. Paradoxically, social movements and the religious opposition have used Islam not only to wage their struggle against the established regimes, but also to challenge the religious claims of the state. By denying the state one of its fundamental bases of legitimacy, radical Islamists in particular have sought to delegitimize the state and the elites in charge of governing the country. For their part, secular movements used Marxism or liberalism to challenge state policies. But the ideologies of the secularist movements had little appeal among the population because their proponents represented minority views. Especially in a society where the rate of illiteracy remains relatively high, Islam and Islamic references, rather than 'imported' foreign ideologies, have been the source of identity and authenticity. Here lies the main reason for the popularity of the radical Islamism of the 1980s and early 1990s.

Unquestionably, radical Islamism emerged as the most important and most potent protest movement in the years following the death of Houari Boumediene in December 1978. Although authoritarian and populist, the Boumediene regime (1965–1978) had succeeded to a large degree in creating a substantial level of legitimacy and support among the masses. The success of the regime stemmed mostly from the overall socio-economic performance it achieved. Regardless of one's opinion with reference to the Islamist movement in Algeria, there is no doubt that neither Islam nor the Islamist phenomenon can be dissociated from the history of the country's nationalist movement. It is thus no exaggeration to assert that the Islamist movement is one of the belated progeny of colonial rule in that country. While the movement is the product of the socio-economic failure of the 1980s, the doctrinal aspects draw partly from the crisis of identity caused by 132 years of colonial rule. The brutality of French rule in Algeria is legendary. The colonial authorities did not content themselves with killing, pillaging, plundering, and exploiting the entire natural and human resources. They also expropriated the principal local religious institutions: mosques and religious schools were closed; religious lands expropriated (Ruedy, 1992); and Islamic culture was projected as inferior to Christian (Western) civilization. Thus, French colonial domination in Algeria went beyond the monopolistic control that French capitalism exerted over commerce, banks, industry, and agriculture. The colonial state operated a systematic uprooting of Arab and Islamic culture. The French Administration exercised almost full control over the cultural and religious activities of the indigenous Muslim population. The people lived in poverty and were denied basic religious, cultural, political, and economic rights, which the Europeans, albeit a minority in the country, enjoyed. On the eve of the War of National Liberation, less than a million Europeans lived in Algeria, accounting for about one-tenth of the population.

Colonial policies left an indelible imprint in the Algerian psyche. Because France resorted to extremely coercive ways to establish its cultural hegemony (Turin, 1983), and because French colonialists treated the native population and values with contempt (Lacheraf, 1965, p. 107), Algerians had no other recourse but to cling to their religion, Islam. Not surprisingly, Islam became—and still is—the most salient component of Algerians' national identity. Although secular in nature, the nationalist movement, too, used Arab-Islamic values as symbols for popular mobilization against colonialists. Most of the leaders of the nationalist movement, whose struggle culminated in the War of National Liberation (1954–1962), were French-educated and carried a secular vision of politics and society. Yet, the war against the French was conducted as a *jihad* and fighters were designated as *mujahidins* (holy warriors). The nationalist movement was not homogeneous: an important component came from religious associations. As pointed out by a keen observer of Middle East politics, in Algeria, like the rest of the Arab world, two antinomic currents, nationalism and the Islamic sentiment, dominated the system. In that system, successive regimes would refer to revolutionary principles. However, the concrete application could not but be severely limited (Abdelmalek, 1972, p. 427).

Upon independence in July 1962, Algeria established an authoritarian regime characterized by the absence of political pluralism in which a small group, backed by the military, held power. The single party, the *Front de Liberation Nationale* (FLN), which led the revolution, controlled civil society and played the role of transmission belt to the clan in power. The post-independence state drew its legitimacy not from any democratic process, but from a historic evolution: the war of liberation and a developmentalist strategy in which Islam held a privileged position. The state's main efforts concentrated on eliciting support for a particular vision of society carried by coopted elites and intellectuals. The unconvincing references to Islam and socialism rested on the notion of social justice, which Algerians were deprived of during the colonial years. Yet, the clientelist system that the authorities instituted did not correspond to the socialist discourse, or with Islamic morality, as trumpeted by state elites, because only small segments of the population truly benefitted from development policies despite some initial successes. Undoubtedly, the original achievements of industrialization in the 1970s and the tangible social benefits[1] it provided did for a time preserve the consensus and save the tacit social contract. In the 1970s, promises for a better future were indeed credible. But when the state failed to deliver the goods it pledged, its legitimacy was inevitably undermined and the whole edifice so painstakingly put together began to crumble. That was particularly manifest in Algeria, where there exists little state tradition. Indeed, the state had always been a foreign entity imposed upon society by outside powers. A fragmented society, made up of self-governing tribes, always resisted foreign states (Roberts, 1992, p. 442). After independence this tradition of resistance changed very little and the mutual suspicion between the state and society has remained intact. The question of Islamism, therefore, cannot be dissociated from the process of nation- and state-building and its failures (Zoubir, 1994, pp. 741–747).

Early on Algerian authorities manipulated Islam for political and ideological purposes. In order to build a modern identity and gain legitimacy, successive regimes sought to integrate what they defined as a modern type of Islam into revolutionary, vanguard perspectives. Thus, Islam, understood in its modernized form, was decreed to be the state religion in the 1963, 1976, 1989, and 1996 Constitutions. The state elites conceived Islam as the foundation of identity of the Algerian citizens. The role of the state, at least in the so-called socialist era (1962–1980), consisted in not only bestowing upon citizens the material benefits of the modern world (work, education, and all kinds of services), but also in promoting Islamic principles and morality. The authorities hoped that they would achieve this objective through the construction of mosques, teaching of the Arabic language, and creation of a multitude of religious institutions. The state established its monopoly over religious life and repressed interpretations which deviated from the official norms that the state propagated. Even though tolerated, *maraboutic zawi'as* (mystical brotherhoods) popular practices were denounced as archaic and in contradiction to the 'rational' vision of Islam defended by the state. In fact, activities of *zawi'as* were closely watched by the state's security services, which viewed them as counterrevolutionary bases.

Because of the monopoly the regime and the single party exerted upon society, Islam was granted an influential role only insofar as the version endorsed the regime's dissemination (Bey, 1978, p. 448) of Islamic socialism. In other words, the authorities decided to incorporate Islam, again in its so-called progressive interpretation, as an essential component of the ideological and political apparatus of the regime. That tactic was part of a large vision to build a modem nation-state through a developmentalist strategy. In this context, Islam as a system of values, or a set of rational principles, would coexist with modernity in a model which a French sociologist defined as *laicite islamique* (Islamic secularism) (Sanson, 1983, p. 8). *Laicite*, in this context, is also understood as the absence of a religious hierarchy. Despite the preponderance of Islam, however, secularist elites held the monopoly of power. More importantly, as suggested previously, Islam played an ever greater role with respect to the legitimacy of successive regimes. The state used Islam not only as an instrument of national integration in an ethnically heterogeneous society, but also as a tool of political legitimization. Indeed, the irreversible character attributed to Islam in the country's different constitutions inevitably paved the way for various interpretations with consequential implications. While some elites saw Islam as a religion open to modernity, others viewed it through a traditionalist prism, thus giving it the most conservative definition. Not surprisingly, conservative forces, including those within the regime itself, construed a discrete interpretation of Islam that was in contradiction with the socio-economic and cultural policies expounded by the state. The state and its various structures were infiltrated by many Islamists—including some influential *ulamas* (religious scholars), such as Tewfiq al-Madani (former minister of religious affairs), whose nationalist wartime credentials were questionable; most of the *ulamas* did not join the FLN until after 1956 (Ben Bella, 1987, pp. 71–74). Faced with an ideological struggle between secular 'Progressives' and Islamists, the regime sought to achieve a balance between two irreconcilable visions, contenting itself with exclusion of the most extremists within opposing forces in order to preserve national unity and depict itself as an indispensable arbitrator.

In sum, the Algerian State and successive regimes that ruled Algeria contributed to the emergence of Islamism. The authorities, with few exceptions, claim ad nauseum that Algerian identity rests solely on Arab-Islamic oneness. Thus, they deny the multiplicity of other contributing factors to that identity—such as Berber, African, and Mediterranean—that the Islamists have used as one of the main tenets in the 1980s and 1990s. For decades state elites did not seem to discern the obvious contradictions of which they were victims. On the one hand, they held a secular, modernist, and socialist discourse. On the other hand, they held a political-religious discourse that rested on an ideologized Islam, which they sought to impose upon the society. Inevitably such contradictions resulted in a multitude of concessions that the state has made to Islamists until today.

Islamist Challenge to the State

The considerable growth of the radical Islamist movement in Algeria is a relatively recent phenomenon. However, a number of Islamist organizations have challenged the regime at various periods to different degrees since the country's independence. This is why it would be erroneous to attribute the emergence of Islamism to socio-economic factors alone, though the latter have undoubtedly contributed to its eruption. The truth is that Islamism can certainly be situated in the context of colonization and decolonization. In other words, one can view Islamism as the latest reawakening against Western domination and Western-inspired modernity following failure of post-independence authorities in creating prosperous Muslim societies.

The first Islamist association, *El-Qiyam al-Islamyya* (Islamic Values), was founded in 1963 and has enjoyed a practically legal existence as of 1964. The organization's aversion to the country's first president Ahmed Ben Bella's socialist policies and to some secular aspects of the policies adopted by the single-party at its April 1964 Algiers Congress, mobilized a few religious figures. The association included individuals, such as Abassi Madani, future leader of the Islamic Salvation Front (FIS) in the late 1980s, as well as some individuals from the wartime FLN, such as Mohamed Khider (Roberts, 1988, p. 563), one of the nine historic founding members of the wartime FLN. *El-Qiyam* also counted among its members the maverick Malek Bennabi, an outstanding, but often ignored, Islamic thinker who had a strong influence among the early French-educated Islamists attending the University of Algiers in the 1960s and early 1970s until Bennabi's death in 1973 (Zoubir, 1998, pp. 107–112). Opposition to socialism was only one aspect of the *El-Qiyam's* mottoes. The organization also put forth other demands which future Islamists would, in due course, include in their agendas. The members of *El-Qiyam* demanded full implementation of the *shari'a* (Islamic law). The association sought closure of stores during Friday prayers, a demand satisfied in 1976 by the Houari Boumediene regime. It also demanded a ban on the sale of alcohol, exclusion of non-Muslims from public jobs, separation of beaches for men and women, introduction of religious teaching in schools—which was instituted in 1964—and interdiction of women's participation in sports, as well as parades celebrating national holidays (Leca and Vatin, 1975, p. 308; Harbi, 1992, p. 134). The 'cultural' association, perhaps reflecting its obstinate rebuff of Ben Bella's attraction to communist and secular groups, declared in *Humanisme musulman* that all non-Muslim organizations (secularist, Marxist-socialist, or nationalist) were dangerous and needed to be banned in Islamic countries (Leca and Vatin, 1975, p. 308).

El-Qiyam—whose leader, Hachemi Tidjani, acknowledged his affiliation with Jamal al-Din al-Afghani, Muharned Abduh, Shakib Arslan, Hassan al-Banna, Sayyid Qutb, Mohamed al-Ghazali, and Abu A'la Mawdudi—was disbanded in 1966. The sanction resulted from the vehement opposition of its members to the death sentence and eventual execution of the Egyptian Islamist Sayyid Qutb by Gamal Abdul Nasser's regime. The Algerian regime forbade the association and its main publication, *Majallat al-Ta'dhib al-Islamiy* (Review of Muslim Education), because of the diplomatic strain that the existence of the organization and continued publication of that review were likely to cause in Algerian-Egyptian relations (Khelladi, 1992, p. 19). The more important reason, of course, was that the Algerian regime never tolerated any form of contestation regardless of the level of threat it represented to its rule (Zoubir, 1999). *El-Qiyam* was definitively dissolved in March 1970. The greatest contribution of this association was in paving the way for future Islamist organizations in Algeria (Deheuvels, 1991). Despite the dissolution of the organization, furthermore, members of *El-Qiyam* never left the political scene. In fact, they remained anchored within the system, exerting pressure to extract further concessions from the state on moral, socio-economic, and cultural issues. More concretely, their demands revolved around economic liberalization, family law based on *shari'a*, generalization in all fields the teaching of Arabic language, and increase of religious programs on television (Lamchichi, 1989, pp. 151–153). In 1970, the state, through Minister of Religious Affairs Mouloud Kassim, launched its own campaign to prevent the degradation of morals. The minister denounced the loosening of mores, alcoholism, and Western influence in the country (Cubertafond, 1979, pp. 88- 91). Clearly, the association reflected a political-religious current outside and within the state and ruling party's structures, which pushed for the 're-Islamization' of Algeria. The underlying argument, which Islamists have maintained to this day, was that Algeria had lost her Arab-Islamic identity because of French colonization. The consequences of such arguments are quite evident: francophone intellectuals and Westernized elites, particularly women, became the main targets of Islamist attacks.

It is noteworthy that *El-Qiyam* was not unique in using Islam as an instrument of resistance against the regime. A traditional current linked to the *Jamaat al-Ulama* (Association of Religious Scholars), successor of the pre-independence 'reformist' association founded in 1931 by Sheikh Abdelhamid ibn Badis, expressed its opposition to government policies on several occasions. *Jamaat al-Ulama* was actually close to *El-Qiyam*. The association criticized what it perceived as Westernization of Algerian society and degradation of Islamic values. Bitter attacks against Boumediene's socialist policies and alleged degradation of morals in Algeria came from one of the forefathers of Algerian Islamism, Imam Abdellatif Soltani. In his book, *Al-Mazdaqiya Hia'asl al-Ishtiraqiya* (Mazdaqism Is the Source of Socialism) published in Morocco in 1974 (Burgat, 1988, p. 147 fn), considered the manifesto of Algerian Islamism, Imam Soltani criticized socialism as a foreign ideology that is incompatible with Islam because Islam does not prohibit private ownership. Although Islam is a doctrine of social justice, he added, it has no relationship with the state's conception of Muslim socialism (Harbi, 1992, p. 137). Sheikh Soltani also attacked the alleged atheism that resulted from secular teaching in public schools. He saw the *shari'a* as the response to all problems faced by society, a perspective still prevalent among most Islamist factions. The regime was forced to reckon with the demands formulated by Islamists by giving in on certain issues, such as outlawing gambling and promulgating Friday as the Muslim weekend in 1976.

Another group of Islamists was comprised of Arabic teachers educated in Middle Eastern universities. Their views are probably best represented by Sheikh Mahfoud Nahnah, leader of the non-violent Islamist association *Al-Irshad wa'l Islah* (Orientation and Reform). In 1990, the association established a political party, *Harakat at-Mujtama' al-Islamiy* (Movement for Islamic Society), known under the acronym HAMAS until it was forced to change its name in 1997. The renamed party, *Mouvement pour la Societe Pacifique* (Movement for a Peaceful Society, MSP) is a major player in today's Algerian political scene. Nahnah's group belongs to the larger *Da'wa wa al-Tabligh* (Proselytize and Communicate), linked to the *Jamaat at-Ikhwan al-Muslimin* (Association of Muslim Brothers). In the 1970s, this group waged a bitter ideological struggle against Boumediene's regime. From 1976 to 1980, Nahnah was imprisoned for participating in minor acts of sabotage. Nahnah resorted to such acts because of his opposition to the 1976 National Charter's leftist orientation. Nahnah's association and party have held a moderate discourse (accepting reference to human rights, non-violence, and work for women). Nahnah's disciples endeavor to re-Islamize Algerian society through persuasion. And only reluctantly did the movement constitute itself as a political party in 1990 (Zoubir, 1997). In the 1970s, Nahnah's followers chose the linguistic and family issues (woman's rights, divorce, and inheritance) as their battleground. The linguistic subject had a utilitarian value. The Arabic-trained students felt that their education was inadequate because it offered few job prospects. In contrast, French-educated groups enjoyed better employment opportunities. Thus, their emphasis on the importance of Arab-Islamic values was motivated primarily by socio-economic considerations. As to the family question, a subject of bitter conflicts between secular and religious groups since Algeria's independence, it remained very complex and was an even more sensitive topic during the accelerated, chaotic economic liberalization and high unemployment of the late 1990s and 2000. Despite his popularity and growing power base, President Abdelaziz Bouteflika only cautiously approached the issue of family law in October 1999.

The Radicalization of Political Islam

Radicalization of the Islamist movement intensified at the end of the 1970s and early 1980s. The phenomenon assumed its importance in the wake of what sociologists, following Max Weber, call the 'disenchantment of the world' (Weber, 1978, p. 129 fn) provoked by modem science. Basing his analysis on Weber, French anthropologist Bruno Etienne argues convincingly that the real detonator of Islamism in Algeria was the disenchantment subsequent to the first twenty years of independence (Etienne, 1987, p. 131). A close analysis shows quite clearly that an Islamist is first an individual who has become conscious of the acute socio-economic inequalities. Second, he is convinced that his situation is hopeless for the current strategies of development, which will not succeed in alleviating them. Finally, he has lost faith in the state and its capacity to provide him with socio-economic and cultural benefits. The frustrations were very strong because expectations were very high (Clement, 1980, p. 46). In September and October 1999, Algerian journalists interviewed armed Islamists who surrendered after the proclamation of the Law on Civil Concord which reduced the sentences of Islamists who laid down their weapons. Most of the reports substantiate the depiction of the Islamists described earlier. Clearly, Islamism is also a consequence of anarchic modernity. The transition from *Gemeinschaft* (continuity) to *Geselischaft* (society) proceeded without the state offering the newly-urbanized, anonymous citizens the societal structures that could adequately replace the old, communitarian ones. Charitable Islamist associations, fulfilling the function of a spiritual community, provided such structures which supplanted and simultaneously discredited the state, undermining its populist discourse. In Islamism, the alienated individual is able to regain a global image of the self within a community of believers who share a similar *Weltanschauung* (worldview). This situation is especially true in a country dominated by youth, where the populist state has increasingly been incapable of feeding, clothing, educating, housing, and employing its continuously growing population. Worse still, in a country where the state has established its almost total domination over the public sphere and hindered, until quite recently, blossoming of the private domain, only the mosque could offer an existential refuge. The mosque also became a moral substitute for alcohol, drugs, and violence, which had constituted the main pursuit hitherto. The state has ceased to be seen as the provider. Instead, the society, especially its youth (Rarrbo, 1995), feels betrayed. Not only does the youth communicate with the state through violence (Carlier, 1992, pp. 185–219), expressed in the form of cyclical riots, especially under Chadli Bendjedid's rule, but also rejects all the founding myths and symbols of the Algerian nation. In other words, the state has lost its legitimacy and its raison d'etre in the eyes of this disenchanted population.

Although the question of Islam in the political system has always been central, the recent phenomenon of Islamism as a radical protest movement resulted from a combination of factors. The first and foremost of these factors has been the almost total failure of social, economic, and cultural modernization. This, however, should always be coupled with the painful colonial history whose effects continue to influence the evolution of Algerian society. Secularist elites in Algeria, like those in many other Arab-Islamic countries, understood modernization in its material sense. Thus, they failed to take into account the necessity for a process of secularization, which, despite Islamist claims to the contrary, is not necessarily antithetical to Islamic values (Ferjani, 1992). Furthermore, the post-independence FLN regime's ineffective developmental policies and the resolute refusal of the party and the state's personnel to acknowledge openly the shortcomings of the overall program, has led to a complete loss of legitimacy and credibility. The regime fared miserably in its attempt to reconcile a Western model of modernization, obviously without its democratic principles, to a traditional, patriarchal society. In many ways, the state helped strengthen Islamism because it perpetuated neopatriarchy[2] that rests on demagogic and equivocal positions on religious and cultural issues. The total corruption and inefficiency of the regime, which hampered genuine development policies, led to intolerable stagnancy. Evidently the blame for failure of the developmentalist strategy cannot be put solely on the state. The demographic explosion contributed a great deal to worsening socio-economic problems. Worse still, the trauma that followed chaotic urbanization, which resulted from the dislocation of traditional society, debilitated the diffident modernization programs, especially in the socio-cultural realm. The result was an identity crisis, which has had disastrous consequences. The fragility of Arab nationalism and concomitant defeats suffered by Arab regimes against Israel, success of the Iranian Revolution, and humiliations by the West, such as the war against Iraq, provided additional ingredients for continued expansion of the Islamist movement.

Even though the political system has been dominated by presumably secularist elites, Islamism has always had a propitious terrain in Algeria. Furthermore, the presence of hundreds of Egyptian volunteers, primarily Islamists, sent by Gamal Abdul Nasser—who wished to get rid of them—to teach Arabic, had a major influence on large segments of Algerian educators. Another factor that facilitated the growth and rapid expansion of Islamism was the state's loss of control over the thousands of mosques that the state had built since independence. The 'volunteers,' often self-proclaimed Islamist *imams* (leaders), progressively took control of mosques from which they propagated their ideology. The existence of thousands of mosques is, of course, only natural in a vast country where the population is 99 percent Muslim. But the mosque was no longer a place of prayer. It became the political base of the Islamist movement and the place where future *amirs* (commanders) of the armed Islamist groups were formed (Azzi, 1999). By then, of course, state-appointed imams had lost their credibility because of their pacifist inclinations and close identification with the regime. In the field of education, the state created its own gravediggers: Arabic-trained teachers with no real future. The state failed—or was not willing—to create adequate structures to provide acceptable jobs for them. In 1975, Boumediene sent home the Egyptian teachers and closed down Islamic institutes, also built by the state. At the same time, however, he encouraged the construction of new mosques under the pretext that socialism helped the promotion of Islam in Algeria. A mosque would be erected in each socialist village. After the 1988 uprising, the FIS, founded in March 1989 following the liberalization process, was already in control of practically all mosques in the country. Those mosques became powerful political forums for the Islamists. They constituted the embryo of a counter-power, a sort of counter-hegemonic power, to the state.

The Algerian regime was instrumental in helping the expansion of the Islamist movement. It is noteworthy that despite its authoritarian nature, the regime never delineated the boundaries for activities by Islamists and their allies within the state. So long as Islamists did not threaten the survival of the system, the regime allowed them to operate freely and even encouraged them to curb the secularist Left which also had its allies, albeit less powerful, within the bureaucracy. Whenever it opposed the Islamists' ideology, the regime did so in the name of Islam because religion was a necessary, even though increasingly contested, component of its legitimacy. The regime, in fact, favored the spread of Islamist ideology by not only allowing the building of thousands of public and private mosques, but also establishing Islamic institutes, flooding television with religious programs, and allocating substantial resources for hosting international seminars on Islamic thought. In other words, secularist elites never had the courage of confining religious activities to the realm of civil society. Obviously, reluctance to permit the existence of a public sphere independent of the state would have curtailed the power of the state and diminished its hegemonic rule. Undoubtedly, with respect to the state's attitude toward Islam, there is no doubt that the state can hardly be accused of being anti-Islamic when most officials insist on presenting themselves in an almost pathological fashion as impeccable Muslims. Islam was, and might continue to be, one of the foundations of the hegemonic discourse and hegemonic rule of Algeria's regimes. It was in fact the state's contradictory policy vis-a-vis Islamists which bolstered the audacious approach of the Islamist movement, especially in the late 1980s and early 1990s. What is paradoxical, of course, is the fact that regardless of the state's investments in the religious sphere, Islamists succeeded in portraying that very same state as an atheistic, anti-Islamic entity.

The ruling FLN party used Islam as part of its ideology in order to legitimize the political system in place. But its attempt to produce a synthesis between Islam and socialism proved futile because the political system continued to generate inequalities, especially under Bendjedid's rule. The egalitarianism that the regime promised to the people proved illusory; the socialist political discourse was in total contradiction with socio-economic reality (Garon, 1993). In many ways, most Islamists were the orphans of Boumediene. Unlike his successor, who lacked any vision of society, Boumediene had at least succeeded in mobilizing the youth around a strategy of development. The strategy had the advantage of being essentially egalitarian in a relatively triumphant era in which corruption and clientelism, though present, never reached the outrageous form that developed under Bendjedid's rule. Islamism in Algeria presented more violent forms in the 1970s and 1980s despite the rather complaisant attitude, if not encouragement at times, of the Bendjedid regime (1979–1992) towards the movement in general. That violence was present in the universities, with bloody encounters between Islamist students—

mobilized around cultural, linguistic and moralistic themes—and leftist or secular students, Berberists, and people who did not share the Islamists' interpretation of Islam. Ironically, it was the state's acceleration of the Arabization campaign that led to further contestation owing to growing cultural distinctiveness and absence of opportunities for Arabic-educated emerging elites. In other words, Islamist groups couched their socio-economic demands within an ideological discourse garbed with religion. In fact, the fifth demand in the Islamist appeal of November 1982, which included, among other things, the full implementation of the *shari'a*, demanded that the citizens be given access to national wealth through legal means, such as agriculture, trade, or industry. They believed that this could be achieved only if opportunities were offered to all without discrimination (al-Ahnaf, et al., 1991, p. 47).

The Iranian Revolution of 1979, which had a much greater impact on Algerian Islamists than observers are willing to admit,[3] bolstered some of the most radical voices of Algerian Islamism. Algerian Islamists used the opportunity—which coincided with the change of regime in Algeria—to make their demands on the new president more forcefully. They demanded the introduction of Islamic teaching from kindergarten to university, creation of specialized Islamic sections in high schools and universities, opening of Islamic universities, teaching of the Qur'an by popular associations, total freedom for religious associations (under the supervision of the ministry of religious affairs), building of mosques, and training of *ulamas* and *imams*. They also called for an increase in religious programs on television and radio, a ban on the sale of any items offensive to Islam, thereby ensuring that the population observe the precepts of Islam, and penalizing those who violate those measures (al-Asala, 1979, pp. 59–67). The regime could ill afford to ignore demands coming from members of the influential *ulama* association who were well-entrenched in important ministries (higher education, justice, national education, and religious affairs) and in the FLN.

The most violent, albeit small, Islamist groups rallied around Mustapha Bouyali, who founded the Armed Islamic Movement (MIA) in 1982 and served as its *amir* until his violent death in 1987 (Merah, 1998). Bouyali's actions epitomized the impulsive response opposed by some Algerians because of a lack of democratic channels to express frustrations and disenchantment with modernization. The forerunner of the MIA was an organization, also created by Bouyali, the Group for the Struggle against the Illicit, which had conducted attacks against bars and individuals. The organization had little impact and soon Bouyali was compelled to seek a more effective method—armed struggle—against the regime. Even though many Islamists were in agreement with Bouyali regarding the foundation of an Islamic state in Algeria, many other Islamist activists did not share the violence he and his followers, such as Ahmed Merah, advocated. Mahfoud Nahnah, in particular, believed that the armed struggle against the regime was, in fact, harmful to Islam (Khelladi, 1992, p. 76). Bouyali resorted to Blanquist tactics: the *amir* believed that a small, well disciplined organization, made up of determined individuals, committing political assassinations and acts of sabotage, could seize power and hold on to it until they succeeded in swaying the population to their cause. That belief was strengthened following the 1982 arrest of Islamist figures—with no links to the MIA—such as Abdelatif Soltani, Ahmed Sahnoun, and Abassi Madani, over incidents that took place at the University of Algiers. The authorities dismantled Bouyali's organization rather quickly. However, it took years before the security forces could trap Bouyali—killed in 1987—and a handful of his followers. In 1989, Bendjedid pardoned Bouyali's hard-core disciples in the hope of preventing further radicalization of the movement. But many of them eventually joined the guerrilla war waged—led by more extremist, well-equipped, and better organized Islamist groups—in the 1990s against the regime. The Islamist movement in Algeria also includes a whole collection of smaller groups with views ranging from the most peaceful to the most fanatic. Although some of them were little known before the bloody riots of October 1988, many have existed since the 1970s. The participation of some young Algerians alongside Afghan *mujahidins* in their war against the former Soviet Union bolstered the prestige of these daring groups, whose reputation was equaled only by their ruthlessness. They seem to act as autonomous bands, owing unconditional allegiance to an *amir*. In the 1970s and 1980s, *Al-Muwahiddun* (Unifiers), *Ansar Allah* (Supporters of God), *Junud al-Allah* (Soldiers of God), *Da'wa* (Proselytism) of Sidi Bel Abbes (a western city in Algeria), *Ahl al-Da'wa* (Members of the Proselytization) of Laghouat (a southern city), *Al-Hijra wa al-Takfyir* (Emigration and Excommunication), and others targeted bars, breweries, police stations, and Soviet citizens and interests in Algeria (Khelladi, 1992, pp. 117–121).

In the 1980s, the Islamist movement remained atomized and spanned from very peaceful fundamentalists to quite extremist groups. Yet, despite the Bouyali affair, the regime seemed oblivious to the growth of radical Islamism and continued to either disregard its grievances or make demagogic concessions, such as the promulgation of the discriminatory Family Law of 1984. The regime made concessions by increasing religious programs, organizing international symposia on Islam, and even 'importing' in 1982 Mohamed al-Ghazali, an Egyptian fundamentalist from the prestigious Al-Azhar Mosque, to give televised sermons. Two years later, he was made head of the Department of Islamic Studies at the University of Constantine (in eastern Algeria). That highly visible super *imam*, held in very high esteem by Bendjedid himself, served as an ideological cushion for the religious pretensions of the regime. Through his ambiguous discourse, al-Ghazali also did much to encourage the diffusion of Islamism in the country (Rouadjia, 1990, pp. 197–208). However, the influence of al-Ghazali and other Islamist figures in Algeria cannot account for the massive Islamist expansion after the tragic riots of October 1988. Well before the disturbances, Islamists were attempting to 're-appropriate' Islam. In taking away Islam from the state, they were undermining one of the essential components upon which the political system has built its legitimacy.

The Expression of Disenchantment

A deterioration of socio-economic conditions of laboring masses was discernible in the 1980s despite the economic reforms and (chaotic) liberalization the regime had introduced. In particular, industrial workers had lost the social benefits that they had garnered under Boumediene's welfare-oriented regime. Unemployment grew as a result of dismantling state enterprises. The growing elimination of food subsidies and liberalization of prices in agriculture resulted in a significant rise in prices of essential goods. That had critical social ramifications, especially for the urban poor. Not only urban poor, but also large sections of the middle class were affected by changing socio-economic conditions. Thus, the chaotic execution of Bendjedid's economic liberalization led Algerian society to resort to unlawful speculation. The crisis of the Algerian economy led to a parallel underground economy (Bennoune, 1992, p. 19). Algerian sociologist, Ali El-Kenz, argued that the predatory gangster-like business led not only to widespread corruption, but also it produced ethical disquiet. This situation provided ammunition for radical sermons in mosques and helped the growth of Islamism (El-Kenz, 1989, pp. 24–25). During Bendjedid's reign, clientelist networks multiplied in a spectacular fashion and reached incredible proportions, illicit business and the informal sector became widespread, and a whole underground, parallel economy—known as trabendo[4]—was instituted. Moreover, due to the corrupt nature of the regime the authoritarian state in its entirety became alienated from society. At the same time as corruption invaded the entire social body, traditional forms of social resistance (strikes, urban riots, and underground struggles) were replaced by more radical religious contestation. For their part, Islamists organized networks of solidarity that brought them indisputable support from a despairing population. This, in part, explains the popularity at the polls of the Islamist movement in the late 1980s and early 1990s. The abandonment of welfare policies, which the regime extended to the educational and health sectors, led to the emergence of additional networks of privileges. A selective schooling system emerged and so did private (much better equipped and more expensive) hospitals, further alienating large sections of society who used to benefit from redistribution of part of the national rent. The regime's reforms amounted to a type of economic liberalization which benefitted only the friends, relatives, and clients of those in power. The marginalization of large segments of society became evident and led to widespread anger, despair, banditry, and utter hatred toward the state and its clienteles.

Opposition to the reforms extended to factions within the FLN party whose members—no longer benefitting from the national income due to reduced distributive capacity of the state (Harbi, 1993, p. 204)—were among its opponents. Even some radical Islamists, linked to the center of power, thus to the national rent (Goumeziane, 1994, p. 276), also expressed their antagonism to the reforms. The unions, communists, and intellectuals constituted yet another section of the anti-reform camp. Popular indignation toward the disengagement of the state, which resulted in conspicuous disarray that cut across the Algerian society, was manifest through a return to the most archaic forms of solidarity (family, clan, tribe, and region). The result was that cultural struggles superseded any ideological or political contest. The rising cultural demands from Islamists, Berberists, and other groups obscured the ideological and socio-economic struggles. In other words, cultural identity issues blurred the socio-economic and political or ideological lines. Those political and ideological trends, in turn, succeeded in rallying social groups with diametrically opposite socio-economic interests. The 1980s were thereby characterized by intense demobilization and persistent atomization of an embryonic civil society (Zoubir, 1999). A double process unfolded and resulted in the emergence of what seemed to be a new type of civil society. The first aspect was the direct result of abandonment of state welfare policies, pursuit of economic liberalization, emphasis on profit, and progressive withdrawal of the state from various sectors. Some of those sectors usually had helped the destitute segments of society. Thirst for profit and easy gain, without regard for rationality, replaced the sense of egalitarianism that Algerians have traditionally cherished. A redefinition of boundaries was drawn, which made necessary the creation of associations standing between state and civil society. The second factor relates to the crisis of legitimacy, which highlighted the erosion of any claims of legitimacy drawn from the Algerian revolution. The new movement away from the state, in favor of associations, accentuated discord within the regime and subsequent mutations that took place. Also, it contributed to calling into question the principle of a single party system (Babadji, 1991, p. 231). The events of 1988 offered the opportunity for the movement to expand to a magnitude hitherto unimaginable.

The Islamists did not initiate the October 1988 riots (Charef, 1990; Boukhoubza, 1991). Yet, they were soon able to play a mediating role between the regime and rioters and fill the political vacuum created by events. Of major relevance here is the speed with which a considerable faction of the Islamist movement was able to constitute itself as a national party and use the opening of the political system to its own advantage (Zoubir, 1995). The so-called democratic parties that emerged following the liberalization of the political system, with few exceptions, enjoyed at best an infinitesimal popular base. In late 1988 and early 1989, members of the *Rabitat al-Da'wa* (League of Preaching) sought to unify the Islamist movement and provide it with a national structure. The objective of the League was to be apolitical, limiting itself to moral issues. It was to be a league that would serve God and Islam and would work for *ijtihad* (interpretation) (al-Ahnaf, et al., 1991, p. 30). But very quickly mutual suspicions, conflicting ambitions, and different backgrounds of the leaders made a unified movement a wishful dream. On the one hand, theologians, such as Mahfoud Nahnah and Abdallah Djaballah, opposed the creation of a mass organization. On the other hand, Abassi Madani, a product of the nationalist movement, endorsed the idea as a strategy for the salvation of the *um'ma* (Muslim nation) and the Algerian people. Nahnah created his own association, which eventually became a political party, Movement for Islamic Society (HAMAS) in 1990. Djaballah, whose ideas are close to those of Hassan al-Banna and Mohamed al-Ghazali, founded his own party in 1989, *Harakat al-Nahda al-Islamyya* (Movement for the Islamic Renaissance, also known as Ennahda). In 1997, Ennahda dropped the word 'Islamic' in order to conform to the law on political associations introduced by the regime. The party has since experienced internal turmoil. Djaballah, a presidential candidate in the April 1999 election, was practically forced out of the party. He created his own party, the Movement for National Reform, which claims to be unequivocally in opposition to the regime.

The Islamic Salvation Front gained immense support, especially among the underprivileged sections of society. The largest component grew out of dislocation of traditional society and from demobilization generated by disengagement of the state. But it also attracted a myriad of individuals who held various grievances against the successive regimes that ruled Algeria. The FIS not only became the main party, but also the most popular and appealing organization to have emerged and gained from liberalization of the political system. This mass party was the most mobilized and best-structured Islamist party in the country. The leadership contended that they expressed the general will of the Algerian people and promised to implement the *shari'a al- Islamyya* (Islamic law) once in power (Project de Programme, 1989). That, of course, implied total disregard for a republican constitution and augured what may be called the divinization of politics. Hence, the promise precluded not only secularist views, but also the existence of a genuine civil society. The FIS was quite successful in presenting itself as the heir of the 'authentic' FLN, the radical nationalist party of the Revolution that, in the eyes of Algerians, incarnated such values as unity of the Algerian people, egalitarianism, dignity, and independence. The FIS, thus, adapted FLN's nationalist-populist discourse to an Islamist vision. The party claimed to be the only force capable of offering salvation to Algeria and absolve it of all the evils that pervaded it. In practice, that meant developing not only a hegemonic discourse which the FIS Islamists could use to fight their foes, mainly the democratic (secularist) parties, but also establishing its hegemony through the courts. By identifying itself with Islam, the FIS succeeded to some degree in discrediting other parties that resisted the movement's hegemonic domination. The FIS inadvertently contributed to further atomization of the society sought by the regime. Furthermore, using an uncompromising ideological discourse the FIS could at the same time discredit moderate Islamists, who could then be accused of collaboration with the regime for failing to call for overthrow of the regime and the secular state.

Even though the military resisted ascent of the FIS, the regime, in violation of its own laws, legalized the existence of that powerful Islamist party in September 1989. The FIS had, by then, already established its popularity among the marginalized youth, promising an immediate solution to their most pressing (earthly) problems. Its power of mobilization could not be matched by the highly discredited FLN. The democratic parties, for their part, were incapable of reaching any agreement about forming a common front to counter the power of the Islamists. Also, the democratic elements were incapable of preventing their own manipulation by the old ruling party. Unlike the FIS, which concentrated its attacks against the state, democratic forces appealed to the state to contain the Islamist wave and protect their interests against the advance of the Islamist mob. Inexorably, the democrats appeared as objective allies of the authoritarian regime. The Islamists had little difficulty discrediting secularist forces in the eyes of the population and prove that democrats were in fact propagating a foreign ideology. The FIS, of course, had the easy task of showing that it was the party of Algerian and Islamic authenticity. But, again, whatever the manipulation of religion by its members, the discourse of FIS was more reminiscent of radical, secular movements than that of, say, Talibans in Afghanistan or mullahs in Iran (at least in the later stages of the Iranian Revolution). In fact, had it not been for the stronger emphasis on religion, the difference between the FIS and FLN would be rather insignificant. Unlike *islah* (reform) movement—a peaceful, intellectual, and small collection of patricians concerned with moral and cultural issues—Islamism is a social phenomenon resulting from modernity. Although the movement seeks a return to the *shari'a*, with the exception of some of its components, it is not interested in a return to an antiquated past. Rather, Islamism, especially in its early stages (before turning into mere 'neofundamentalism'), is a revolutionary movement that strives to re-appropriate society and modern technology through political means. It wants to seize power in order to re-Islamize a society allegedly corrupted by Western values (Roy, 1994). The movement is therefore not theological, but essentially sociological. There ensues, at least for important sections of Islamism, an ideologization of Islam whereby Islam is not simply a religion but also an ideology which regulates the whole community (Merad, 1981, p. 38). In this sense the FLN was not much different because the FLN's so-called secular elites used a good dose of religious beliefs in the organization of society.

Like the FLN, the FIS was by no means a monolithic organization; it had composite membership and structures. From its creation in February 1989 until its ban in March 1992, the FIS comprised a variety of groups and ideological currents. The heterogeneous leadership of the FIS, combining radicalized salafists and new activist militants (Labat, 1994) never really agreed on the means to achieve power—their principal preoccupation— in order to establish a vaguely defined Islamist state. Aspirations of the different groups included in the FIS diverged greatly. Some upheld a millenarian vision of which recourse to violence—whose major aim was dismantling the nation-state in its current format—was an intrinsic part. For others the objective was limited to a mere substitution of the Islamist elite for the one currently in charge of the state, which is perceived as having failed in both its modernizing tasks and preserving Islamic values. Still others had no clear strategy whatsoever. What is certain, however, is that the main objective of the party was the appropriation of the state by legal (electoral) means for some, or through violence for others. This explains the contradictory statements concerning the necessity of or refusal to participate in the electoral process. Yet, in spite of its heterogeneous nature, the FIS succeeded in developing a dominant ideological discourse in dealing with important political and social issues. But because of the ideologization of Islam, which unavoidably shifted the core of the debate from theological concerns to norms and values of the socio-political domain, the core beliefs of Islam either retrograded or were entirely cloaked. Like many other movements in the Middle East and North Africa, FIS leaders came under the influence of Egyptian and Indo-Pakistani Islamists such as Hassan al-Banna, Sayyid Qutb, Abul A'la Mawdudi, and Mohammed al-Ghazali. The major components of the discourse were around those 'ills' that have plagued modern society and led to its 'decadence.' In their view, contemporary secular ideologies—such as liberalism, socialism, communism, and feminism—have replaced religion and corrupted societies. Like the chief Islamists who inspired them, many FIS leaders believed that the evils of the *jahilyia* (pre-Islamic society) have plagued not only the Western world, but also have been blindly emulated in Muslim societies. Islam, in their opinion, is the only solution to such grave problems (Benhadj, n.d.). The state in Muslim societies has failed to carry out its duties and has thus deviated from the divine commandments. In fact, the state has contributed to the *jahilyia*. The regimes should be considered infidels and must therefore be fought through *jihad*. By the same token, *qital* (assassination) of political leaders would be perfectly *halal* (permissible).

Radical Islamists in Algeria developed an interpretation of Islam that refuted any liberal interpretation of Islam. They bitterly opposed any attempt to justify the separation of politics from religion. *Laicite*—the separation of state and religion—constitute in their eyes the biggest threat to Muslim societies. The objective underlying such interpretation was quite functional. The appeal from radical Islamists derived particularly from a critique of the secular regime, which failed in its tasks precisely because it had stayed away from Islam. One can easily see how the same arguments could be used successfully against the democratic forces that based their arguments on secular principles. Consequently, democratic values become, in their conception, sacrilegious and totally antithetical to Islam. Secular values, upon which democracy is said to rest, lead to *fitna* (disharmony) within Muslim societies. The irony is that these conclusions regarding secularism and democracy do not derive from any theological or serious political analysis of the concepts. The whole discourse regarding those concepts serves one purpose: propaganda within the context of a strategy of conquest for power. But there is evidence from their own speeches that had radical Islamists come to power in Algeria, they would probably have discarded the republic constitution and outlawed secular political parties altogether (al-Ahnaf, et al., 1991, p. 87 fn). It is interesting that the economic plan of the FIS confirms the similarity of vision with its 'father,' the FLN. A close examination shows that the FIS economic program was a concoction of rhetorical statements of economic nationalism (economic independence, social justice, and self-reliance), economic liberalism, Islamist principles of morality in trade and human relations, and basic economic principles found in the *shari'a*. They were elements of social justice meant to curb the ramifications of liberalism: pleas to Algerians to mobilize around a program that would help them 'reestablish [their] identity' and doubtful propositions concerning various fields of agriculture, industry, trade, finance, and so on. The economic project, which occupies about one-third of the entire program, contains a lot of banalities due mostly to the framers' arduous job of reconciling a utopian scheme with complex realities. That was further complicated by their aspiration for a third road between capitalism and socialism. Even though the economic program betrays the party's preference for a mercantilist economy, it resorts to a populist language to answer the grievances of its rank and file.

The radicalism of FIS and the perceived threat it posed to the regime and armed forces resulted in annulment of the legislative election in January 1992. The slow decomposition of the party and imprisonment of its political leaders led eventually to emergence of small, armed groups that threatened the very fabric of Algerian society. In fact, the state itself came to the brink of collapse during 1993–1995. Although by far the most powerful popular Islamist political party in Algeria, the FIS, banned since March 1992, was not the only Islamist party and always had its Islamist challengers. Two other parties have a relatively sizable following because of their proclaimed 'moderation' and their middle class membership. Also, they may have succeeded in coopting former members of FIS. Both continue to survive and have played an important role in the political and social life of the country. The MSP (formerly HAMAS) and Ennahda (now split into two parties) owe their comparative popularity to their long standing in the mosque and *Da'wa* (Proselytism) movements.

Political Islam since the Early 1990s

The period since cancellation of the legislative elections in January 1992 was marked, until quite recently, by a savage war between Islamist guerrilla groups and state security forces. The new brand of Islamism that emerged defied all logic. The question as to whether the FIS had a legitimate right to resort to violence divided the leadership of the party (Willis, 1996, p. 272 fn). The inability of the regime to devise a clear strategy following cancellation of the election, the imprisonment of FIS leaders, and persecution of FIS militants, many of whom opposed violence, gave the upper hand to the factions who always believed in armed struggle. Leaders of FIS who favored the armed insurrection sought to create a unified command. They organized it around MIA, the armed group created by Bouyali in the 1980s, involving FIS and the so-called Afghans.[5] The disparate nature of the Islamist movement, however, led to emergence of the Armed Islamic Group (GIA), which held an exceedingly radical ideology. Central to that ideology was the rejection of any constitutional means to create an Islamic state. The group, which eventually multiplied into smaller, autonomous factions, held democracy in contempt, describing it as pure and simple *kofr* (blasphemy). The attitude toward democracy and pluralism was well summed up by Abdelhak Layada, the founder of the GIA, who argued that political pluralism was equal to subversion. He explained that his cohorts never intended to participate in elections or enter parliament because the right to legislate belongs solely to God (Willis, 1996, p. 282), an argument that Ali Benhadj, the second ranking FIS leader, repeated ad nauseum. The GIA launched a campaign in 1993 that has lasted to this date. The GIA campaign, which reached its apogee during 1994–1996, has lessened considerably in intensity, due mostly to increased effectiveness of the security forces and a changing political situation since 1997.

There is much confusion about the exact nature of the armed factions committing acts of violence. Those factions seem to act as autonomous bands, owing unconditional allegiance to an *amir* and obeying no other logic but their own. Although further research is needed to determine the exact nature of the relationship they have established with the FIS's Islamic Salvation Army (AIS), there is evidence that GIA and FIS maintained, at least until 1997, close links despite differences over tactics and targets (*Nouvel Observateur*, September 1995). The entente, however, should not obscure major differences in political goals and tactics between the two groups. There is good reason to believe that the major objective of AIS tactic has been to induce the regime to make concessions, including allowing the FIS to re-enter the political arena through one form or another. For the GIA, the principal goal, if there really is one, is to overthrow the regime and to establish some mystical 'Islamist state.' That nirvana's main inspiration stems from the writings and recorded speeches of Ali Benhadj, FIS's fiery leader, imprisoned since July 1991. Undoubtedly, the differences which since 1995 have divided the FIS leadership over negotiations with the regime, elections, and tactics, have also affected FIS's relationship with the GIA. One can hypothesize that the brutal attacks which followed Madani's liberation in July 1997 have been the work of extremist Islamist factions opposed to any negotiation with the regime. This hypothesis is plausible in view of the countless sect-like factions that have emerged since 1996. The *Ghadibun a'la Allah* (Those Upset with God), a sect whose brutality defies any sociological or anthropological analysis, appeared in the Mitidja area near Algiers. Other factions, just as vicious, appeared in various regions of Algeria. The GIA claimed to be the only legitimate Islamist movement in the country. The various factions calling themselves armed Islamic groups intensified their bloody attacks against the regime, members of the moderate MSP, leaders of secular parties, and the civilian population, which no longer supported them and was armed by the state to defend themselves. Also, the GIA launched deadly attacks against the AIS (*Financial Times*, January 12, 1996), the armed wing of the FIS, which the GIA accused of treason because the AIS negotiated a cease-fire with the authorities on October 1, 1997, rather than continue the armed struggle. One should point out, however, that it has become quite problematical to refer to the GIA in the singular because of the proliferation of armed factions. In view of the evolution of the situation on the ground and the absence of ideological justification for at least some of the massacres, the term 'bandits' would be more appropriate. Even though one should not discount the reality of the sects and intriguing armed groups that have mushroomed in various parts of the country (*La Tribune*, January 13 and January 25, 1998).

The political evolution of the situation in Algeria, bloody massacres that the armed groups committed against the population, increased effectiveness of the security forces and their auxiliaries, and the international context have all had an impact on Islamism and its initial popularity. From the 1980s till the mid-1990s, Islamism had strong support among large sections of the population. The most obvious explanation, of course, is that the rise and expansion of Islamism has been a response to policies of the 'secular' state and its failure to satisfy the socio-economic and cultural needs of the people. The support that

Islamism garnered at the polls often indicated a desire for change on the part of the population. The Islamic Salvation Front's victory in June 1990 municipal elections and December 1991 legislative elections represented a vote of retribution against the FLN rather than the desire for an Islamic state. Undoubtedly, the promises that the FIS made to the people were extremely appealing, especially to the youth, the largest component of the population. The armed struggle itself found support among important segments of the population because of hatred toward the regime. The perception of an infidel state that has abandoned the people, and whose policies have benefitted only friends and relatives of the rulers, was widespread and quite credible. Villagers, for instance, provided shelter, food, and other support to the so-called *mujahidins* of GIA and AIS. The GIA and AIS had little difficulty finding new recruits among the unemployed, marginalized youth either in urban centers or the countryside. Membership in the GIA brought important benefits: a weapon that provided a sense of power, respect from the local population for fear of punishment or genuine admiration (Gacemi, 1998), and financial gains for the fighter and his family. Attacks against the state sectors helped advance the private sector, often dominated by shadowy individuals. Many analysts have focused on ideological aspects of the quasi civil war. They often overlooked the economic gains (and losses) that took place behind the turmoil (Martinez, 1998).

Algeria is, perhaps, the only country in the Middle East and North Africa where the rise of Islamism not only has been the most tragic, but also has undergone the most fateful evolution. Indeed, the situation brought about considerable changes at several levels. While still trying to maintain itself in power, the regime was compelled to open, albeit incrementally and cautiously, the political system. Constitutional and institutional reforms have been put in place since late 1995. Regardless of their limitations, those reforms have allowed the rise of an increasingly combative civil society. Algerian authorities initiated an institutional process aimed at allowing a degree of participation, including moderate Islamists, while at the same time guaranteeing continuity for the old elite (Bouandel and Zoubir, 1998, pp. 177–190). The whole process has yet to create the legitimacy needed to provide the necessary push for a rehabilitation of the state and the indispensable mobilization for a definitive end to the crisis. The economic liberalization initiated by successive regimes has led to further unemployment and even to an impoverishment of the middle class. It is conceivable that the instability due to the warfare between armed Islamist groups and state security forces has delayed any benefits from economic transformations. But what is certain is that socio-economic conditions have worsened in recent years despite positive macroeconomic results, acknowledged by international financial institutions such as the International Monetary Fund. The socio-economic situation has re-shifted the focus from issues of security to every-day economic concerns. Those concerns have lessened the debate over Islamism. In fact, Islamism has itself undergone an important transformation. The most consequential has been the emergence of a more moderate Islamism acceptable to the regime. Indeed, the MSP has participated in various institutions since 1994. Abdallah Djaballah, for instance, was one of the candidates in the April 1999 presidential election.[6] Moderate Islamists are allowed to conduct political activities and occupy seats in the National Assembly as well as the Council of the Nation—the legislative bodies.

The methods that the armed groups have used against innocent civilians and families of the security forces alienated major segments of the population. During 1995–1996, the government decided to give arms to the population in remote villages, a policy that helped dissuade Islamist armed groups from committing atrocities at least in some areas. Resentment against armed groups, which have become mere bandits in many cases, has led to a much more cautious attitude toward Islamism. Undoubtedly, Islamism in Algeria, at least its extremist version, is in sharp decline. However, many of the grievances the movement highlighted in the 1980s and 1990s are still compelling. The difference with the past is that today Islamists could express those grievances through institutional channels. The lawful participation of Islamists in Algeria's political life means that their views will impact the political system. This is precisely why the military, for instance, continues to view activities of Islamists with suspicion. Unlike what had happened in the late 1980s, however, the authorities have incorporated in the institutional framework measures—such as proportional representation—that would prevent Islamists from winning a vast majority in any election. Interestingly, in recent years, Islamism has become a trump card for political parties. For instance, while the regime has successfully co-opted moderate Islamists, some political parties (such as the Front of Socialist Forces, FFS), and prominent political figures such as Mouloud Hamrouche (former prime minister) and Ahmed Taleb Ibrahimi (former foreign minister) have sought to rehabilitate the FIS or, at least, its more moderate leaders. The presidential election of April 1999 showed very clearly a division of the political class into those who supported the Sant'Edigio process (FFS, part of the FLN, Djaballah's MRN, and FIS) and those opposed to it (majority of the FLN, RND, MSP, Ennahda, and others). A governmental coalition between nationalists and moderate Islamists, the so-called national-conservative coalition, is now a disparate group that includes independents, some democrats, and radical Islamists. The disbanding of the AIS in December 1999 and the application of the Civil Concord policy have facilitated the progressive return to normalcy. Undoubtedly, an extremely weakened armed movement and a greatly divided political leadership will have little weight in the face of a reinvigorated state. Clearly, the moderate, tamed Islamists are more likely to benefit from the political system than those whose radical views led directly or indirectly to the near-civil war in Algeria.

The April 1999 presidential election presented an opportunity for Algeria to see an end to the crisis. Compared to his predecessors, Abdelaziz Bouteflika demonstrated all the attributes of a statesman. His political experience as Algeria's long-lasting foreign minister (1963–1979), knowledge of the system, good relations with the military, and negotiation skills were looked upon favorably by the military, whose support he succeeded in securing. Within a few weeks after his election, the security situation in Algeria witnessed marked improvement. The reasons for this evolution rest primarily on the new president's effective management of the crisis, especially the Islamist question. Indeed, Bouteflika made some radical moves. He succeeded in securing the total capitulation of the AIS, albeit a cease-fire had been in place since October 1, 1997. While some of the details of the trade-off remain secret, it is clear that the AIS obtained partial pardon for those of its members who have not committed assassinations, rapes, and other violent crimes. The agreement obtained the support of most of the leadership of the banned FIS at home and abroad. Bouteflika's main objective has been to reconcile Algerians with and among themselves. To this end he had submitted a text on 'Civil Concord' that was approved by the parliament in July 1999. Bouteflika offered a discourse, which combined views from the opposition, those inside the regime—the so-called 'conciliators'—and abroad, especially the United States. All encouraged Algerian authorities to achieve a negotiated solution rather than rely on eradicationist policies alone. The president seemed to hold two intertwined objectives: restoration of civil peace and economic recovery. Indeed, without civil peace, economic recovery or foreign investments would be impossible while dire socio-economic conditions would continue feeding the ranks of the armed insurgents. The goal of his trip in late June 1999 to Crans Montana, Switzerland, aimed at both publicizing his program abroad and attracting foreign investors. Although foreigners have invested billions of dollars in the hydrocarbon sector, Algeria needs approximately $1 to $2 billion annually in foreign direct investments in other areas to stimulate growth and reduce unemployment.

Bouteflika's policies, which have undoubtedly been endorsed by the military, large segments of the population, the political opposition, and foreign governments, have produced some positive effects. On September 16, 1999, the population voted overwhelmingly in favor of Civil Concord. The security situation since that referendum has improved substantially. Killings of civilians in remote villages have continued, but they have dramatically diminished in terms of scale and frequency and are in no way comparable to those committed in 1997 and 1998. The GIA and the Salafist Group for Preaching and Combat (GSPC), challengers of the AIS, rejected Bouteflika's proposals and will no doubt continue their terrorist activities. But, they have had more difficulty finding logistical or moral support among a population they have largely succeeded in alienating. In fact, the authorities hope that the AIS and other Islamist groups seeking an end to the crisis would help them eradicate the groups that have rejected calls for national reconciliation. In order to obtain further support from so-called moderate Islamists, Bouteflika has suggested that the state would not discount the reconstitution of the FIS, albeit under a different name. Such assurance in allowing the resurrection of the FIS relies on the stringent conditions regarding the existence of political parties stipulated in the 1996 Constitution, which are more explicit than those contained in the 1989 Constitution. Bouteflika's decision to provide Islamists with the possibility of repenting within six months resulted in the surrender of hundreds of Islamist combatants who wish to reintegrate into the society. A few thousand imprisoned Islamists have been freed on Independence Day (July 5), and thousands more were liberated on November 1, 1999, a move that has encouraged more Islamists to surrender to the state authorities.

Conclusion

At the close of 1999, the security situation in Algeria had improved substantially. But the diehard Islamists refused to give up the fight. In some parts of the country, armed Islamist groups have accentuated their attacks against gendarmes, soldiers, policemen, and auxiliaries. Officially, 1,175 members of the GIA had surrendered four months after the adoption of the law on Civil Concord (*Le Matin*, November 9, 1999). Those who surrender receive reduced sentences, as stipulated in the law. However, reports—refuted by government authorities—have indicated that a dozen GIA members who surrendered to the state authorities eventually decided to renew their previous activities. Clearly, the most extremists among the Islamists will continue their campaign of terror. However, the nature of their activities—racketeering, rape, fake roadblocks to extort passengers, and assassinations—demonstrate that the ideological dimension has given place to pure banditry. The authorities had vowed that after January 13, 2000, expiration date for the law, those groups who refuse to surrender would be fought with all the means at the disposal of the state, notwithstanding the opinions of non-governmental organizations, such as Amnesty International or Human Rights Watch. While the state authorities may be justified in fighting the criminal activities of armed groups, it is evident that terrorism will survive as long as the state has not tackled the deep-seated problems (corruption, injustice, and marginalization) that have led to the armed insurgency in the first place.

Notes

1   Free medical care and education as well as little taxation made possible by the oil rent.
2   This concept is used in the sense conceived by Hisam Sharabi. Accordingly, in a modernized patriarchy 'material modernization' shaped 'patriarchal structures and relations' and strengthened them by giving them a semblance of modernity (Sharabi, 1988, p. 4).
3   Author's interviews with Islamist students at the University of Algiers in 1979, 1980, and 1983. Yet, in the literature on Algerian Islamists, emphasis is put on the fact that the Islamist movement is homegrown with little or no reference to outside influence. Noteworthy exception is Abderrahim Lamchichi, who argues that the Iranian Revolution contributed to the radicalization of the Algerian Islamist movement (Lamchichi, 1992, p. 69).
4   *Trabendo* refers to illegal imports of foreign goods—especially those unavailable in the country—and their re-sale at prohibitive prices at home. Individuals involved in such a market have made huge fortunes. Their connection with the Algerian bureaucracy and with barons of successive regimes is certain (Bouzourene, 1994). It should also be pointed out that the Islamists, too, were heavily involved in *trabendo* activities.
5   'Afghans' refer to those Algerian Islamists who fought the Soviets alongside the *Mujahidins* in Afghanistan in the 1980s.
6   Abdallah Djaballah later joined five other candidates in withdrawing from the race for alleged fraud.

References

Abdelmalek, Anouar (1972), *La Renaissance du monde arabe* (Renaissance of the Arab World), Editions du Culot: Gembloux (Belgium).
Al-Ahnaf, Mustafa; Bernard Botiveau; and Franck Fregosi (1991), L'Algerie par ses islamistes (How Algerian Islamists See Algeria), Karthala: Paris.
Al-Asala (1979), Nos. 65–66, January-February, pp. 59–67.
Arkoun, Mohammad (1988), 'Algeria,' in Hunter, Shireen (ed.), *The Politics of Islamic Revivalism: Diversity and Unity*, Indiana University Press: Bloomington, pp. 171–186.
Azzi, Mohamed Farid (1999), 'Algerian Youth: Between Alienation and Integration,' in Zoubir, Yahia H. (ed.), North Africa in Transition: State, Society, and Economic Transformation in the 1990s, University Press of Florida: Gainesville.
Babadji, Ramdane (1991), 'Le phenomene associatif en Algerie: genese et perspectives' (The Associations Movement in Algeria: Origins and Perspectives), *Annuaire de l'Afrique du Nord 1989*, Vol. 28, CNRS: Paris.
Ben Bella, Ahmed (1987), *L'Itineraire* (The Itinerary), Editions Maintenant: Alger (Algeria).

Benhadj, Ali (n.d.), Sheikh Abu a'bd al-Fatah Ali Ben Hadj, *Fasl al kalam fi muwajahat zul al hukkam (al jabha al-islamyia lil inkkad)*, FIS.

Bennoune, Mahfoud (1992), 'Notre derniere chance: Comment on fait le lit de l'integrisme, I' (Our Last Chance: Comment on How the Ground Is for Islamism), *Algerie-Actualite*, No. 1376, February 27-March 4, p. 19.

Berque, Jacques and J. Paul Charnay (1966), *Normes et valeurs dans l'Islam contemporain* (Norms and Values in Contemporary Islam), Payot: Paris.

Bey, Mohamed-Cherif Salah (1978), 'La Constitution et la theorie generale du droit' (The Constitution and the General Theory of Law), *Revue algerienne des sciences juridique, economique, et politique* (Algerian Review of Law, Economic, and Political Sciences), Vol. 15, No. 3, September.

Bouandel, Youcef and Yahia H. Zoubir (1998), 'Algeria's Elections: Prelude to Democratization?' *Third World Quarterly*, Vol. 19, No. 2, pp. 177–190.

Boukhoubza, M'hammed (1991), *Octobre 88-Evolution ou rupture?* (October 88-Evolution or Break?), Editions Bouchene: Algiers (Algeria).

Bouzourene, Karim (1994), 'L'economie informelle de distribution en Algerie' (Informal Economy of Distribution in Algeria), DEA Thesis, Institut d'Etudes Politiques: Paris.

Burgat, Francois (1988), L'Islamisme au Maghreb: La voix du Sud (Islamism in the Maghreb: The voice of the South), Karthala: Paris. This book is also available in English as Burgat, Francois and William Dowell (1993), *The Islamic Movement in North Africa*, Center for Middle Eastern Studies: Austin, TX.

Carlier, Omar (1992), 'De l'islahisme a l'islamisme: la therapie politico-religieuse du FIS' (From Islahism to Islamism: The Political-Religious Therapy of the FIS), *Cahiers d'etudes africaines* (African Studies Notebooks), Vol. 32 (2), No. 126, pp. 185–219.

Carre, Olivier (1993), *L'Islam laique ou le retour a la grande tradition* (Secular Islam or the Return to the Great Tradition), Armand Colin: Paris.

Charef, Abed (1990), *Octobre 1988*, 2nd ed., Editions Laphomic: Alger (Algeria).

Clement, Jean-Francois (1980), 'Pour une comprehension des mouvements islamistes' (For an Understanding of Islamist Movements), *Esprit*, Vol. 1, January.

Cubertafond, Bernard (1979), *La Republique algerienne democratique et populaire* (The Democratic and Popular Republic of Algeria), P.U.F.: Paris.

Cubertafond, Bernard (1981), *L'Algerie contemporaine* (Contemporary Algeria), 2nd ed., Presses universitaires de France: Paris.

Deheuvels, Luc-Willy (1991), *Islam et pensee contemporaine en Algerie: La revue al-Asala, 1971–1981* (Islam and Contemporary Thought in Algeria: The Authenticity Review, 1971–1981), CNRS: Paris.

El-Kenz, Ali (1989), 'La societe algerienne aujourd'hui: esquisse d'une phenomenologie de la conscience nationale' (Algerian Society Today: Outline of a Phenomenology of National Conscience), in El-Kenz, Ali (ed.), *La Modernite et l'Algerie* (Modernity and Algeria), CODESRIA: Dakar (Senegal).

Etienne, Bruno (1987), *L'Islam radical* (Radical Islam), Hachette: Paris.

Ferjani, Mohamed-Cherif (1992), *Islamisme, laicite et droits de l'homme* (Islamism, Secularism, and Human Rights), Editions l'Harmattan: Paris.

Financial Times (1996), January 12, p. 5.

Garon, Lise (1993), *L'Obsession unitaire et la nation trompee: La fin de l'Algerie socialiste* (Obsession with Unity of a Cheated Nation: The End of Socialist Algeria), Presses de l'Universite Laval: Sainte-Foy, Quebec (Canada).

Gacemi, Baya (1998), *Moi, Nadia, femme d'un emir du GIA* (I, Nadia, Wife of an Amir of the GIA), Seuil: Paris.

Goumeziane, Smail (1994), *Le Mal algerien: Economie politique d'une transition inachevee, 1962–1994* (The Algerian Ailment: Political Economy of an Unfinished Transition, 1962–1994), Fayard: Paris.

Harbi, Mohammed (1975), *Aux Origines du FLN* (To the Origins of the FLN), Editions Bourgois: Paris.

Harbi, Mohammed (ed.) (1992), *L'Islamisme dans tous ses etats* (Facets of Islamisrn), Editions Rahma: Alger (Algeria).

Harbi, Mohammed (1993), *L'Algerie et son Destin: Croyants ou citoyens* (Algeria and her Destiny: Believers or Citizens), Editions Arcantere: Paris.

Khelladi, Aissa (1992), *Les Islamistes algeriens face au pouvoir* (Algerian Islamists in the Face of Power), Editions Alfa: Algiers (Algeria).

Labat, Severine (1994), 'Islamism and Islamists: The Emergence of New Types of Politico-Religious Militants,' in Ruedy, John (ed.), *Islamism and Secularism in North Africa*, St. Martin's Press: New York.

Lacheraf, Mostefa (1965), *L'Algerie: Nation et societe* (Algeria: Nation and Society), Editions Maspero: Paris.

Lamchichi, Abderrahim (1989), *Islam et contestation au Maghreb* (Islamism and Contention in the Maghreb), Editions l'Harmattan: Paris.

Lamchichi, Abderrahim (1992), *L'Islamisme en Algerie* (Islamism in Algeria), Editions l'Harmattan: Paris.

Leca, Jean and Jean-Claude Vatin (1975), *L'Algerie politique: Institutions et regime* (Political Algeria: Institutions and Regime), Presse de la Fondation des Sciences Politiques: Paris.

Martinez, Luis (1998), *La guerre civile en Algerie* (The Civil War in Algeria), Karthala: Paris.

Le Matin (1999), November 9.

Merad, Ali (1967), *Le mouvement reformiste en Algerie, 1925–1940, essai d'histoire religieuse et sociale* (The Reformist Movement in Algeria, 1925–1940, An Essay on Religious and Social History), Mouton: Paris.

Merad, Ali (1981), 'The Ideologization of Islam in the Contemporary Muslim World,' in Cudsi, Alexander S. and Ali H. Dessouki (eds.), *Islam and Power*, The Johns Hopkins University Press: Baltimore.

Merah, Ahmed (1998), *L'Affaire Bouiali telle que vecue par Ahmed Merah ou comment un pouvoir totalitaire a conduit a la revolte* (The Bouiali Affair as Witnessed by Ali Merah and How a Totalitarian Regime Led to Rebellion), El-Oumma, BEK: Algiers (Algeria).

Nouvel Observateur (The New Observer) (1995), No. 1608, International Edition, August 31-September 6.

Projet de Programme du Front Islamique du Salut (Draft Program of the Islamic Salvation Front) (1989), March 7: Algiers (Algeria).

Rarrbo, Kamel (1995), *L'Algerie et sa jeunesse: Marginalisations et desarroi culturel* (Algeria and Its Youth: Marginalizations and Cultural Turmoil), Editions l'Harmattan: Paris.

Roberts, Hugh (1988), 'Radical Islamism and the Dilemma of Algerian Nationalism: The Embattled Arians of Algiers,' *Third World Quarterly*, Vol. 10, No. 2, April.

Rouadjia, Ahmed (1990), *Les Freres et la Mosquee: Enquete sur le mouvement islamiste en Algerie* (The Brotherhood and the Mosque: Investigation on the Islamist Movement in Algeria), Karthala: Paris.

Roberts, Hugh (1992), 'The Algerian State and the Challenge to Democracy,' *Government and Opposition*, Vol. 27, No. 4.

Roy, Olivier (1994), *The Failure of Political Islam*, I.B. Tauris: London.

Ruedy, John (1992), *Modern Algeria: The Origins and Development of a Nation*, Indiana University Press: Bloomington.

Sanson, Henri (1983), *Laicite islamique en Algerie* (Islamic Secularism in Algeria), Editions du CNRS: Paris.

Sharabi, Hisham (1988), *Neopatriarchy: A Theory of Distorted Change in Arab Society*, Oxford University Press: New York.

La Tribune (1998), January 13 and 25, p. 5 and pp. 1, 5, respectively.

Turin, Yvonne (1983), *Affrontements culturels dans l'Algerie coloniale: ecoles, medecines, religion, 1830–1880* (Cultural clashes in colonial Algeria: schools, medicine, religion, 1830–1880), Entreprise nationale du livre, ENAL: Algiers (Algeria).

Weber, Max (1978), 'Science as a Vocation,' in Gerth, H.H. and C. Wright Mills, *From Max Weber: Essays in Sociology*, Oxford University Press: New York.

Willis, Michael (1996), *The Islamist Challenge in Algeria: A Political History*, New York University Press: New York.

Zoubir, Yahia H. (1994), 'Algeria's Multi-Dimensional Crisis: The Story of A Failed State-Building Process,' *Journal of Modern African Studies*, Vol. 32, No. 4, December, pp. 741–747.

Zoubir, Yahia H. (1995), 'Stalled Democratization of an Authoritarian Regime: The Case of Algeria,' *Democratization*, London, Vol. 2, No. 2, pp. 109–139.

Zoubir, Yahia H. (1996), 'Algerian Islamists' Conception of Democracy,' *Arab Studies Quarterly*, Vol. 18, No. 3, Summer, pp. 65–85.

Zoubir, Yahia H. (1997), 'Islamist Political Parties in Algeria,' *Middle East Affairs*, Vol. 3, Nos. 1 and 2, pp. 95–122.

Zoubir, Yahia H. (1998), 'Islam and Democracy in Malek Bennabi's Thought,' *The American Journal of Islamic Social Sciences*, Vol. 15, No. 1, Spring, pp. 107–112.

Zoubir, Yahia H. (1999), 'State and Civil Society in Algeria,' in Zoubir, Yahia H. (ed.), *North Africa in Transition: State, Society, and Economy Transformation in the 1990s*, University Press of Florida: Gainesville, pp. 29–42.

7 Palestine: HAMAS and Religious Extremism

FRANK J. TRAPP

The emergence of HAMAS[1] has thrust religion onto the Palestinian political stage. As a driving political force for the *intifada* (shaking off—Hunter, 1993, p. xi—or uprising), HAMAS initially threatened decades of Palestinian Liberation Organization (PLO) dominance within the Palestinian communities in the West Bank and Gaza strip. Although the breakthrough peace agreements, Oslo I and Oslo II, have restored the PLO's dominance, HAMAS remains an important third voice in Israeli-Palestinian relations. This chapter analyzes the explosive interactions of religion and politics between the PLO and HAMAS through an examination of the evolution of HAMAS and its protracted relations with the PLO.

Genesis

Although HAMAS formally came into existence in 1988 during the *intifada*, its ideological and spiritual roots can be traced to the revolutionary pole of the broad social movement referred to as Islamic fundamentalism. This movement is based on the following tenets: Islam embraces all aspects of life and offers solutions for all situations; shortcomings found in Muslim societies are the result of deviation from the straight path as indicated in the *Qur'an*, *sunnah* (Prophet Mohammad's examples), and *shari'a* (Islamic law), which has been replaced by Western-inspired secularism and materialism; a renewal of Muslim society is dependent on a return to Islam and obedience to the earlier practices of Islam (Esposito, 1991, pp. 163–164). According to Oliver Roy (1994, pp. 77–80), there are two branches of Islamic fundamentalism: reformist and revolutionary. The reformists pursue a bottom-up approach aimed at re-Islamizing the society through social action. In contrast, the revolutionaries advocate political action, including *jihad* (holy war), against non-believers. Prior to the emergence of HAMAS, the message of Islamic fundamentalism was spread among Palestinians by a group of Islamic clerics belonging to the Muslim Brotherhood, originally a reformist movement. The Muslim Brotherhood was founded in 1928 by Hassan al-Banna, a charismatic cleric who preached that Islam was the way to overcome the social injustices of the Egyptian monarchy (Bill and Springborg, 1994, p. 78). As al-Banna's message gained broad accepted among the Egyptian peasantry, the Brotherhood's membership grew in strength to a point where the monarchy perceived it to be a threat. Consequently, the movement was banned in 1949. Following the 1952 Free Officers Revolt, which was led by Gamal Abdul Nasser, the Muslim Brotherhood enjoyed a brief resurgence. However, religious differences between these two groups polarized relations, culminating in a 1954 assassination attempt on President Nasser. A crackdown that followed induced the movement to assume a more discreet posture, weakening its influences throughout Nasser's Egypt. It was during this period that foundations for the

Brotherhood were laid in the Gaza strip, eventually giving rise to HAMAS.

The ideological and spiritual head of the HAMAS is Sheikh Ahmad Yassin. During his youth, he studied at Ein Shams University in Cairo, Egypt. Sheikh Yassin's involvement with political extremism did not start with the *intifada*. Rather, he, along with other members of the Muslim Brotherhood, was arrested and deported from Egypt, following a failed 1965 coup attempt. Upon his return to the Gaza strip, Sheikh Yassin and other Islamic leaders joined together to form a leadership core which espoused an Islamic lifestyle for Palestinian residents of Gaza (Kurz and Tal, 1997, p. 1). The Brotherhood applied for registration as a non-profit organization under the name *Al-Mujamma al-Islami* (The Islamic Association). Because *Mujamma's* platform did not contain nationalistic clauses, Israeli authorities hoped it would act as a counterweight to the nationalistic—but secular—PLO. And in 1978 *Mujamma* was approved by the Israeli Civil Administration (Schiff and Ya'ari, 1989, pp. 222–228). Up to the *intifada*, the focus of *Mujamma* was to educate Palestinians and maintain Islamic institutions. Its activities included building mosques, running schools, and efforts to unify the Palestinian population through its Islamic message (Mishul, 1999, pp. 3–4). In the aftermath of the 1981 assassination of Egyptian President Anwar Sadat, the group was energized when Palestinian students studying at Islamic universities in Egypt were deported to Gaza. These students, under the leadership of Sheikh Yassin, gradually mobilized a sizable proportion of the Muslim Brotherhood's membership from its reformist pole to the revolutionary pole of Islamic Fundamentalism. This shift was crystallized when Israeli authorities increasingly used force in the early stages of the *intifada*. The message of these revolutionaries was later codified into the *Charter of Allah* (Charter of God), a document which serves as a guide and blueprint for HAMAS.

The *Charter of Allah*, which appeared in August 1988, contains thirty three articles outlining the main goals and functions of HAMAS (Israeli, 1992). HAMAS describes the Charter as an extension of the Muslim Brotherhood in Palestine. Muslims who accept the *Charter of Allah* are expected to commit to its plan of action, defend against external threats to the Muslim world, and engage in any actions called for by its leaders. While inspiring others to join its ranks, HAMAS members are expected to keep the leadership of the organization a secret. The ultimate goal of HAMAS is to raise the banner of *Allah* over every inch of Palestine, an area which would include all land from the Mediterranean Sea to the Jordan River, bordered by Lebanon in the north and the Red Sea in the south. HAMAS regards *wataniyya* (nationalism) as part and parcel of its religious faith. For HAMAS followers, nothing is more nationalistic than the belief that *jihad* is necessary when confronting non-believers threatening the Muslim world. In addition to provisions on education, art, and women, the *Charter of Allah* addresses relations with the PLO. HAMAS leaders concede that the PLO has kept the ideal of a Palestinian state alive, but hold that the secular PLO is doomed to failure. This is because Islam is not only a spiritual force, but also a patriotic force. And the PLO lacks the ideological tools to achieve its goals. Following the declaration of the *Charter of Allah*, which espoused political actions, HAMAS undertook a revolutionary course. As the organization has evolved, a loose organizational structure emerged.

Organizational Structure

Although HAMAS has a discernable structure, it has remained in a constant state of flux. This evolving structure results from Israeli attempts at eliminating HAMAS and PLO efforts to absorb HAMAS members. Consequently, only the general structure and components of HAMAS have been identified. Mosques controlled by HAMAS leaders serve as central organizations. These places of worship facilitate recruitment of new members and dissemination of information. Furthermore, they serve as schools, libraries, and venues in promoting HAMAS' influence. In addition, HAMAS is active at clubs and universities where its leaders project the idea of a Jewish plot against the Muslim nation.

Sheikh Ahmad Yassin not only authored the *Charter of Allah*, but also had been actively involved in HAMAS political activities. In 1984, he was arrested by Israeli authorities and later sentenced to 13 years in prison for weapons possession with the intent to commit terrorism. However, he was released the following year as part of a prisoners exchange agreement between Israel and the PLO (Kruz and Tal, 1997, p. 2). During the *intifada* he was again arrested by the Israeli Government on charges of developing the *Charter of Allah*, passing on extensive financial assistance to HAMAS, and ordering the death of three Palestinians accused of collaborating with Israeli authorities. In October 1991 he was convicted of these charges and sentenced to life imprisonment. Because of his deteriorating health, and as part of a goodwill gesture following a blotched assassination attempt on another HAMAS leader residing in Jordan, Sheikh Yassin was released from prison in October 1997. In addition to Sheikh Yassin, other members of the present leadership core include Ibrahim Yazouri, Abd al-Aziz al-Rantisi, Mahmoud al-Zahar, Jamil Hammami[2] (a member of the West Bank Brotherhood), Ibrahim Ghawshah (official spokesperson), and Muhammad Nazzel (head of HAMAS in Jordanian). This core leadership coordinates the various wings of the organization: military, security, political and information, and special events.

Mujahedim a-Falestinin, the military section of HAMAS began its operations in the 1980s. It is responsible for terrorist attacks against Israeli targets within the 'Green Line'. The military section operates under considerable secrecy and employs a variety of methods for hiding and providing arms to its activists. It was headed by Sheikh Salah Shahadeh. Following Shahdeh's arrested and imprisoned in 1989, Khaled Meshal assumed control of the military wing from his office in Jordan. In 2000, the Jordanian Government issued orders for Meshal's arrest on charges of sedition. At that time, Meshal was in Iran; he avoided arrest by not returning to Jordan. Israeli authorities attribute the deaths of 132 Israeli civilians and 70 Israeli soldiers to the military wing (Mishal and Sela, 1997, p. 6). *Al-Majd* (Glory), the security wing, was founded in 1987 (Kurz and Tal, 1997, p. 3). It has two primary tasks. First, it is responsible for uncovering and punishing Palestinians suspected of engaging in activities inimical to the principles of Islam such as the sale and use of drugs. Second, it has targeted Palestinians suspected of collaborating with Israeli authorities. Suspected collaborators have been abducted and interrogated. In some cases, the accused have been executed. The political and information section is the third component of HAMAS. Its main role is to publicize HAMAS political doctrine and objectives through leaflets and bulletins. It is noteworthy that HAMAS first revealed itself on December 14, 1987, with the issuance of a leaflet which decried the sale and use of drugs by Palestinians. In addition, the information wing is responsible for various publications such as the *Falestine al-Muslimah*, which is published in the United Kingdom. The political section also is thought to have strong ties with pro-HAMAS newspapers published within the 'Green Line' by Moslem activists. The last component of HAMAS is the events unit. Established during the *intifada*, its primary role is to organize opposition activities. It initiates and enforces strike calls by the HAMAS leadership. It is also responsible for organizing demonstrations and roadblocks, often resulting in violence. Although Palestinians have abandoned their mass political protests, the events unit is still active in painting nationalist and religious graffiti on walls and buildings.

In terms of its membership, there are important differences within HAMAS, especially between the West Bank and Gaza strip branches. Since it emerged from the Islamic Association, with its independent support structure, the Gaza strip branch was not dependent on the PLO leadership living outside Gaza. As the local Islamic establishments in the West Bank were supported by the Jordanian Royal House and, later, the PLO, that branch was initially influenced by nationalist forces. Both branches are governed by a *Shurah* (Council) consisting of HAMAS members residing both inside and outside the West Bank and Gaza strip. With imprisoning of the leadership by Israeli authorities during the *intifada*, the *Shurah* was relocated from the West Bank and Gaza strip to Amman, Jordan. In recent years, HAMAS has also established missions in Sudan and Iran. Although politically outspoken in the West Bank, Gaza strip, and Jordan, HAMAS has acted cautiously in Sudan and Iran to avoid the appearance of intervening in the domestic affairs of these two allies. Apart from money raised in the West Bank and Gaza strip, HAMAS has sought support from local Islamic associations in the Gulf states. These money is used primarily for educational, social, and cultural centers. A large proportion of this money comes from Saudi Arabia. When Iran assumed leadership of the rejectionist camp opposed to the Arab-Israeli peace negotiations, HAMAS developed close ties with Iranian authorities. This led to the opening of a HAMAS office in Tehran, noted earlier, and the establishment of training centers in Iran, staffed by Iranian Revolutionary Guard members, and Hizbullah camps in Lebanon. The Iranian Government has pledged $30 million annually to HAMAS. Although HAMAS has a identified structure and links to other Islamic Resistance camps in the Middle East, it remains financially weak compared to the PLO. Nevertheless, HAMAS has challenged the PLO leadership in opposing the Oslo Agreements.

Evolving Relationship with the PLO

Relations between the PLO and HAMAS have gone through different phases. Their interactions have been influence by specific events such as the *intifada*, Oslo Agreements, and Wye River Memorandum (Mishal and Sela, 1997, pp. 6–9). At times these relationships have been explosive; at other times they have been conciliatory. From an ideological standpoint, it is easy to conclude that the political doctrine espoused in the *Charter of Allah* provides little room for a dialogue between HAMAS and the PLO. In fact, HAMAS holds that Palestine is an inalienable *waqf* (endowment) and thus there is no room for negotiation regarding a Palestinian state. Despite such rhetoric HAMAS can be characterized as a rationally-motivated actor which considers both the costs and benefits of its relations with the PLO when determining its course of action. Because of these calculated actions HAMAS has remained a voice in Palestinian politics though the organization has splintered into two different factions. One group takes a moderate position; the other advocates a confrontational approach. The first period of PLO-HAMAS relations was one of solidarity within the ranks of HAMAS. During the *intifada*, HAMAS was able to challenge the PLO's claim to leadership within the Palestinian community.

The *intifada* was a watershed event in the Middle East. Although the level of confrontation between the Israeli Government and Palestinian community became intense, the seemingly spontaneous street violence in the Gaza strip caught both Israeli authorities and Palestinians living abroad by surprise. The rock throwing, burning of tires, and physical attacks of the *intifada* qualitatively differed from bombings, armed assaults, infiltrations, and hostage-takings of the past forty years. As Israeli police and soldiers became engrossed in pitched battles with rock and bottle-throwing youths, stern measures—including the firing of metal-jacketed bullets—radicalized the Palestinian population. It also led to intense debates within Israel and among Israeli supporters abroad. In that environment, HAMAS flourished while the PLO floundered. Even though the causes of the *intifada* are many and complex, there is a general agreement that feelings of despair and hopelessness, broadly held by Palestinian refugees, produced the mass eruption of anger. For Palestinians living outside Israeli-controlled territories, the fast-moving events of the *intifada* seemed beyond their influence and control. In contrast, because of its linkages to the Islamic community in the West Bank and Gaza strip, HAMAS was able, at least initially, to orchestrate the flow of these events. That influence stemmed from HAMAS leaflets which exhorted the Palestinian population to undertake both violent and non-violent actions. The violent activities included stone throwings, building barricades of burning tires, wielding knives and axes, and violent attacks on those considered to be collaborating with Israeli authorities. Non-violent activities included calls to sever economic ties with Israel, building alternative local institutions to provide social services, civil disobedience, and activities to promote solidarity. Because HAMAS acted independently of the PLO, HAMAS directives ordered actions that often differed from those ordered by the PLO. By the end of the second year, however, the PLO leadership regained control over the uprising through the PLO-affiliated Unified National Command (UNC). Eventually, the PLO came to dominate the *intifada* and the debate for a Palestinian state.

For the Palestinian people, the presence of two task-masters was particularly tiresome and bewildering. The *intifada* fizzled out partly because of a profound weariness among average Palestinians. Exhausted by years of violence and counter-violence, many were unwilling to continue the struggle. It was also during the winding down of the *intifada* that the PLO underwent an extraordinary transformation from a revolutionary organization bent on the destruction of Israel to a conciliatory organization willing to negotiate the framework of a Palestinian state. This dramatic doctrinal shift was evident as early as 1988 when a draft declaration of Palestinian independence was announced in Algiers, Algeria. For the first time in its history the PLO, represented by Faisal Husyaini, took a conciliatory position towards Israel in accepting United Nations Security Council Resolution 181 as well as an international peace conference on the basis of Security Council Resolutions 242 and 338. That document produced an intense debate within the leadership circles of the Palestinian community and sparked violent clashes between the PLO and HAMAS supporters on the streets of Gaza. The draft 'statement of independence' was totally unacceptable to HAMAS because it did not envisage an Islamic state outlined in the *Charter of Allah*. As the proposal for a negotiated settlement with the Israeli Government gained momentum in the Palestinian community in late 1989, the PLO began a campaign to incorporate HAMAS and its members into its large umbrella organization. In its first major initiative, the PLO called on HAMAS members to accept the UNC as the sole authority to call general strikes, organize demonstrations, and prosecute collaborations. HAMAS leaders rejected these initial overtures, especially following the exclusion of HAMAS operatives from PLO lists for prisoner committees in Israeli prisons and detainee camps (Bill and Springborg, 1994, p. 345).

Apart from a weariness with the *intifada*, the PLO's decision to embrace a conciliatory posture towards Israel was stimulated by changes in international and domestic environment. First, the collapse of communism in the former Soviet Union and Eastern Europe had deprived the PLO of an important ally for economic support and ideological endorsement. Second, the decision to support Saddam Hussein during the 1990–1991 Persian Gulf Crisis cost the PLO dearly, both in terms of remittance earned by Palestinians working in Kuwait and direct financial aid given by the governments of Kuwait and Saudi Arabia. Following the expulsion of Iraqi forces after the 1991 Operation Desert Storm, the Kuwaiti authorities expelled some 400,000 Palestinian workers to Jordan. Later, both the Kuwaiti and Saudi Governments ended subsidies to the PLO. In the wake of this financial loss, PLO leaders softened their position about a negotiated settlement with Israel. In addition, the incorporation of HAMAS, especially its militant wing, was a necessity for a successful peace with Israel. To that end, the Palestinian National Council (PNC), which would include representatives of HAMAS, was created as a representative body for the Palestinian people. On the eve of preparatory meetings, however, HAMAS sent a list of demands that the PLO found unacceptable. First, HAMAS insisted on a formula whereby 40 percent of the seats in the new PNC would be appropriated to HAMAS, insisting that its proven electoral power in public institutions in the West Bank and Gaza strip justified allocation of 40 percent of the seats. Second, it called for a general election that would include all Palestinians, both those living in the West Bank and Gaza strip as well as Palestinians in diaspora throughout the Middle East. Third, HAMAS insisted on changes in the *Palestinian National Charter* to incorporate *jihad* as the sole means for liberating Palestine. Fourth, a proportion of the financial contributions to the PLO should be shared with HAMAS. Finally, HAMAS representatives would be incorporated into PLO's bureaucracy. In countering these stipulations, Yassir Arafat, Chairman of the PLO, offered HAMAS 20 percent of PNC seats. However, he declined to concede to the other demands made by HAMAS. With the start of the October 1991 Madrid Conference, sponsored by the United States, initial efforts to bring HAMAS into the PNC fold were halted. Over the next two years, PLO-HAMAS relations ebbed and flowed as Arafat assessed HAMAS electoral gains in public institutions in the West Bank and Gaza strip.

Following the Israeli Government's expulsion of 415 HAMAS activists to southern Lebanon in response to the kidnapping and murder of an Israeli border guard, Palestinian public pressure induced the PLO to attempt another dialogue with HAMAS. Although the deportation initially boosted HAMAS' popularity within the Palestinian community, it paralyzed the organization in the West Bank. The immediate result of the resumption of a PLO-HAMAS dialogue was an ad hoc agreement between *Izz al-Din al-Qassam*, the military wing of HAMAS, and *Al-Fatah* the PLO counterpart. This agreement called for coordinated actions against Israel. Also, pressure from within the Palestinian community induced HAMAS to participate in a December 1992 meeting at the PLO headquarters in Tunis, Tunisia. At that meeting Arafat repeated his earlier proposal to include HAMAS as the 'second largest faction' in the PNC. The HAMAS delegation rejected the offer and demanded PLO's withdrawal from the Madrid peace talks. Although HAMAS and the PLO were unable to find common grounds, the Tunis meeting was important. HAMAS' participation at the PLO's headquarters, in spite of internal discord and Iranian protest, was a tacit recognition of the PLO's status as the 'major representative' of the Palestinian people. The event undercut HAMAS' claim as the representative body for the Palestinian people. This series of offers, counter-offers, and meetings became indicative of the interplay between the PLO and HAMAS during the 1990s. Following the PLO's decision to open direct negotiations with Israel and the resulting landmark agreements, HAMAS legitimacy and standing within the Palestinian community was further eroded, eventually causing the organization to splinter.

The signing of the 'Declaration of Principles,' also know as the Oslo I Agreement, was a second major watershed event in the Middle East. On September 13, 1993, Yassir Arafat and Yitzuah Rabin had a historic meeting on the south lawn of the White House in Washington, DC, where they not only signed an agreement ending fifty years of hostilities, but also shook hands in a very symbolic gesture between the two former antagonists. HAMAS remained committed to its ideology in rejecting the agreement and took measures to preserve its influence within the Palestinian community (Kurz and Tal, 1997, p. 1). The most important feature of Oslo I was the establishment of an autonomous Palestinian National Authority (PNA). Negotiations in May 1994 in Cairo, Egypt, produced further protocols which placed Jericho and the Gaza strip under the PNA's control. One of the first goals of the PLO following the Cairo Agreement was to convince HAMAS to accept the authority of the PNA. Second, the PLO sought to get the HAMAS leadership to renounce terrorism against Israel. Publicly HAMAS expressed a position of coexistence with the PNA. It was a strategy designed to preserve its political power and ideological appeal to the Palestinian population. Internally, however, confusion and dissension emerged within the ranks of HAMAS. Some factions expressed a fear that the longer they remained opposed to the Israeli-Palestinian peace negotiations and allowed HAMAS militants to perpetrate acts of terrorism, the more vulnerable they would be to the PNA police and Israeli reprisals. That was particularly so given the extent of cooperation which was developing between Israeli authorities and the PNA (Kurz and Tal, 1997, p.3). While the political and security wings of HAMAS explored avenues of moderation and accommodation, the militant wing reiterated its commitment to the *Charter of Allah* and decided to expand the level of *jihad* to *istish-had* (self-sacrifice). This meant attacks on Israeli citizens in the heart of their cities where escape was not possible and capture, if not death, was a certainty. In April 1994, *Izz a-Din al-Qassam* squads carried out terrorist attacks in Afula and Hadera coinciding with the signing of the May 1994 Cairo Agreement establishing the PNA. In July and October 1994, there were kidnappings and murders of Israeli soldiers.

This HAMAS campaign of terror was an effort not only to derail support for the peace negotiation within the Israeli population, but also it was designed to weaken the PNA in the eyes of the Israeli Government and Palestinian community. In the latter case, the terrorism campaign initially produced the intended effect. As the PNA sought to establish its authority over the newly-transferred territories, tensions between PNA and HAMAS supporters resulted in violence. On November 18, 1994, there was a violent clash between HAMAS supporters and PNA loyalists when Palestinian police fired upon HAMAS worshipers at the Filastin Mosque in Gaza City, killing 16 worshipers and wounding 200 others. Because of the deadliness of the incident, leading Israeli Arabs and Palestinian Gazans attempted to renew discussions between the PNA and HAMAS. As a result, HAMAS and the PNA agreed to refrain from armed acts of provocations. Furthermore, HAMAS agreed to recognize the authority of the Palestinian police as the only force authorized to bear firearms in the Gaza strip. The agreement applied only to the Gaza strip, not the West Bank. *Izz a-Din al-Qassam* squads remained active in the West Bank, attacking Israeli citizens and targets. The agreement was important because it showed a willingness on the part of moderate HAMAS members to engage in political accommodation with the PNA. Following this spate of terrorism, Israeli authorities imposed new restrictions and sanctions reminiscent of the extreme measures undertaken by Israeli authorities during the height of the intifada.[3]

The signing of the second major Israeli-Palestinian peace agreement on September 25, 1995, the so-called Oslo II Accord, produced further divisions within HAMAS. One important provision of the agreement was setting an agenda for elections to the PNA's legislative Council. Within HAMAS, a struggle arose between the Gaza strip leadership and external leadership comprised of HAMAS members in Israeli prisons and those living in Jordan. The rift was evidenced by two meetings which explored the possibility of modifying the HAMAS rejectionist position regarding the peace negotiations. On October 7, 1995, there was meeting in Khartoum, Sudan, between four Gazan HAMAS activists and members of the external leadership. The goal of the meeting was to mitigate growing intra-organizational differences. The following issues were discussed at the meeting: recognition of the Oslo Agreements as a fait accompli; appointment of HAMAS activists to secondary positions in the PNA; cessation of military operations by HAMAS against Israeli targets presently under PNA control; and a prohibition against preparing for such operations in PNA controlled areas when aimed at Israel. In exchange for acceptance of these proposals by the militant faction of HAMAS, its members currently under PNA detention would be released. Despite a HAMAS leaflet which claimed that the four Gazans who met with the external leadership did not have the authority to acticulate a formal agreement with the PNA, a second meeting with the PNA took place. The following October 13, nine HAMAS activists from the West Bank, headed by Jamil Hammani, and the four member delegation returning from Sudan, met with Yassir Arafat. The response by the external leadership to this meeting was a second leaflet which stated that the HAMAS position towards the Oslo process would remain unshaken and the organization would continue its *jihad* against Israel. Despite efforts by the external group to influence the flow of events, on December 7 a 13-member HAMAS delegation—eight from the earlier Gaza meeting and five from the external leadership— headed by Haled Mish'al met with a 15-member PNA delegation headed by Salim Za'noun, Chairman of the PNC. The PNA proposal included suggestions that HAMAS participate in the upcoming election, become a political party, and discontinue terrorism. Although the HAMAS delegates declined the strategy, the meeting was a tacit acceptance of PNA authority—by the moderate faction of HAMAS—on the Gaza strip and newly acquired autonomous areas of the West Bank.

The elections for the PNA, which took place on January 20, 1996, were perceived by local Gazans and foreign observers as a vote of faith for the Oslo Accords. The HAMAS position regarding the elections was influenced by two factors. First, HAMAS was faced with having to decide whether or not to participate in the PNA elections. The decision would, in turn, link HAMAS to the Oslo principles and legitimize the PNA, or risk the possibility of being marginalized by boycotting the elections. Second, even if HAMAS boycotted the elections, the organization would have to decide whether or not it would, or could, play a more significant role within the PNA. Although HAMAS publicly reiterated its opposition to the 'shameful and humiliating accord,' efforts to seek reconciliation with the PNA rekindled an intra-HAMAS debate regarding its stand on the forthcoming election. In November 1995, HAMAS officially announced its decision to boycott PNA elections. However, HAMAS made clear that the boycott would not prevent indirect participation by its members, hinting at the possibility of forming an Islamic bloc of names to be placed on the ballot. Adhering to this strategy of an 'unofficial presence,' HAMAS was able to put forth seven candidates, six of whom were elected. HAMAS also supported a number of independent candidates and several *Fatah* candidates known for 'their good relations' with the Islamic opposition (Mishal and Sela, 1997, p. 20). The series of meetings between HAMAS moderates and the PNA, along with indirect participation in the PNA elections, signaled a mellowing of the internal leadership's opposition to the PNA. The external leadership, living outside the PNA controlled areas, continued its strategy of *jihad* against Israel. Eventually, a renewed campaign of violence threatened the position of the moderates and the PNA's ability to deliver on a pledge to end Palestinian sponsored terrorism. After the elections—which HAMAS officially boycotted but pledged to accept—the PNA undertook yet another effort in inducing HAMAS members to join the PNA. As dialogue between the PNA and HAMAS resumed, unfortunately a series of suicide bombings inside Israel ended those discussions. On February 25, 1996, a suicide bomber on the No. 18 bus in Jerusalem detonated a bomb which killed 26 Israelis. Less than two weeks later, on March 3, a second suicide bomb detonated in another Jerusalem bus, killing 19 persons. The immediate effect was not only an end of negotiations between the PNA and HAMAS, but also a rise in tension between Israel and the PNA.

At the heart of the Palestinian-Israeli-HAMAS triad is the issue of security. From the Israeli perspective, the Oslo I and II Accords were designed to end years of terrorism and the uncertainty which this violence has inflicted upon the life of the average Israeli citizen. Despite its efforts to curtail terrorism perpetrated by HAMAS, the PNA was unable to stop these activities for a number of reasons. First, HAMAS leadership structure was divided between the internal moderates in the West Bank and Gaza strip and the militant external branch dominated by individuals residing in Amman, Damascus, Khartoum, and Tehran. On the one hand, this external leadership has persistently advocated an uncompromising *jihad* as the only way to confront Israel. Despite occasional statements that the PNA's acceptance of a limited Palestinian state is a treason, on the other hand, the moderates claim that HAMAS exists only inside the occupied territories because this is the arena where Palestinian people are suffering under Israeli occupation (Kurz and Tal, 1997, p. 8). Second, the structure of the military wing of HAMAS makes it a difficult component to control. Also, the perpetrators believe that their self-sacrifice will be rewarded with eternal paradise. Furthermore, the suicide bombers appear to be primarily recruited by the external leadership. In addition, the inability of the PNA to corral the military wing of HAMAS stems from the continued Israeli policy of collective punishment, discredits the PNA and engenders another group of suicide bombers who clearly see the state of Israel as the oppressor. Third, since 1967, the Palestinian community has had dependent relationships with Israel. Prior to the start of the *intifada* an estimated 120,000 Palestinian laborers, many from the Gaza strip, were working inside Israel, (Kurz and Tal, 1997, p. 9). These workers have been an important source of cheap labor for Israel. In turn, the wages earned by Palestinians working in Israel are an important component of the Palestinian economy. Although security restrictions resulting from the *intifada* reduced that number of laborers to 80,000, including 30,000 from the Gaza strip, these wages remain important—especially after the expulsion of Palestinian workers from Kuwait—to the Palestinian community. Following the February and March 1996 suicide attacks, Israeli authorities again closed its borders with Gaza and imposed a general curfew over the West Bank. The measure led to an unemployment rate of 45 percent and 30 percent among workers in Gaza strip and the West Bank, respectively. Lacking an independent infrastructure, Palestinian raw materials sent through Israeli ports were especially hard hit because of the curfew and closures. In total, these measures were estimated to have cost the Palestinian economy $1–2 million a day (Kurz and Tal, 1997, p. 9).

For the PNA, the closure of borders was particularly troublesome. While Palestinians initially vented their anger against HAMAS, over time that frustration shifted to the PNA and Israel. According to Ibrahim Ghawshah, a HAMAS spokesperson in Amman, the terror campaign of 1996 was successful, despite the hardship imposed on the Palestinians, because it was designed to influence Israeli public opinion into rejecting the Oslo Accords. Ironically, the strategy helped Benjamin Netanyahu and the conservative Likud party win the May 1996 Israeli elections. It was also interesting that the HAMAS militants believed the Likud party would bring an end to the Oslo process and thus discredit the PNA and Arafat. However, the external HAMAS leadership miscalculated Likud's response regarding the peace process. Whereas Shimon Peres suspended further redeployment of Israeli forces in Hebron, the Netanyahu Administration reached an agreement on new redeployment with the PNA in January 1997. The Israeli Government hoped that PNA to could eventually bring HAMAS under its control. In fact, polling data of the Palestinian population has indicated that HAMAS popularity dramatically dropped following its campaign of suicide bombings. Support for terrorist attacks against Israelis dropped from 57 percent in November 1994 to 46 percent in February 1995, and declined further to 21 percent by March 1996.

Despite efforts by the PNA and Israeli Government, terrorist actions attributed to HAMAS continued through 1997 and 1998. Those attacks not only brought the Oslo process to a standstill, but also further strained relations between the PNA and HAMAS. The July 1997 suicide bombings of the Mahane Yehuda market in Jerusalem, which killed 13 people and wounded 170 others, led the PNA to arrest HAMAS members. The following September three additional suicide bombs killed four persons and wounded 180 others as Israelis were strolling along a popular shopping promenade in Jerusalem. In the aftermath of the attack, Palestinian security forces arrested 20 additional HAMAS members on the West Bank and Gaza strip. The continued pace of suicide attacks in Israel severely strained Israeli-Palestinian relations. Members of the Netanyahu Government expressed concern over the ability of the PNA to combat terrorism assumed to be originating from PNA controlled territory. In numerous incidents members of the *Knesset* (Israeli parliament) openly criticized Arafat's leadership of the PNA. Following these bombings Netanyahu declared that political dialogue was not possible as long as Israelis were being blown up in the streets of Israel. Despite those recriminations, efforts under the sponsorship of the Clinton Administration led to three rounds of talks at the Wye River Conference Center. While not as dramatic as the Oslo Accords, those discussions produced a breakthrough agreement between the PNA and Israeli Government. The Wye River Memorandum was an attempt to facilitate the implementation of the Oslo II Agreement and other related understandings reached earlier between the Israeli Government and PNA. Central to the Wye Memorandum was a tacit understanding that the PNA would participate with Israel and the United States in a combined effort to end the campaign of violence by the military wing of HAMAS. Under this agreement, Israel and the PNA recognized that it was in their interest to combat terrorism through a joint program that entailed attacking both terrorists and their support structure. To that end, the Israeli Government and PNA would share information, strategies, and actions. Furthermore, the PNA would outlaw terrorist-based organizations, prohibit illegal weapons imports, and prevent violent incitements by Palestinian groups. The United States Central Intelligence Agency was authorized to assist the PNA with its antiterrorism campaign and evaluate PNA's efforts in combating terrorism. Although attacks attributed to the military wing continued, the success of the Wye Memorandum was felt in terms of bungled terrorist attacks and renewed pressure by the PNA on HAMAS to end these activities. Arafat condemned these actions in public statements because they not only jeopardized the Wye River Agreement, but also threatened to undermine the progress already made under the Oslo process. In an effort to combat terrorism, he ordered the detention of dozens of Islamists in PNA controlled territory, including placing Sheikh Ahmed Yassin under house arrest. Increasingly, Gazan HAMAS leaders renounced the distribution of leaflets claiming the 'struggle' against Israel will never stop.

In 1999, the rift between the internal and external elements of HAMAS continued as each side vied for support from Palestinians. Apart from the campaign of suicide bombings, the competition was in the form of statements and leaflets aimed at the Palestinian people. Following a meeting between HAMAS and the PNA in April that year, Ibrahim Ghawshah announced that the HAMAS delegation from the Gaza strip—led by Sheikh Yassin—that met with the Central Council of the PLO was 'a local decision.' According to Reuven Paz, the phrasing of the language was in important because Ghawshah was no longer describing Sheikh Yassin as 'the founder' and spiritual leader of HAMAS, but as one of the local brothers who made a decision based on purely local consideration. The response to the step taken by Sheikh Yassin was indicative of the conflict taking place between the local and external leadership of HAMAS. Shortly after the meeting and the Ghawshah statement, Khaled Meshal, leader of the military wing, declared that HAMAS remained strongly opposed to interim peace agreements with Israel. He added that the lack of attacks since October 1999 was not evidence that HAMAS had bowed to pressure to halt attacks against Israel.

Conclusion

The Palestinian-Israeli peace initiatives represent a unique phase in Arab-Israeli relations. Not only have these two protagonists reached an accommodation with one another, but also have attempted to engage in negotiations for a peaceful future. One important obstacle to realizing this peace is the militant arm of HAMAS. While a fruitful dialogue appears possible with the Gazan and West Bank leaders, the external leadership has steadfastly remained committed to the *Charter of Allah* and *jihad*. Interestingly, both Israel and the PLO have concluded that terrorism and brute force will not produce desired results. Thus, the former adversaries have gradually abandoned violence in favor of coexistence. Although sensitive issues—the status of Jerusalem, borders, and refugees—have stymied further progress toward a permanent settlement, HAMAS remains yet another hurdle that must be overcome. As noted in this chapter, the origin of HAMAS can be traced back to the broader notion of Islamic Fundamentalism. The organization is a manifestation of the revolutionary zeal and militant thought process associated with Islamic Fundamentalism. Despite efforts by the PLO to incorporate HAMAS into its folds, HAMAS remains a prominent third voice in Palestinian politics. However, division between the internal and external leadership has weakened HAMAS and, over time, its role in Palestinian politics may be marginalized.

Notes

1   The formal name is Harakat al-Muqawama al-Islamyya (Islamic Resistance Movement).
2   Subsequently, Jamil Hammami has publicly disavowed membership in HAMAS. In the late 1990s, he actively participated in a number of Israeli-Palestinian peace negotiations (Mishul, 1999, pp. 45–46).
3   It is noteworthy that in addition to military actions and the imprisonment of PLO operatives, since 1967 the Israeli Government had waged a campaign of collective punishment against the Palestinian community. The operation included demolishing homes of people suspected of terrorism, mass curfew in camps and towns, and closure of borders between Israel and the occupied territories.

References

Bill, James A. and Robert Springborg (1994), *Politics in the Middle East*, 4th ed., HarperCollins, New York.

Esposito, John L. (1991), *Islam: The Straight Path*, Oxford University Press: New York.

Hunter, F. Robert (1993), *The Palestinian Uprising: A War by Other Means*, rev. and expanded, University of California Press: Berkeley.

Israeli, Raphael (1992), translator and annotator, *The Charter of Allah: The Platform of the Islamic Resistance Movement*, The Hebrew University: Jerusalem (Israel).

Kurz, Anat and Nahman Tal (1997), *Hamas: A Radical Islam in a National Struggle*, Memorandum No. 48, Tel Aviv University: Tel Aviv (Israel).

Mishal, Shual and Avraham Sela (1997), *Hamas: A Behavioral Profile*, Tel Aviv University: Tel Aviv (Israel).

Mishul, Muhammad (1999), *The Foreign Policy of Hamas*, Council on Foreign Relations: New York.

Roy, Oliver R. (1994), *The Failure of Political Islam*, Harvard University Press: Cambridge, MA.

Schiff, Ze'ev and Ehud Ya'ari (1989), Intifada: *The Palestinian Uprising: Israel's Third Front*, Simon and Schuster: New York.

8 Chechnya: Islam and Political Insurrection

ALYNNA J. LYON

Chechnya, lying on Russia's southern border, in the North Caucasus region between the Black and the Caspian Seas, has engaged Russia in a bloody and destructive war for almost an entire decade. In 1999, reports of Russia's invasion of Chechnya with armored tanks and air strikes shocked the world and undermined the legitimacy of the newly formed democratic Russian Federation. The conflict began in 1992 when Chechen nationalist leaders rejected the Russian Federation Treaty and initiated a secessionist campaign. In response, Moscow attacked Chechnya and was met by a significant, organized, and unanticipated resistance. The conflict escalated from 1994 to 1996 and, after years of civil war, approximately 500,000 people were displaced from their homes and 25,000 to 100,000 people died ('Chechnya,' 1997, pp. 17–18). Furthermore, the two largest cities in Chechnya, Grozny and Gudermas, were devastated and the local economy was shattered. Then, in the fall of 1999, the conflict again escalated as Russia threatened to obliterate the capital of Chechnya and expel its residents. Scholars have looked to the Caucasus for years and tried to explain the Chechen conflict in both primordial and instrumentalist terms (Bitov, 1992; Burney and Lang, 1971; Goldenberg, 1994; Layton, 1986; Nichols, 1994; Suny, 1983). This debate considers whether the Chechen ethnic identity is enduring and responding to external threats, or largely manufactured and manipulated for political gain. Although the questions are important, often there is something missing in these works (Damrel, 1995, p. 10). Most studies, in their quest to explain the origins of ethnicity, tend to downplay the influence of religion in their analyses of the Chechen secessionist movement and the civil war that followed. The Chechens are 'deeply Muslim peoples' and Islam has provided the foundation for Chechen nationalism for centuries (Avtorkhanov and Broxup, 1992, p. ix). During the 18th and 19th centuries, Islam united the people of the North Caucasus in a common cause against the Russian, Tzarist Empire and, in the early part of the 20th century, it mobilized them against the Soviet Union. After 70 years of marginalization under Soviet rule, Islam has reappeared in Chechnya. In fact, the Chechen secessionist movement must be understood in historical context: 250 years of religious-based insurrections against Russia. The Chechen Muslim identity was an important component that shaped the insurgency and fueled the flames of war in the 1990s.

This chapter explores the role of the tenets and symbols of Islam in the hostilities between the breakaway republic of Chechnya and Russia. Also, the work examines whether the Chechen conflict is indicative of what Mark Juergensmeyer (1993) has identified as a 'new Cold War:' religious nationalism confronting the secular state. Furthermore, in discussing several ways in which religion can influence political life, this chapter raises questions about the continued role of Islam in Chechnya and the recent controversial adoption of the *shari'a* (Islamic law). In particular, is the Islamic model shaping a political system and judicial administration, or is it peripheral and private? When one looks at Chechnya through a religious lens, the depth of the recent conflict with

Russia is revealed. The case illustrates how Chechen nationalist leaders invoked religious history and Muslim identity in this struggle with Russia and transformed the demands for autonomy into a violent secessionist movement. Islamic discourse—built on Sufi symbolism, religious warriors, and an established tradition of *jihad* (holy war)—enhanced three essential components of the Chechen conflict with Russia: unity, organization, and mobilization. This approach highlights the process whereby Islam took on political significance: religion became intertwined with politics as the tenets and symbols of Islam challenged Russian authority and prescribed a new social order. Also, the politicization and repression of Islam during the Soviet period, recent development of the Chechen secessionist movement, and events of the war with the Russian federation are explored. What is particularly interesting here is how Chechen political leaders adopted religious rhetoric, which allowed them to transform political agendas into a *jihad*. The symbol of *jihad* and the Islamic Sufi orders created political power, defined a national group, and mobilized the Chechens to violence and civil war. Here, religion and politics came together: the sacred and spiritual became relevant for the 'authoritative allocation of values' (Easton, 1965, p. 50). Thus, in the tradition of Max Weber (1965), this study is an analysis of socio-political processes and religion.

Islam and *Jihad* in Historical Context

Within Chechnya, there are three primary ethnic groups: Chechens, Ingush, and Russians.[1] In 1936, these peoples were legally united in the Autonomous Chechno-Ingushetia Republic. Census data from 1989 reported that among the 1.2 million people in Chechnya, 57.8 percent of the population were Chechen, 23.1 percent Russian, and 12.9 percent Ingush (*National'nyi sostav naseleniia SSSR*, 1991, pp. 34–40, cited in Huskey, 1992, p. 255). The Chechen and Ingush peoples are Sunni[2] Muslims; most Russians are Eastern Orthodox Christians. Historically, economic inequalities and disproportionate ethnic concentrations in industrial enterprises within the Chechnya territory have strained relations between these three groups. Although the republic has been rich in agricultural resources and oil reserves, recent fighting has destroyed most of its agricultural sector and industrial infrastructure. When Moscow invaded Chechnya in December 1994, Chechen political leaders used religious rhetoric and impressed on the Chechen people that the Russians were infidels who threatened their religious autonomy. The character of Chechnya's historical experience with Russia and the connections with Islamic tradition— specifically the glorious image of *jihad*—helped to frame the secessionist issues and justified the resort to violence in the Chechen mindset. In examining the above questions, with specific focus on Chechnya's secession and Islam, it is necessary to understand the concept of *jihad* or *gazavat* (holy war). As will be discussed in more detail below, many Chechen people believe that *jihad* against Russia is both necessary and legitimate.

The term '*jihad*' is itself very potent and loaded with political and religious connotations. Benjamin Barber recently used the term to portray dogmatic and violent behavior emerging from local identities in their responses to the uniformity of consumerism and modernization, or the imposing 'McWorld' (Barber, 1995). *Jihad* has also been caricaturized in the Western media as an irrational and fundamentally aggressive crusade against Western civilization, and it is frequently associated with terrorists, ambitious tyrants, and heedless mobs. Therefore, it is important to clarify *jihad* as a religious tenet of Islam. It is noteworthy that *jihad* is not synonymous with war. It is derived from the word *jahad*, which refers to 'exerting oneself' to one's fullest potential, or from *mujahed*, an individual who exerts himself to support *Allah's* (God's) cause (Hassan, 1981). Islamic doctrine is not inherently hostile to non-Islamic states or peoples; *jihad* does not refer to war against Jews or Christians. In fact, Islam wages tolerance to non-Muslims, particularly to the 'People of the Book' (Jews and Christians). In fact, the Qur'an proclaims that to each is his own religion (Qur'an 109:6). The Western stereotype, portraying Islam as an antagonistic force in which all believers irrationally seek to confront and ultimately conquer the non-Muslim world, is inaccurate and myopic. However, historical glory is an essential component of Islamic heritage and that leads some Muslims to aspire for an Islamic state (Hassan, 1981, p. 250). At the same time, the Qur'an articulates that *jihad* should not be fought for evangelical purposes; it can only be undertaken in defending and protecting a religious community. However, when a legitimate Islamic authority declares a *jihad*, all Muslims are expected to participate in that struggle. The call of *jihad* is an appeal to the Muslims, both as individuals and as an Islamic community to take it as a duty of the righteous to 'forbid evil' (Qur'an 3:104) and is therefore a 'just' cause undertaken out of necessity and with reverence.

Around the 8th century the Arabs brought Islam to the Caucasus. The region became an arena for clashing empires as Ivan the Terrible fought the Persians and Ottomans for control of the Caucasus in the 16th century. During that time Russia used Christianity to facilitate its expansion and counter Ottoman imperialism; Islam became an antithesis to Christian Russia in the struggle for empires. As those political-religious identities became rigid, the seeds were sown for centuries of antagonism. The relationship between Chechnya, religion, and the Russian political establishment intersect through *jihad* in three periods: the eighteenth, 19th and 20th centuries.

An invasion by Peter the Great in the early 1700s only confirmed for many Chechens and their neighbors that Russia was intent on destroying their religion, autonomy, and way of life. Consequently, the Chechens have fought tzars, dictators and presidents for over 250 years. In order to understand what one author calls the 'politico-religious' environment within Chechnya (Splidsboel-Hansen, 1997, p. 1505), we must look to the past. A review of the historical development of encounters between Chechnya and Russia, as it was defined by religion, helps to explain the process by which religion became intertwined in the political life of Chechnya. The emergence of religious nationalism can be traced back to the 1800s, when a *jihad* was fought by two formidable Chechen historical figures, Sheikh Mansur and Sheikh Shamil. The first, Sheikh Mansur, was an *imam* (religious leader) who received a vision from Prophet Mohammad asking him to declare *jihad* and expel the approaching Russians. Mansur's calls for piety and his declarations against infidels unified many of the mountain tribes under the umbrella of Islam. At one time he led more than 12,000 men into battle and had several triumphant campaigns against Russia (Dunlop, 1998, p. 11). He was captured in 1791 and, after appearing in front of Catherine II, spent several years in a prison in St. Petersburg before he died. Mansur popularized the Naqshabandi Sufi *tariqat* (path or way)—the clan-based brotherhoods—in Chechnya and he is remembered as a messiah and martyr (Spencer, 1839, p. 380). The *jihad* against the Russian Empire was again embraced a few decades later by Sheikh Shamil who led an insurgency against Russia for almost thirty years, ending in 1859. Although Shamil was from neighboring Daghestan, he was widely supported by the people of Chechnya. Like Mansur, Shamil used Islam and strict interpretations of *shari'a* to overcome tribal divisions and unite the peoples of the Caucasus in a robust alliance. After a massacre of 400,000 Chechens by tzarist forces in the 1860s, Shamil's *jihad* and his legacy continued till the end of the 19th century, including rebellions in 1865, 1877, 1879, and 1890 (Damrel, 1995; Lyons, 1994). The legend of these warriors and their gallant outmaneuverings in warding off Russia's shadow in the Caucasus Mountains remains with the people of Chechnya today. The legacy of resistance to infidels, enshrined by Mansur and Shamil, is both powerful and rich in symbolism and myth.

The Chechen struggles against Russia continued into the 20th century. During the October Revolution in 1917, the Bolsheviks originally appeared sympathetic to Chechen calls for autonomous political control. The revolutionaries' program of self-determination led the Chechen people to believe that Tzarist Russia would melt away, leaving autonomy for Chechnya. In May 1918, Chechnya formed the independent North Caucasian Republic ('The Mountain Republic') and declared itself a sovereign state. However, once in power, the new Soviet regime did an about-face and occupied the area, taking over local administration and imposing an ethnically neutral, atheistic state. In response, the Chechen nationalists lifted the Islamic banner and declared another *jihad* to fight the Soviet Army. Moscow answered the *jihad* with an aggressive campaign to destroy Islam in the Caucasus. Mosques were demolished, Islamic weddings and funerals outlawed, and religious schools closed. In 1929, after Soviet attempts to confiscate private property, the Chechens retaliated in a bloody insurrection. Subsequently, in 1944, Josef Stalin removed the boundaries indicating a territory of Chechnya from Soviet maps. Islamic images were systematically destroyed and mullahs arrested; religious monuments, remaining mosques, and cemeteries with Islamic tombstones were dismantled stone by stone. Whereas the Soviets 'imported' Russian settlers into the region, a million Chechen people were deported—forced onto cattle trains and relocated in prison camps—that culminated in scattering the Chechen people throughout the Soviet Empire (Lyons, 1994, p. A14). In the aftermath of Stalin's death, the Khrushchev regime, from 1957 to 1960, allowed repatriation of the Chechens back to the Caucasus. Nonetheless, that also aggravated Russian-Chechen relations as the return of the Chechens—after 15 years of exile— resulted in confrontations with Russians residing in the region, many of whom had occupied former Chechen homes. Islam, however, remained suppressed during most of the Soviet regime; religious ceremonies were clandestine activities, performed only in the shadows. One indication of the success of the anti-Islamic campaign by Moscow was the reduction of mosques in Chechnya from 806 in 1913 to only nine in the early 1960s (Bennigsen & Wimbush, 1985, p. 14).

When *glasnost* (openness) was promulgated in the late 1980s in the former Soviet Union under the Gorbachev Administration, there came a revival of Islam in the Caucasus. With the combination of religious resurrection and open media, new Islamic schools were built, the Qur'an became available, and Lenin Square in Grozny was renamed Sheikh Mansur Square. Slowly, Chechens began making the pilgrimage to Mecca and relearning their Islamic religion.[3] Political parties also came to the foreground and began advocating an independent Islamic Chechen state. In early 1990, a nationalist group emerged that demanded autonomy and a repeal of the Soviet bans on the practice of Islam (Dunlop, 1998, p. 91). At the same time, Boris Yeltsin, in a political maneuver designed to gain support in his power struggle with then President Mikhail Gorbachev, encouraged a debate on the issue of the republics and called on the republics to be as independent as they 'can handle' (Kober, 1993, p. 68). That led the Chechen nationalists to believe that Yeltsin was an advocate of their rights and would promote their autonomy. When Moscow came under siege during an attempted coup, the Chechen secessionists began their move for independence. In November 1990, the Chechen All-National Congress designed an independent Chechen Republic and declared 'State Sovereignty' for the Chechen-Ingush Republic. The following September, Dzhokhar Dudayev, a former Soviet General and Chechen native, forced the Supreme Soviet of the Chechen-Ingush Autonomous Republic to disband and declared Chechnya independent from Russia. A month later, Dudayev became the first president of the independent Chechen-Ingush Republic as he took his presidential oath (with one hand on the Qur'an). Like the Bolsheviks in the past, once Boris Yeltsin came into power, he abandoned his previous position on Chechnya's autonomy and declared a state of emergency in the Chechno-Ingush Republic. He dispatched troops to Chechnya to 'restore order' and relieve Dudayev of his position. However, the Chechen National Guard forced the Russian troops to withdraw and, in 1992, the Russian forces abandoned their post within Chechnya, leaving behind a treasure trove of military hardware. For a time there was a peaceful hiatus, but in the spring of 1993 there followed an internal political struggle between Dudayev and his opponents. The General used force to dismantle the Chechen National Congress and suppress his opposition. Preferring a secular state, Dudayev originally rejected incorporating Islam into the institutional structure of the Chechen Republic. However, in 1993, political pressure from Islamic factions within Chechnya—specifically 'Mehk Khel' or the Council of Elders composed of Muslim clergy and chieftains—forced him to adjust this position and embrace Islamic principles and political organizations (Malashenko, 1995, pp. 46–47). In February 1993, the Constitution of Chechnya acknowledged Islam as the official state religion.

In the final days of December 1994, Yeltsin ordered a full-scale military invasion of Grozny complete with air raids, ground soldiers, and tanks. However, much to Russia's surprise, the Russians were engaged in fierce combat as Chechen sniper fire confronted them in the streets of Grozny. The Russian Army had not anticipated a diligent and determined opponent. Even after extensive bombing of Grozny, the secessionists refused to relinquish the city. What was intended to be a brief cleanup mission, turned into a disaster for Russia. Internally, Yeltsin was extensively criticized in Moscow and many international governments—primarily Islamic states—harshly condemned the military invasion. Despite numerous attempts at peace settlements and cease-fires, Russia and Chechnya fought a bloody war from 1994 to 1996. In April 1996, Dudayev was reportedly killed; the following December, several humanitarian personnel from the International Committee of the Red Cross (stationed in Chechnya) were brutally murdered while they slept.[4] In January 1997, a peace agreement was signed and the Federal Army withdrew, leaving Chechnya a quasi-independent state. According to Russian General Alexander Lebed, casualty estimates for the Chechen 1994 to 1996 conflict were between 70,000 and 90,000 people (Fowkes, 1998, p. 182). In addition, the conflict in Chechnya placed a heavy economic burden on the fragile Russian economy and undermined the credibility, rule of law, and political processes of the emerging democratic state.

Chechnya gained *de facto* autonomy from Russia through the 1997 cease-fire agreement. However, Chechnya's official legal status remained controversial. A final decision on the status of Chechnya's independence was postponed till 2001 to allow a 'cooling off' period for both parties. In Chechnya, self-government meant a little more than anarchy. Even after the fighting with Russia ceased in 1997 much of the population remained militarized with an agile and profitable Chechen Mafia. For Chechnya, independence proved to be somewhat impractical (as it has essentially been a Russian colony for two centuries); it was difficult to sustain political autonomy without commensurate autonomy in the economic sphere. Despite attempts to diffuse the situation, in September 1999 Chechen insurgents attacked neighboring Dagestan with the intention of promoting the establishment of an Islamic state (Rashid, 1999, p. 22). Russia responded with airstrikes and the bombing of an oil producing facility in Djohar. By early October the Russian Government recommitted ground operations in Chechnya and on December 15, 1999, Russian tanks penetrated the Chechen stronghold in Grozny. The fighting forced over 240,000 civilians out of Chechnya and in February 2000, the insurgents began fleeing to the mountains while Russian Federal forces brutalized what was left of the capital city.

Identity Politics and Secessionist Struggle

Most Western scholars hold that the conflict in Chechnya was primarily a political-economic one (Smith, 1998). Indeed, from Russia's standpoint maintaining political control over the territory was very important to prevent the new Russian Federation from falling apart. Chechnya had the potential of precipitating a 'falling domino' in the Caucasus. The loss of Chechnya could result in the secession of Tatarstan and other former autonomous republics. For Russia, Chechnya was also important for access to and control of oil. Yeltsin wanted to ensure that the strategically vital Baku-Novorossiisk pipeline that runs through Chechnya was intact and would continue to transport Russian oil and gas to Europe (Smith, 1998, p. 71). In addition to subduing a national uprising, Yeltsin's advisors also viewed military intervention in Chechnya as a way to send a strong message to the Chechen Mafia, one of the most visible and active organized crime groups within Russia. From the Chechen perspective, there were also political-economic issues driving the insurgency. Within Chechnya, the mixture of ethnic discrimination, economic inequality, and religious resentment became an explosive compound that led to insurgency and ultimately to civil war. The political unrest was partially a symptom of the severe economic conditions as Chechen Muslims were consistently in the lowest economic sectors in the region. In 1991, approximately 30 percent of Chechnya's population was unemployed (Kazikhanov, 1991, p. 21). Poor health services, heavy environmental pollution, forced economic migration, and the fact that Russians dominated the lucrative oil industry all contributed to discontent within Chechnya. At the same time, the 1991 income for state farm workers (mostly Chechen) averaged only 74.8 percent of the Russian Federation wage (Dunlop, 1998, p. 87).

However, for the Chechen people, the secessionist movement went far beyond a call for socio-economic equalities; they also wanted political autonomy and religious self-determination. Thus, the conflict became Muslim Chechens versus Christian Russians. In order to understand the fierce conviction of the Chechen insurgents, one must consider the role of Sufi mysticism and religious tenets in the secessionist movement. One powerful way politics becomes non-secularized is by incorporating the structures of religious associations and rituals into political discourse. A political movement's leadership can use preexisting religious establishments as the foundation for recruitment and participation. Religion can provide 'fertile soil' for the 'birth and growth' of political movements because a community of people with similar beliefs is already present. Religious communities share normative views and consensus building is easy to establish (Zald and McCarthy, 1987). Politics and religion can become intertwined with symbols, creating social order and defining power relationships. Jan Kubik (1994), in his work on the Solidarity movement in Poland, explains that cultural symbols are real and provide meaning to political life. Also, he explores how cultural symbols can lend legitimacy to political power struggles. Kubik finds that symbols usually take on a dichotomous nature, defining and separating communities as well as reifying cultural, ethnic, and religious boundaries. Symbols include both language and images and, when connected with political values, they can be very powerful (Eickelman & Piscatori, 1996, p. 9). When the symbols of history, religious tenets, and practice are brought together, they influence political tactics by constructing 'strategies of action' (Kubik, 1994, p. 126). Furthermore, the use of religious symbols serves as an effective and persuasive force that encourages people to implement these strategies.

Islam played a formative role in the secessionist movement and mobilization towards civil war with Russia. In Chechnya, the use of symbolic language appealed to the collective memories of *jihad*, and the myths of religious warriors Mansur and Shamil created the dichotomous social reality that Kubik describes. Muslim religious identity, practice of Sufism, and the notion of *jihad* fanned nationalist flames in Chechnya as they were braided together into powerful symbols that inspired violence. The process of combining the symbols of Islam with Chechen history and struggle against Russia strengthened Chechen unity, facilitated military organization, and enhanced mobilization. The following section explores what Alexei Malashenko (1995, p. 47) has called the 'islamicization' of Chechnya and how Islam was diffused into Chechen politics through history, myth, and political rhetoric as well as its influence on Chechen politics in the 1990s in three areas: unity, organization, and mobilization.

Although the Communists used a number of tactics, including colonization, assimilation, deportation, and even genocide, they never successfully coopted the Chechens into their corps. The Chechens retained their ethnic and religious identity, and, today, Chechnya is a fortification of Islam (Avtorkhanov and Broxup, 1992, p. 7). The irony of the anti-religious Russification policies of the Soviets was that they served to both solidify and then politicize Islam in Chechnya (Nekrich, 1978, pp. 51–52). Three generations of Chechens remember the shared experience of exile and attempted genocide. The physical detachment from their homeland combined with ethnic and religious repression pushed the Chechen people to find solace in Islam and a purpose in their Muslim roots. The national homeland became a powerful symbol, and the legends of Mansur and Shamil engendered a cult of personality that would resurrect Chechen nationalism. Paul Henze (1995, p. 25) argues that Chechen clan loyalty and family solidarity sustained Islam as it was forced into the shadows of Soviet society. The continued reverence for and rebuilding of Chechen Islamic holy places during the Soviet regime points to one indication of Islam's endurance in spite of Moscow's attempts at asphyxiation. The strength of this ethno-religious identity was also apparent in the 1980s when Chechens strongly resisted conscription during the Soviet invasion of Afghanistan—

Chechens did not want to kill fellow Muslims (Broxup, 1992, p. 12).

Subsequently, in the early 1990s, the nationalists used religious discourse to overcome regional factionalism—smoothing the fragmented points of diverse social cleavage and, at the same time, sharpening the socio-political division between Russia and the North Caucasus. General Dudayev used religious rhetoric to portray Russians as infidels. His political speeches were replete with religious images in describing Russia as riddled with 'satanism' and 'full of sin' (FBIS-SOV, 1995, p. 10). Henze also observes that, for the anti-Russian cause, Islam supplied the Chechen people with an ideology that promoted 'unity of purpose' in transcending tribalism (1995, p. 11). Another indication of the growth in Islamic identity is found in the fact that the number of Muslim associations (mostly in the North Caucasus) increased from 870 to 4000 between 1991 and 1992 (Malashenko, 1995, p. 42). Competing factions within the region found a common enemy and solidarity in their struggle against Russia. The Islamic symbols and historical images of Mansur and Shamil provided the needed legitimacy to the secessionist political agenda. The nationalists wanted their cause to have broad popular support and moral justification. In fact, according to Sebastian Smith (1998, p. 154), the Islamic identity deepened as the conflict progressed. As they had mobilized against the Russian Tzars and the Soviets, the people of the North Caucasus put aside their tribal difference and united as a Muslim nation fighting for independence.

The religious roots of Chechen society also contributed to the organization of tactical military operations. The infrastructure of Sufi orders was an important foundation for establishing and sustaining the fighting force that cost the Russians over a billion dollars to fight. Islam promoted the recruitment of soldiers. Dudayev hung a large picture of Sheik Mansur in his office and organized the Chechen military force in the tradition of Mansur and Shamil, with national guards and decree (de Waal, 1994, pp. 22–23). In fact, the Chechen army or the *boyeviks* (fighters of the war) were mostly volunteers and included Muslims from Ukraine, the Baltics, and Tatarstan. Many came from as far as Azerbaijan to fight the Russians because, for generations of Muslims in the North Caucasus, the Sufis have historically taken up arms in anti-Russian wars (Smith, 1998, p. 78). The Chechen army was largely a people's army composed of farmers and industrial workers, who in many cases supplied their own weapons and ammunition. By September 1992, the Chechen rebel force was over 10,000 strong (Soldatova, 1993, p. 63). Sufism also contributed to the organization of the fighting force through the practice of the *zikr*, a ritual intended to bring those involved in the ceremony in union with God. It is characterized by repetitive prayer and—in the Qadiriyya order—song, dance, clapping, and movement. The *zikr* creates a sense of being close to *Allah*. With the perception that one is an instrument of the divine, there is little fear of death. Thus, Sufism promoted a courageous warrior culture in Chechnya. Alexandre Bennigsen and S. Enders Wimbush (1985, p. 83) note that it is common for the images of Shamil and Mansur to be invoked in *zikr* in the North Caucasus. Because the *zikr* is a collective ceremony with intense affective ends, it produces profound collective emotional ties. In relying on *tariqat*, small groups reinforce notions of brotherhood and purity. Furthermore, the Sufi brotherhoods brought organization, direction and grounding to the loosely organized insurgents. The Sufi orders easily became guerilla units with unofficial networks and a cohesive organization. Bennigsen and Wimbush (1985, p. 70) describe the Sufi brotherhoods as 'well-structured', 'well-disciplined', and 'inherently capable' of underground struggles. Because Sufism did not require buildings and religious artifacts, it was easily taken onto the battlefield. One author calls the Sufi *tariqat* an 'ideal' religious form for facing external cultural and military foes (Smith, 1998, p. 40). Together, Sufism and Dudayev's rhetoric swelled nationalist emotion into a mass-based, well-organized insurgency. The *zikr*, preformed in the streets of Grozny and in high mountain ravines, proved to be a powerful weapon on the battlefield as religious ideas and symbols were combined with a struggle for political power.

Mobilization, as defined by Charles Tilly (1978, p. 69), refers to the process in which a quiescent group of people become active participants in public life. Before insurgency, there is mobilization; it is the steam or wind that provides momentum and lifts the wings of rebellion. People become inspired to protest in the streets, establish paramilitary groups, and take up arms against complete strangers and close neighbors. Sufi mysticism, to borrow a metaphor from John Dunlop (1998), was the spark that set off the timbers of discontent among the Chechen population. In addition to providing a significant moral intensity and designing a military force, religion was also a mobilizing impetus that guided the Chechen people into combat. In many ways, the legacy of Mansur and Shamil as well as centuries of *jihad* against Russia propelled Chechen people from their homes to the battlefield. Sergei Arutiunov explains that in Chechnya 'even the smallest boy' is familiar with Chechen history under the Tzars and the deportations in 1944 (Arutiunov, 1995, p. 16). The legends of Mansur and Shamil helped boost morale and sent men with poor training and little organization to fight for *Allah* and for freedom. In fact, it was common for the anti-Russian insurgents to call out '*Allah Akbar*' (God is Great) before fighting and in combat. War cries, for the fighters, became prayers to *Allah* in the service of *Allah*.[5]

Jihad is a war for the protection of an Islamic way of life and, because it is only permissible under these threats, it is powerful and evokes emotion and mobilization. When President Dudayev got wind of Yeltsin's plan to invade in 1994, he used Islam as a political tool and called for an Islamic state and incorporation of the *shari'a* to counter Russian infidels (Dunlop, 1998, p. 148; Malashenko, 1995, pp. 46–47). In mid-December, as Russian forces began to invade Grozny, Chechen Vice President Zelimkhan Yandarbiyev gave a national broadcast proclaiming that *Allah* would protect the Chechen people from the evil of Russia (FBIS-SOV-94, 1994 p. 36). Dudayev played on the religious attachment of the Chechen people, with particular focus on the mountainous regions of Chechnya, to bring them into the civil war. On December 22, in a television address, he called on the Chechen people to rise up, exhorting them that they could either become slaves or die in a holy war (FBIS-SOV-94, 1994, p. 17). The separatist campaign against Russia was projected as a just war; the Chechen leaders called for a *jihad* to protect their nascent Republic. One observer claimed that Islam was used as an instrument to promote the 'manipulation of mass awareness' (Kul'chik, 1994, p. 4). Ultimately, the Chechen fighters were motivated by 'national mythology' and the desire to defend 'freedom' (Smith, 1998, p. 153). One indication of this sentiment was visible in the green bands many Chechen fighters wore on their hats that symbolized their commitment to die in protecting Islam, a custom established in the 1800s with Mansur and Shamil (Lieven, 1994, p. 14). An understanding of *jihad* also provides insight into how the Chechen rebel forces prevailed against the comparatively vast resources of the Russian Federation. Islam provided the secessionists with a sense of unity, purpose and inspiration. Islam was the spiritual food that produced highly energized and enthusiastic soldiers. Chechens *boyeviks* were defending their homes and religion on the same battlegrounds that Sheiks Mansur and Shamil had fought. While the Russian Army was greater in number and military resources, it was a poor match for the highly mobilized and dedicated Chechen conscripts. Many branches of Russia's military refused to become involved in Chechnya and the morale was extremely low for those that did. The Russian Army had little enthusiasm to fight a controversial war in which they received poor training and little or no monetary compensation. In fact, there were reports of Russian soldiers selling their weapons and other military equipment to Chechen rebels (Smith, 1998, p. 186; Siren, 1998, p. 123). Overall, the Russians faced substantial problems of recruitment and insubordination. And they were constantly plagued by deserters, some of whom reportedly joined the Chechen cause (Siren, 1998, pp. 123–125).

Therefore, the Sufi brotherhoods brought organization, direction, and grounding to the insurgents. A well-established militant history repeated itself against the Russian infidels in 1994 and, again, in 1999. Moreover, the Islamic tradition of *jihad* provided a 'tool kit' in which the Chechen secessionists could form a 'strategy of action' (Kubik, 1994, p. 126). The tradition of holy war is an illuminating component of the Chechen secessionist movement. The Sufi orders once again took on their historical role and fought a *jihad* against another imposing force from Moscow. What is intriguing here is that Duyadev, a former secularist, successfully drew a link between Shamil, Mansur, *jihad*, and centuries of struggle against Russia. That process of coupling symbols brought Islam into the political realm in Chechnya. The Islamic history and concept of *jihad* was as powerful a weapon as the tanks and weapons captured from the Russian Army. When the separatist call echoed through the breakaway Chechen Republic in the Russian Federation, the voice that mobilized Chechens towards battle was that of Islamic religious nationalism. Unlike much of the developed world, where religion is bracketed to the private and personal realm, after *glasnost* religion became public and political in Chechnya. As Kubik describes, and noted earlier, symbols and rituals were incorporated to build political reality. Islam in the North Caucasus gave credence to a military tradition and cultural autonomy: its ceremonies provided stability in chaos and historical figures proscribed reactive measures. The symbol of *jihad* was very persuasive when combined with political uncertainty, economic instability, an invading Russian force, and a history of religious insurgency.

Islam played a unifying role in the quest for independence. In contrast, it became a point of discord for governance after 1996. While the Chechen Constitution recognized Islam as the state religion, it also created secular governing structures and institutions. In the 1997 presidential elections each candidate included the incorporation of *shari'a* law in their platform (FBIS-SOV-97–042, 1997, p. 5) and Aslan Maskhadov, the former Chief of Staff of the Chechen military, was elected President. Since his acquisition of power, tensions in Chechnya between fundamentalism and secular political life are increasing. While the political voices within Chechnya remain full of staunch Islamic and anti-Russian rhetoric, there are increasing factional tensions between the vocal and fervent fundamentalists and more mainstream Muslims. Many are also wary of the *Wahhabi*[6] movement from Saudi Arabia and the extensive role the *Wahhabis* believe Islam should play in governing Chechnya and Dagestan. Many Muslims in Chechnya are opposed to the incorporation of Islamic law and argue that seventy years of atheism has left the Chechens without the religious training and knowledge or the *kazis* (religious judges) to implement the *shari'a* legal doctrine correctly. Ikhvan Gerikhanov, the Chairman of the Chechen Constitutional Court, rejected the full adoption of Islamic law in Chechnya and remarked that the people of Chechnya are 'Chechens first and Muslims afterwards'. He added that the women would refuse to wear the *hijab* (veil) and men would not give up their sheep fur hats for the turban (FBIS-SOV-97–323, 1997). Yet, the following November Vice President Vakha Arsanov declared (on Chechen television) that women must adopt traditional Islamic dress and banned the production and sale of alcohol. This discord is also apparent within the Chechen separatist movement itself.   President Maskhadov's repeated calls for *jihad* and unity against Russia is evidence of attempts to smooth internal contentions. In fact, Shamil Basaev, a political competitor of the Chechen president stated that he was 'very grateful' for the 1999 Russian offensive because it re-ignited Chechen unity ('Russia and Islam,' 1999, p. 24).

The nationalist issue is so explosive that it is spilling over outside Chechnya, and affecting Russia. In September 1997, a *shari'a* court in Chechnya sentenced two people to death. They were shot and killed in a public square in Grozny and the executions were broadcast over a local television station. These actions brought world attention to Chechnya with protests from international human rights agencies. Along with criticism, however, religious identity also brings external supports. As hostilities escalated in the Fall of 1999, the Chechen plight raised sympathies in other Muslim countries. Jordan's Islamic Action Front party, the governments of Saudi Arabia, Pakistan, and Iran have all made pleas for Muslim unity and criticized the Russian Government. Still, another instance of the transnational connection established by religion is found in reports that Osama bin Laden, the Islamic fundamentalist leader, may be contributing weapons and training facilities to the Chechen separatists (Rashid, 1999, p. 22). In fact, the Islamic component has become so potent that Russia now views the presence of Islam as a serious threat to its national security (Splidsboel-Hansen, 1997, pp. 1501–1503). How Islam influences the Chechen political environment in the future remains to be seen. At present, it appears that religion will continue to be a source of contention in Chechen political life, a cloak worn in the ongoing battle with Moscow.

Conclusion

After seventy years of religious repression, it is not surprising that in the wake of *glasnost* opposition movements within the former Soviet Union should assume a religious character. The Muslim heritage and the mystical Sufi brotherhoods of the Chechen people provided a sense of identity that reemerged during the turbulence and uncertainty of the late 1980s, early 1990s, and again in the Fall of 1999. Dzhokhar Dudayev and the Chechen secessionists used the Islamic tradition of *jihad*, Sufi orders, and Chechen Muslim historical figures to mobilize the people and incite them to resist Federal troops. Unemployment and ethnic nationalism combined with Islam to provide an explosive concoction. It is important to point out that the instrumental use of religion in this situation does not diminish the strength of conviction of the Chechen people. While it is clear that Dudayev manipulated the historical and symbolic power of Islam for political gain, at the same time it is noteworthy that the reemergence of Muslim identity and the Sufi orders are not a sham: popular sentiment concerning Islamic affinities is manifest and sincere. Even though the conflict between Russia and Chechnya is not solely a religious one, Islam is an important variable in the hostilities. Islam serves to magnify the separatist conflict between the Chechens and the Russians. One cannot capture the reality of the Chechen secessionist struggle without considering the religious symbolism of *jihad* and *zikr*. Many theorists see secessionist movements in purely institutional (statehood) terms and fail to incorporate the social and religious identities that are often intrinsically tied to political movements. In fact, social identities often resemble a kaleidoscope—with multiple horizontal and vertical variables (religious, ethnic, economic, territorial, and historical) that change with changing political circumstances. As illustrated in this case study, the role of religion in the Chechen struggle did not dismiss ethnic affiliations of the insurgency, nor did it discard the desire for independence from Russia. Religion and politics are never completely separate: the relationship is dynamic and fluctuating, at different times more entangled and visible than others. Donald Horowitz (1985, p. 50) reminds us that in many developing areas religion is an ascriptive affiliation that forms a core component of an ethnic group's identity. Religious symbolism and Islamic history enrich our understanding of the recent conflict in Chechnya.

The Chechen case also offers an example of the explosive combination of religion and politics. The relationship between Islam and the Chechens has both fed and defined much of the violence against what have been time and again viewed as Russian attempts to conquer the people of Chechnya. Islam intensified this struggle—by defining, legitimizing, and invigorating it—and creating potential international alliances. It is potent and destabilizing. At the same time, it is undeniably nascent and there is little agreement about the shape and form of Islam that will guide the struggle in Chechnya. This study illustrates how religion can act as a vessel for transporting political ideas from generation to generation. Furthermore, the implications go beyond the region: Islam in Chechnya may influence geopolitical relations between Russia and other Muslim countries like Turkey, Afghanistan, Iran, and Saudi Arabia. This is especially relevant as globalization is folding local, regional, and global politics into one contextual sphere and demanding that our ontological visions include 'local' conflicts in an international political context. The scenario is not one of Juergensmeyer's 'new Cold Wars,' with holy allegiances confronting a secular state; it is more complex. Religion was not the only cause of the conflict between Russia and Chechnya. The situation, as illustrated in this study, is complicated and cannot be explained by a single factor. However, as David Little (1994, p. xi) points out, religion does not need to explain everything to be an important component in contemporary violent conflicts. Islam played a significant role in the Chechen civil war against Russia and will continue to be influential in whatever future government emerges from the ashes of Grozny.

Notes

1   It is important to note that the minority Russian population is not homogenous. In Chechnya, the Russian Cossaks are composed of Ossetians, Cherkess, Nogais, and Kabanties.

2   The Chechen and Ingush Muslims belong to the Naqshbandiyya and Qadiriyya Sufi orders.

3   Sebastian Smith (1998) describes a strange mix of practicing Muslims comprised of the very old and the very young. At the same time, there is an entire generation of middle aged Chechens that are unfamiliar and uncomfortable with the practice of religion.

4   Many argue that the act was deliberately aimed at Western media and the humanitarian

presence. However, there is controversy over whether the operation was Chechen or Russian.

5   Derived from Imam Shamil's hymn (Smith, 1996, p. 74).
6   Wahhabism is an interpretation of Islam that directs followers to adopt the strict religious teachings established 1,400 years ago.

References

Arutiunov, Sergei (1995), 'Ethnicity and Conflict in the Caucasus,' in Wehling, Fred (ed.), *Ethnic Conflict and Russian Intervention in the Caucasus*, Policy Paper No. 16, University of California: California, pp. 16–17.

Avtorkhanov, Abdurahman and Marie Bennigsen Broxup (eds.) (1992), *The North Caucasus Barrier*, St. Martin's Press: New York.

Barber, Benjamin (1996), *Jihad vs. McWorld*, Ballantine Books: New York.

Bennigsen, Alexandre and S. Enders Wimbush (1985), *Mystics and Commissars*, University of California Press: Berkeley.

Bitov, Andrei (1992), *A Captive of the Caucasus*, Farrar, Straus and Giroux: New York.

Burney, Charles and David Marshall Lang (1971), *The Peoples of the Hills: Ancient Ararat and the Caucasus*, Praeger: New York.

'Chechnya' (1997), *The Current Digest*, Vol. 49, No. 47, pp. 17–18.

Damrel, David (1995), 'The Religious Roots of Conflict: Russia and Chechnya,' *Religious Studies News*, Vol. 10, No. 3, p. 10.

De Waal, Thomas (1994), 'Al Calm in Dudayev's Breakaway Chechnya,' *Moscow Times*, December 18, pp. 22–23.

Dunlop, John B. (1998), *Russia Confronts Chechnya*, Cambridge University Press: Cambridge (United Kingdom).

Easton, David (1965), *A Framework for Political Analysis*, Prentice Hall: Englewood Cliffs, NJ.

Eickelman, Dale F. and James Piscatori (1996), *Muslim Politics*, Princeton University Press: Princeton, NJ.

Foreign Broadcast Information Services—SOV-94–247 (1994), 'Dudayev Urges Fight Against "Satanic" Russia,' December 23, p. 17.

Foreign Broadcast Information Services—SOV-95–082 (1995), 'Commentary of Situation in Chechnya,' *Holos*, April 22, p. 10.

Foreign Broadcast Information Services—SOV-97–042 (1997a), 'Mufti Council Chairman on Role of Islam,' *Moscow Literaturnaya Gazeta*, February 12, p. 5.

Foreign Broadcast Information Services—SOV-97–323 (1997b), 'Chechen Constitutional Judge: Chechnya Will Remain Secular,' Moscow Interfax, Transcribed Text, November 19.

Fowkes, Ben (ed.) (1998), *Russia and Chechnia: The Permanent Crisis*, St. Martin's Press, New York.

Goldenberg, Suzanne (1994), *Pride of Small Nations: The Caucasus and Post-Soviet Disorder*, Zed Books: London.

Hassan, Farooq (1981), *The Concept of State and Law in Islam*, University Press of America: London.

Henze, Paul B. (1995), *Islam in the North Caucasus: The Example of Chechnya*, RAND: Santa Monica, CA.

Horowitz, Donald L. (1985), *Ethnic Groups in Conflict*, University of California Press: Berkeley.

Huskey, Eugene (1992), *Executive Power and Soviet Politics*, M.E. Sharpe: New York.

International Herald Tribune (1995), January 10, p. 1.

Juergensmeyer, Mark (1993), *The New Cold War: Religious Nationalism Confronts the Secular State*, University of California Press: Berkeley.

Kazikhanov, Ali (1991), 'Victors in Confusion,' *The Current Digest of the Soviet Press*, Vol. 43, No. 44, pp. 21–22.

Kober, Stanley (1993), 'Revolutions Gone Bad,' *Foreign Policy*, No. 91, pp. 63–85.

Kubik, Jan (1994), *The Power of Symbols Against the Symbols of Power*, Pennsylvania State University Press: University Park.

Kul'chik, Yurii (1994), 'Dva islamam: odna Chechnya' (Two Islams: One Chechnya), Smena (Transformation), May 12, p. 4.

Layton, Susan (1986), 'The Creation of an Imaginative Caucasian Geography,' *Slavic Review*, Vol. 45, pp. 470–485.

Lieven, Anatol (1994), 'Dudayev's Raggle-Taggle Army,' *London Times*, December 14, p. 14.

Lyons, Richard D. (1994), 'Explosive Mix in Chechnya: History, Hatred and Oil,' *New York Times*, December 14, p. A14.

Malashenkil, Alexei (1995), 'Islamic Fundamentalism in Russia,' in Ro'i, Yaacov (ed.), *Muslim Eurasia: Conflicting Legacies*, Frank Cass and Co.: London.

National'nyi sostav naseleniia SSSR (National Composition of the Population of the USSR) (1991), *Finansy i statistika* (Finance and Statistics), Moscow, pp. 34–40.

Nekrich, Alexander (1978), *The Punished Peoples*, Norton and Co.: New York.

Nichols, Johanna (1994), 'Chechen;' 'Ingush,' in Smeets, Rieks (ed.), *The Indigenous Languages of the Caucasus*, Vol. 4: *Northeast Caucasian Languages*, Caravan Books: Delmar, NY, pp. 1–77; 79–145.

Rashid, Ahmed (1999), 'The Taliban: Exporting Extremism,' *Foreign Affairs*, November/December, pp. 22–35.

'Russia and Islam: Action Replay in Chechnya?' (1999), *The Economist*, October 9, p. 24.

Siren, Pontus (1998), 'The Battle for Grozny: The Russian Invasion of Chechnia, December 1994–December 1996,' in Fowkes, Ben (ed.), *Russia and Chechnia: The Permanent Crisis*, St. Martin's Press: New York, pp. 87–169.

Smith, Sebastian (1998), *Allah's Mountains: Politics and War in the Russian Caucasus*, I.B. Tauris: London.

Soldatova, G. U. (1993), 'The Former Checheno-Ingushetia: International Relations and Ethnic Conflicts,' *Russian Social Science Review*, Vol. 34, No. 6, pp. 52–72.

Spencer, Edmund (1839), *Travels in Circassia*, Vol. II, Henry Colburn: London.

Splidsboel-Hansen, Flamming (1997), 'The Official Russian Concept of Contemporary CentralAsian Islam: The Security Dimension,' *Europe-Asia Studies*, Vol. 49, No. 8, pp. 1501–1517.

Suny, Ronald Grigor (1983), 'Transcaucasia: Nationalism and Social Change,' in Suny, Ronald Grigor (ed.), *Transcaucasia: Nationalism and Social Change*, University of Michigan Press: Ann Arbor.

Tilly, Charles (1978), *From Mobilization to Revolution*, McGraw-Hill: New York.

Weber, Max (1965), *The Sociology of Religion*, translated by E. Fischoff, Eyre Methuen: London.

Zald, Mayer N. and John D. McCarthy (eds.), (1987), *Social Movements in an Organizational Society*, Transaction Publishers: New Brunswick, NJ.

9 Bangladesh: Muslim Identity, Secularism, and the Politics of Nationalism

MOHAMMAD RASHIDUZZAMAN

The unyielding polarity between secularism and a widely shared Muslim identity in Bangladesh has unfolded itself through at least three historical waves with no closure in sight! Soon after independence, the secular doctrines marked the overwhelming wave of patriotism in the new nation. For all practical purposes, political Islam then faced an ideological decapitation at the hands of the euphoric Bangali (Bengali) nationalists, who offered the new state a fresh sense of awareness that few dared to question openly. The linguistically driven secular identity was essentially different from the religiosity during the pre-independence era. But the new secular state of Bangladesh did not turn into a passionately secular Bangladesh society; the persisting disjunction between the non-religious compulsions of the new elite and the Muslim-majority civil society became the backdrop of future identity battles. The 1975 bloody coup that assassinated President Sheikh Mujibur Rahman, acclaimed by many as *Bangobandhu* (Friend of Bengal, and popularly called Mujib), and the military-led regimes that followed the tragic event, signaled the second wave of identity politics. The identity struggle softened, but it did not dismantle the earlier secular stance. Bangladesh did not veer to religious orthodoxy under the military and the military-turned-civilian authorities from 1975 to 1990. However, during that period, Islam and the search for a Muslim consciousness, based on its strength from the majority religion and its perceived difference with secularism, gained a political voice.

The Bangladesh Nationalist Party (BNP), an offshoot of the regime under General Ziaur Rahman (henceforth, Zia) created a synthesis between the Muslim identity and Bangali nationalism that readily attracted wide support in the country: it claimed that Bangladeshis were Muslims first, and Bangalis second. That was qualitatively different from the Awami League (AL)-led Bangali nationalists' strident belief that they were Bangalis first, and Muslims second. On March 24, 1982, General Hussain Muhammad Ershad overthrew Justice Abdus Sattar, who had earlier succeeded Zia as the country's president. But the regime change was not a turnaround on identity questions until the AL came back to power in 1996. After a 21-year hiatus, Mujib's daughter Sheikh Hasina Wazid (henceforth, Hasina) heralded the third wave of identity search. She pulled the nation more toward the 'lingo' (language)-nationalism of the early 1970s. Yet, Hasina so far failed to reinstate secularism as one of the constitutional goals that Zia had modified, which the AL resented. Meanwhile, the political dynamics have changed qualitatively; any sudden reversal to a harsh non-religious appeal will face a stiff and pervasive resistance not only from the Islamists, but also from their centrist partners. Twenty-nine years have passed since Bangladesh became independent, but in the standoff between the secularists and adherents of collective Muslim consciousness continues. This is a political reality that few could deny.

Conceptually, identity politics is a search for recognition and a struggle for power between competing sensibilities. In an age of multiculturalism, it is no longer acceptable to discriminate against people on the ground of personal identity—be it religion, ethnicity, place of origin, language, or gender. If individuals or a group get a sense of gratification because of their faith (Islam or any other religion) and express that feeling in public life, such predilections cannot be denied even if they defy state-imposed secular doctrines. It is that new vision of equal space for religion along with other identities, which is demolishing the vaunted arguments of secularism. When identity and culture are threatened, people often react by going back to their roots. In the process, they use metaphors that magnify the differences and revive their ancestral anxieties. The formidable acrimony between non-religious Bangali nationalism and Muslim exclusiveness deserves attention from the preceptors of nationalism in general, students of political Islam, and scholars of Bangladesh. This chapter is largely limited to the moderate—and ubiquitous but non-monolithic—religio-political stance among the Muslims in Bangladesh. Those holding moderate Muslim identity may establish tactical alliances with the more militant Islamic groups in order to confront the secularists. But many of the moderate Muslims are believed to have recently voted for the BNP and the Jatiya Party (JP), the two centrist political organizations. Because of certain gentler postures of Sheikh Hasina before the poll, it is believed that segments of the Muslim identity supporters also swung towards the center-left AL that brought the party to power in 1996.

Identity Politics

The perceived Muslim identity[1] in Bangladesh has not been coherent. It has meant different things to different individuals and groups, at different times. Muslim identity has a broad connotation. One could be a proud Muslim—and refuse to be homogenized—without being a strict adherent of the faith or an advocate of an Islamic state. It is a subtle self-consciousness that is not unique to the Muslims, but also characterizes the Christians, Jews, and Hindus, to mention a few. Such self-definition is the common link between the upholders of a *shari'a* (Islamic law)-based orthodox state and those who want a governance under which Muslims would be allowed political expression, including Islamic symbolism and the pride of living in an independent and sovereign Muslim-majority state. But the demands for an Islamic state and the desire for a Muslim self-consciousness are not identical. Those who seek a distinctive recognition for the Muslims may not support the purist Islamic parties, but they would not join in outlawing them as was done in the early years of Bangladesh. Muslim identity had flourished as a protest against British colonial rule, but also manifested itself as a voice for preservation of rights and privileges against the domination of a Hindu majority in pre-partition (pre-1947) India. The Muslims in Bangladesh strongly opposed the sudden secular impositions after 1971 and did not hesitate to speak against the perceived hegemonic role of New Delhi. The resurgent Muslim identity in Bangladesh is a reaction to the lingo-centric secularists; it is a resistance to the surging secular anchor in the years immediately after independence. Those who support Muslim identity, and particularly those who work with the Islamic parties in Bangladesh, are not endowed with adequate organizational and leadership skills. It is noteworthy that no Khomeini-type messianic

Islamic leader had mobilized the diffused Muslim identity in Bangladesh. The resurrected group consciousness of the Muslims had little to do with religious bigotry. Its regrouping had only a limited debt to the military-led regimes, which, in fact, acknowledged the already embedded Muslim identity in Bangladesh. Nor was it a communal storm against non-Muslims, though it may be perceived as such. It is worth mentioning that even in the Indian context, scholars have tried to separate religious identity from communalism. The latter thrives mostly on fear and suspicion about other religious groups (Bahadur, 1996, pp.1–8). The Muslim identity in Bangladesh has a broad configuration. It can be traced back to Hindu and Muslim nationalisms in British India (Van der Veer, 1998, p.9). However, its imprecise rubric has so far failed to become a formidable catalyst leading to a spectacular political victory in Bangladesh.

Pro-Muslim political activities were clandestine in Bangladesh in the early 1970s; they spawned without any institutional arrangement. Ironically, the well-known leftist leader Maulana Abdul Hamid Khan Bhasani tacitly blessed an underground 'Muslim Bengal' movement that did not survive for long (Khan, 1973). Allegations abound that the Pakistan Government secretly supported the shadowy Muslim Bengal movement (Murshed, 1997). Bhasani was too old and sick, and later died. Ghulam Azam, the *Jamaat-i-Islami* (Islamic Association) leader, was out of the country in the earliest years of independence, returning only when General Zia liberalized the restrictions on the Islamic parties. Because of restrictions imposed upon them, and both the government and the freedom fighters openly criticizing them, the leaders as well as activists of the Islamic parties went underground when open political rallies were banned. Arguably, Bangali nationalism was an 'anti-colonial' expression against the perceived domination by the West Pakistani bureaucratic and military elite. Contrary to most predictions, the old Muslim nationalism that was a force in the creation of Pakistan resurfaced in secular Bangladesh. Even though the 'us-them' dichotomy is unavoidable in identity politics, the Muslim reckoning had little to do with disparaging any particular religious community. It is noteworthy that the confrontation between Muslim identity and secularism has not yet turned into zealotry or a bloody civil war. But there were occasional outbreaks of anger and sporadic violence, mainly between the *Shibir*—*Jamaat* student front—and secular student organizations. On a number of occasions during the recent past, clandestine Islamic extremists were blamed for terrorist-style bombings that the *Jamaat* and other Islamic groups emphatically denied. In the aftermath of the Babri *Masjid* (Babr Mosque) demolition by Hindu extremists in India, there were scattered reactions in Bangladesh. But those were not spillover from the raging identity dispute. Bangladesh intermittently had established democratic institutions, and the identity battle was soon intertwined with mainstream politics (Shehabuddin,1998, p. 148). Even Sheikh Hasina, the Awami League chief, acknowledged that the Jamaat was a political reality in Bangladesh (Kabir, 1995, p. 179).

Those Bangladeshis inspired by a sense of Muslimness generally dispute the homogenizing assumptions of Bangali nationalism. It confirms, in some way, Peter Van der Veer's thesis that 'centralization and homogenization'(as we find in secularism) created their 'own counterforce' (Van der Veer, 1998, p. 23). The AL-inspired secular agenda aroused skepticism among the Muslims who refused to surrender their religious separatism in the private as well as public spheres of life. To the chagrin of the secularists, the Muslim nationalists generally wanted a privileged status accorded to Islam. But the Muslim nationalists did not ask for an Iranian-style Islamic state; only the *Jamaat* and other Islamic parties overtly called for an orthodox Islamic state. The regrouping of the Muslim nationalists was by no means an easy task against the unremitting hostility of Bangladeshi secularists. Actually, the dispute between secularism and religious nationalism was not new for the Muslims in Bangladesh. The 'Bengaliness and Muslimness' really 'coexisted uneasily' in what was undivided Bengal in South Asia (Chatterjee, 1996, p.16). Until 1955 the AL's official title was the Awami Muslim League, and its first general secretary was Shamsul Haque, known for his radical Islamic views. Before 1971, the Awami League had no conspicuous desire for secularism or socialism (Rashiduzzaman, 1970). As a post-1971 phenomenon, the lingo-nationalism sought to legitimize the secession of Bangladesh from Pakistan, and it was also used to validate the AL's hold on power. Except that it dropped 'Muslim' from its name, the AL did not overtly campaign for secularism in the 1960s and it was not a core issue in the 1970 election. Instead, the economic disparity between the two wings of Pakistan was the pivot of the AL offensive. But what the AL did in independent Bangladesh amounted to a secular coup. It banned all the Islamic parties, deleted the Qur'anic symbol from the University logo, and even discouraged simple Islamic rituals at public meetings and official functions, a tradition carried over from the Pakistani period. During the 1971 anti-Pakistan drive, there was no well conceived secular paradigm; it was not the moving force for the independence struggle. Mostly, the freedom fighters and their Calcutta-based leaders dodged the question of the future ideological configuration of independent Bangladesh. The leftists even avoided calling the breakaway state Bangladesh—some called it independent East Pakistan and others called it free East Bengal. The AL assumed an uncompromisingly secular stance only when Bangladesh became a sovereign nation, and the new government enforced it without open deliberation on the subject. The Awami League did not even define secularism in operational terms. Even Sheikh Mujibur Rahman seemed unclear about it on a number of occasions, and an air of ambivalence confused the nation.[2]

Nationalism, secularism, democracy and socialism—collectively called Mujibism— became the new ideological gospel for independent Bangladesh. And *Joi Bangla* (Victory to Bengal) became the patriotic slogan of the new nation. The new government as if in vengeance, erased the names of Mohammad Ali Jinnah and Mohammad Iqbal from the streets and public institutions that had been named for them. Bangladesh, for all intents and purposes, was out to avenge the Pakistani military brutalities by brushing off the last symbols of its Pakistani past. But the Bangali nationalists failed in the exercise of rearranging history. The banishment of Islam in public discourse was, for many Bangladeshi Muslims, a cultural exile in their own country where they were a majority (Rashiduzzaman, 1994, pp. 974-98). The Mujib Government was initially hostile to any political wave of Islam; it was (and still is) feared as a retrieval of Pakistani nationalism. The hate and hysteria towards Pakistan and the memories of military atrocities were effectively used to demonize even the semblance of Muslim nationalism. Pakistan's failure to achieve national integration that relied on religion as the glue was considered a further justification for secularism in Bangladesh. In the immediate post-independence period, numerous people were charged with alleged Pakistani collaboration under the 1972 Collaborators Act (that made helping Pakistan in 1971 a punishable offence with retrospective effect). Many were dismissed from jobs, some sent to jail, and others fled into exile. Pakistani collaboration was not only a scornful accusation, but also such allegations resulted in indiscriminate punishment. As many as 37,000 persons were arrested on charges of collaborating with Pakistan military in 1972, but no more than 7,500 were found guilty, most of whom were also released later (Kabir, 1995). There was a xenophobic thunder of retribution among the Bangali nationalists, some of whom arbitrarily extorted, looted, kidnapped, blackmailed and killed the remnants of the Pakistani militia (known as the *Razakars* or *Al-Badars*), non-Bangali Biharis, and Bangladeshis with pro-Pakistani loyalty. Members of Islamic parties that allegedly collaborated with Pakistan in 1971 were the immediate targets of the government's wrath, but the post-1971 historical narratives in Bangladesh excluded such incidents. As a matter of reality, the distrust and dispute between the avowed secularists and Muslim identity seekers in general, and the scorn for the Islamic parties in particular, has never ended. From time to time Dhaka and even the district towns are rocked by the vociferous confrontations between the religious right and the secularists, and deep down the cultural and political divide was never bridged. In 1999, the *Jamaat* failed to move a writ petition in the Dhaka High Court challenging the validity of the state-sponsored school textbooks that accused the Islamic party of killing the Bangali intellectuals towards the end of the 1971 civil strife (*Daily Star*, 1999). Also, 10 *Jamaat* leaders, including Ghulam Azam, filed a defamation suit against a group of 18 people (including journalists) for spreading unverified allegations against them (*Independent*, 1999). The schism created by the issue of national identity which has divided Bangladesh from the dawn of its statehood continues to exist and is reinforced by the charges by 'patriots' against alleged 'collaborators'.

Secularism in Bangladesh was partly the fruit of its wounded history: it symbolized the pain that many Bangladeshis had suffered and the hatred for Pakistan generated by such suffering. Although there are no reliable statistics, it is estimated that in 1971 three million people had been killed and the Pakistani soldiers raped 300,000 women (Novak, 1993, p. 168; Siddiqi, 1998, p. 209). The nine-month long repression and killings of intellectuals barely hours before the Pakistani forces surrendered created a lasting disdain for Pakistan and anyone suspected to be its supporter. For millions, however, the creation of Bangladesh was the end of a nightmare, and a new beginning after a horror-filled year. There has not been any serious rethinking or historical reassessment about cessation from Pakistan. Hatred for Pakistan became the first step in defining nationalism and inscribing the future consciousness in Bangladesh. Regrettably, Pakistan so far has not assuaged that Bangladeshi anger by apologizing for all the known atrocities perpetrated by the Pakistani military on the people of former East Pakistan. Not unexpectedly, the Bangali nationalists' vengeance was reserved for those believed to be Pakistani sympathizers. Influenced by new slogans—*Joi Bangla* and *Sonar Bangla* (Golden Bengal)—the angry nationalists and their intellectual supporters challenged the 'two-nation theory' that had brought about the religious division of India in 1947. Historians, journalists, teachers, and writers picked up where the politicians paused. Contrary to what Jinnah and the Muslim League claimed during the Pakistan movement, it was argued that the Hindu-Muslim differences in Bengal were simply banal (Ahmed, 1988).

Linguistic Construction of Identity

For the Bangali nationalists, Bangla (Bengali) is more than a language; it is a non-sectarian national symbol and a vehicle of patriotism. The lingo-politics identified language with political empowerment (Lelyveld, 1994, p. 191). To some in Bangladesh, Bangali national consciousness was close to *Bangalitva* (Bangaliness): a 'linguistically pure' imagined identity that proposes the 'oneness' of all Bangla-speaking people. Interestingly, the term *Bangalitva*, though never fully explained, is frequently used in the Bangla books, journals and newspapers in Bangladesh. A popular historical prognosis is that the confrontation over the Bangla language that started in the early years of Pakistan marked the beginning of Bangali nationalism, ultimately culminating into a separate state in 1971. But there was no hard evidence that the language movement was a consciously separatist agitation to break away from Pakistan. Indeed, the *Tamaddun Majlis* (Cultural Forum), a pro-Islamic cultural organization, was among the leading activist groups in the language movement. Even the Muslim League members in the former East Pakistan Legislative Assembly supported the demand to make Bangla one of the national languages. In fact, they made a formal motion requesting the central government of Pakistan to accept Bangla as one of the national languages (Ahad, 1980, p. 137). However, the Karachi-based national Muslim League leaders did not like the idea. The linguistic divide between the two wings started in 1948 when the non-Bangali Pakistani elite proposed to make Urdu the sole national-language. It sparked a widespread agitation in the former East Pakistan. In 1952, the lingering dispute flared into a police-student confrontation on February 21, killing six demonstrators (of which two were known to be students). That particular incident exploded into an unprecedented movement in the then East Pakistan. Finally, the tumult ended in the Pakistani central government's recognition of Bangla as one of the national languages in 1956. Nevertheless, the police action of February 21 became an icon of Bangali nationalism and served as a symbol of resistance to Pakistani authorities. The *Shahid Minar* (Martyrs Tower) is the hallowed ground for the Bangali nationalists.

The selection of Rabindro Nath Thakur's (Rabindro Nath Tagore) poem *Amar Sonar Bangla* (My Golden Bengal) as the national anthem for Bangladesh was a distinctive cultural and political victory for the lingo-nationalists that successfully put their stamp on the national ethos. No definitive explanation of the selection of a *Rabindro Shongit* (Rabindro Nath's song) as the patriotic hymn is known, but certain circumstantial evidences are not difficult to trace. Muslim nationalists complained that the 'outsiders,' a euphemism for West Bengali intellectual and cultural influence, set the parameters of new nationalism in Bangladesh. The fact that the armed struggle was mostly based in India, and generally led from Calcutta, was another contributing factor. Rabindro Nath Thakur, a Hindu poet, was accepted as a non-religious symbol that signified the larger 'we-feeling' of all the Bangla-speaking people in South Asia. The dream of *Sonar Bangla* signified in Rabindro Nath's song was nostalgic; it was an exoticization that inspired the nationalistic imagination.[3] The linguistic identity was further legitimized when the 1972 Constitution stipulated that the citizens of Bangladesh would be known as Bangalis (*Constitution of the People's Republic of Bangladesh*, 1972). The emerging Bangali nationalism confidently appealed to all the Bangla-speaking people. From the early stage of Bangladesh, however, the new stream of vernacular consciousness came into conflict with other sub-national identities. Bangali nationalist slogans caused concern among the

Urdu-speaking Biharis and ethnic minority tribes in the Chittagong Hill Tracts (CHT). In fact, the latter did not identify with either Bangali lingo-consciousness or Muslim nationalism. While visiting the CHT in 1972, however, Mujibur Rahman asked the tribal people to merge with Bangali identity. That marked the beginning of two decades of separatist violence plaguing the southeastern part of the country. Nevertheless, many ardent Bangali nationalists looked upon Bangladesh as an opportunity to revive the dream of using the mother tongue in all stages of education, business, and administration (Rashiduzzaman, 1998). Actually, it turned into a historiography of isolationism. But the lingo-nationalists failed to recognize that the national consciousness in pluralistic Bangladesh could not be determined either through language or religion.

Ironically even Rabindro Nath, whose writings are believed to have inspired the Bangali nationalists, gradually took a universalist position and argued against divisive nationalism (Sen, 1997). Indeed, the linguistic nationalism in Bangladesh coincided with a perceptible indifference to other languages. Since 1971, the standard of English teaching has steadily fallen behind in Bangladesh and, with that, the general quality of education suffered a disastrous decline except for those who could afford the English medium private schools or hire private tutors (Novak, 1995, pp.114–115). Arabic, Persian, and Urdu—languages linked to the history and culture of Bangladeshi Muslims—commanded little respect in the secular intellectual forums. There was also a trend of puritanical writing in Bangla that replaced Urdu, Persian and Arabic words traditionally popular among the Muslims in Bangladesh. The overemphasis of language had a secular ambiance which embraced all Bangla-speaking people irrespective of communal differences. In the final analysis, the linguistic nationalism was hardly broader than the religious, Muslim identity.

Religious Construction of Identity

The pursuit for a Muslim identity as an anti-secularist quest is making its appearance in many countries, including Bangladesh. However, the diffused Muslim identity, observed by Samuel Huntington (1997, pp.174–176), is a consciousness without cohesion. While the liberal advocates of secularism argued convincingly for their cause, they often demonstrated zero-tolerance and ignorance about Muslim self-consciousness, Islamic jurisprudence, religious fundamentalism, and other compelling questions of the political divide in Bangladesh. Ironically, the Bangladeshi secular thinkers displayed an intellectual mood similar to Western Orientalist contortion about Islam and Muslim consciousness that Edward Said had incisively analyzed in another context (Said, 1979). Worst of all, the same brush paints the religious identity seekers, fundamentalists, Pakistani collaborators, and social reactionaries. To judge the Islamic-right in Bangladesh in the 21st century by what happened in 1971 is both unfair and unrealistic. There is a deep reservoir of spontaneous Muslim sentiments. It is a sense of belonging to a monotheistic faith and a nexus of history, values, customs, and rituals. Above all, it is a sense of satisfaction that holds the Bangladeshi Muslims together. Delineation of the Muslim exclusiveness is not easy, but its undeniable presence, mostly subtle in nature, is felt in the political arena and civil society. The general feeling of togetherness among the Muslims—a continuing entity—is not just about religion; its goals are also very mundane, including the security concerns for Bangladesh. A sense of pride uniting a predominantly Muslim country, held together by common beliefs and a shared history, is projected as an important strategic resource for the country. The *Jamaat* and other pro-Islamic groups no longer preach the old slogan that Islam is in danger, but they insist that Islam and Muslim identity are essential for Bangladesh in maintaining its independence vis-a-vis India's domineering influence (Sangram, 1997). Behind the Muslim identity search there is an embedded memory that whenever the Muslims lost political power as a community, they not only suffered humiliation, but also deprivation, discrimination, and injustice. The Indian Muslim consciousness that burst into Hindu-Muslim political acrimony in the 1920s and 1930s reached the climax in the 1940s (Chaudhury, 1987, pp. 458–499). The Muslims were a majority (54 percent) in Bengal during the British rule, but their political power was notable only after the 1937 provincial legislative elections. Since then, the Hindu elite refused to accept what was perceived as the future Muslim political domination in what was then (united) Bengal, and that has been identified as one of the core reasons for the division of Bengal in 1947 (Chatterjee, 1994).

Long after the separation of Bangladesh from Pakistan, the fear about Hindu-majority India has not dissipated. Secularism has failed to relieve that apprehension. And that is not necessarily an expression of communal bent of the Bangladeshi Muslims; it is a combination of negative rhetoric and a fear of Indo-centric Bangladesh (Dixit, 1999, p.174). From 1948 to 1998 as many as 8,000 Hindu-Muslim communal riots took place in India, and hundreds were killed and injured on several occasions (Misra, 1998). The secular constitution in Bangladesh was of little relief to fellow Muslims in India. The sharp rise of the *Bharatiya Janata Party* (BJP) with an agenda of *Hindutva* (Hinduness), that defined nationalism primarily by its dominant Hindu religious teachings, outraged many Muslims. Much to New Delhi's disappointment, the fear of Indian hegemony has replaced the traditional ideological battle in Bangladesh. This has recently manifested in the opposition to natural gas export to India. Also, there is vehement objection to allowing India transit access to India's northeastern provinces through Bangladesh territories. Muslim exclusiveness is not always a question of steering between the two extremes of purely religious and purely linguistic identities; many Bangladeshis take delight in being both a Muslim and a Bangali. Yet, the debate over who is a Bangladeshi has simmered for over two decades. Muslim identity has demonstrated a resilience that few could deny. Whatever happened during the nine months of independence struggle in 1971, the historical and cultural reality of the country—its Islamic affiliation—cannot be dismissed. In the eyes of those who focused on the Islamic ingredient of nationalism in Bangladesh, a new Muslim homeland was born in what was the then East Pakistan in December 1971 (Zaheer, 1994). Soon after Bangladesh's independence, the Islamic sensibility became a yardstick for suspected collaboration with the Pakistani military authorities. However, the mainstream Muslim identity supporters did not propose a return to the pre-1971 Islamic sentiment. Furthermore, most advocates of Muslim exclusiveness did not want to establish a fundamentalist state in Bangladesh. Here, it is noteworthy that the *Jamaat* did not enjoy overwhelming loyalty of the Bangladeshi Muslims. Yet, the secularists did not distinguish between Muslim nationalism and *Jamaat* orthodoxy. The widespread re-awakening of Muslim consciousness was noticeable in both political and cultural spheres. Whereas the orthodox Islamic groups ask for strict adherence to the *shari'a*, they do not reflect the widely dispersed moderate Muslim identity. The latter is more an emblem of protest against secular forces that ignore their sentiments. It is a dissension against the cultural ascendancy of the Calcutta-centric as well as pro-Western secularists in post-independent Bangladesh.

The *madrassas* (religious education institutions), *maktabs* (community religious education facilities), *masjids* (mosques), and *ulamas* (religious scholars) provided the institutional nexus for a sustained Islamic differentiation. In the 65,000 Bangladeshi villages there were about 140,000 *masjids*, 5,766 *madrassas,* and 58,126 *maktabs* that keep the Muslim tradition alive (*Statistical Yearbook of Bangladesh*, 1991). More than 300 *madrassas* are fully funded by the government.[4] Even though thousands of other *madrassas* receive only partial government grants, thousands more operate without any government support. There are orphanages, hospitals, banks, publishers, research organizations, and private voluntary associations with Islamic affiliation. Thousands of listed and unlisted *waqfs* (endowments) throughout Bangladesh run religious schools and voluntary services for the disadvantaged in the cities and rural areas. The *Tablighi Jamaat's* (Association of Communicators) annual *iztema* (prayer congregation) that meets in the outskirts of Dhaka City is believed to be the largest Muslim gathering in the world except the *hajj* (pilgrimage) in Mecca. However, the non-political *Tablighi Jamaat* is not affiliated with the fundamentalist *Jamaat-i-Islami*. This demonstrates that Muslim identity can survive outside the conventional political arena and government patronage. In both the 1991 and 1996 elections, the exclusive Islamic groups received only about 10 percent of the popular votes. It is noteworthy, however, that during the 1991 elections, the *Jamaat* won several *Shangshod* (Bangladesh parliament) seats in the districts bordering India. That was because those constituents believed that only the *Jamaat* would take a bold stand against Indian influence in such areas (Baxter, 1992). From the number of mosques, Friday *Jumma* prayer attendance, *Tabligh* (prayer communication), and *madrassas*, it is generally assumed that the proportion of practicing Muslims in Bangladesh is on the rise, both in rural and urban areas. In contrast to the Islamic orthodox faction, however, the Muslim moderates are a larger segment of the population and cut across party lines. Even though a 1983 survey found 50.6 percent and 62.1 percent of rural and urban respondents, respectively, adhering to orthodox religious beliefs (Banu, 1992, p. 175), they are not members of the orthodox Islamic political parties. Perhaps, the numerous practicing Muslims who resent virulent secularism voted for moderately secular parties.

Interestingly, in 1999 it was alleged that a few Muslim fanatics tried to kill poet Shamsur Rahman, a well-known champion for secularism. The *Talibans*, backed by Osama Ben Laden, were believed to be in league with the *madrassa*-based Islamic militants to assassinate the secular intellectuals in Bangladesh. When President Bill Clinton visited Bangladesh in March 2000, he cancelled part of his itinerary because of security reasons. In the aftermath of a controversy following that cancellation, it was reported that the Hasina Administration had earlier distributed a leaflet accusing the opposition of harboring Islamic militants. Consequently, the country was galvanized by an unfolding power struggle between the Muslim nationalists and secularists. Many Bangladeshis believed that outside supporters sustained the Islamic groups and that large resources, including arms, flowed from several Muslim countries. Different Islamic groups and their supporting organizations do not deny international assistance, but their secular contenders often exaggerate political motivation in that relationship. Saudi Arabia does provide financial assistance for *madrassa* education. *Rabita* (World Muslim Congress) is also active in building mosques, distributing funds for Islamic education and relief to the needy. From time to time the Saudi role in promoting and sustaining Islamic cultural and religious values comes under fire from the secular intellectuals, Bangali nationalists, and the pro-Western liberal elites. By the same token, there are several non-government organizations (NGOs), the cultural contestants of Islamic groups in Bangladesh, that receive overseas funding. In recent years, the orthodox Muslim groups and their religious leaders have raised voice against the externally funded NGOs (Rashiduzzaman, 1997).

A Fragile Systhesis?

Secular presuppositions are no longer deemed to be the only progressive ideas. Even in neighboring India, modern secularism of the upper elite has been challenged (Duara, 1991). And for the first time since Indian independence in 1947, the Hindu nationalists came to power in 1998-99 in New Delhi (Rashiduzzaman, 1999). The first constitution of Bangladesh was secular, and the government also claimed itself to be the same. However, many Muslims abhorred this as a rejection of the Muslim identity. It was also viewed as capitulation to Indian political influence. In the eyes of the orthodox Muslims and *ulama*, secularists and anti-Islamic cohorts were 'atheists' and 'apostates'(Ahmed, 1994). The new level of Islamic consciousness in Bangladesh is not a victory for the zealots. Surely the secularists still dominate the universities, media, and intellectuals, but the new middle class also assimilates the basic Islamic values. More significantly, Islamic activism is by no means confined to the illiterate rural people in Bangladesh, as has been often suggested by secular observers. There is a generation of educated, but unemployed young men who are increasingly attracted to Islamic militancy. The Islamic activists complain that their voice of protest has been deliberately suppressed or stigmatized by the secularists. However, the Taslima Nasreen controversies of 1994 and 1999 galvanized a new sense of buoyancy and confidence in the traditional Muslim groups. Furthermore, introduction of the democratic process—despite a relatively low electoral gain—has increased the bargaining power of the Islamic groups and the visibility of their leaders.

Stirring up the fundamentalist bogey against the orthodox Muslims has been the standard tactic of most secular groups in recent years. In the eyes of the Islamists, a handful of secular leaders and intellectuals are active in their denunciation of Islam and Muslim identity. There is an Islamic counter-press comprised of a few Bangla newspapers—*Sangram, Inquilab, Purnima*, and *Bikram*—which promote the cause of Islam and stress the Muslim heritage in Bangladesh. A group of pro-Islamic authors regularly write on the distinctive culture and history of Muslims in Bangladesh. Muslim nationalists observe Bakhtiar Khilji Day (marking the beginning of Muslim conquest of Bengal in 1199) and Nawab Sirajuddaulah Day (signifying the end of Muslim rule in 1757). Strapped under the ban of Islamic parties in the early 1970s, the manifestation of Muslim identity first took the form of a whispering campaign against Bangali nationalism and rejection of political Islam. The underlying Muslim consciousness was put to use by both the Zia and Ershad Administrations for expanding their political support base. Interestingly, shortly before his assassination in 1975, Mujib demonstrated some flexibility in dealing with the alleged collaborators of Pakistan. In 1974, he participated in the Organization of Islamic Conference. Also, he reinstated funding for *madrassa* education and established the Islamic Foundation, a government sponsored autonomous research body. While Mujib supported a secular political process, the AL claims, he was not opposed to Islam and recognized the Muslim legacy in Bangladesh. There are reasons to believe that Mujib understood that most Bangladeshi Muslims refused to forsake their religious identity. Perhaps, he acknowledged the reality of a predominantly Muslim Bangladesh. And he began steering away from New Delhi's hegemony. An Indian diplomat revealed in his autobiography that Mujib was cognizant of Bangladesh's status as an Islamic country in the subcontinent (Dixit, 1999, p. 72).

What the BNP claimed to achieve, and what the succeeding Ershad regime accepted, was a blending of lingo-nationalism with Muslim ethos. According to Zia, language should not be the only criteria of citizenship, but the BNP never fully elaborated this point. It was closer to what was often described as 'civic nationalism': a kind of umbrella recognition rather than exclusively concentrating on language, religion, or ethnicity. The concept of nationalism that does not specify a single source of identity was a positive step in Bangladesh (Ahsan, 1999). Those who disliked the sole emphasis on language and secularism as the hallmark of nationalism favored the BNP's reconceptualization of national identity. Moreover, those who feared that the secularists were the conduits of Indian hegemony preferred the BNP's approach to nationalism that distinguished between the Bangalis in Bangladesh and the Bangla-speaking people in India. The *Jamaat* and the Islamic groups, seeking a doctrinaire Islamic state, were not pleased with BNP's Bangladeshi nationalism, but they found it more acceptable than the virulent secular nationalism. The BNP's Bangladeshi nationalism was an Islamic 'communal' expression in the eyes of the advocates of secularism. Not only the AL, but also its front organizations, attacked the BNP's notion of nationalism (Choudhury, 1994).

Zia's deletion of secularism from the constitution was disliked by the Bangali nationalists. Even some of his own supporters did not relish it. However, he stopped short of calling Bangladesh an Islamic state. Two major political currents flow through the BNP: one secular and the other affiliated with Islam. The BNP leadership frequently called upon the 'nationalists' to unite. Still, neither the late Ziaur Rahman nor Khaleda Zia (henceforth, Khaleda)—the party leader after her husband's assassination—delineated the staples of Bangladeshi nationalism. Their ideological stand has not been articulated.

The strategic ambiguity in Bangladeshi nationalism is a deliberate posture. If the BNP explicitly favors Muslim nationalism, the secularists assault the party for forging an alliance with the 'anti-liberation forces' that opposed the independence struggle in 1971. Another charge by the secularists is that the BNP was sheltering Islamic fundamentalists and fomenting *communalism* (conflict between religious communities). By the same token, if the BNP closely identifies with the secular configuration, people would find little difference between the AL and BNP. Yet, Khaleda hopes that the Muslim nationalists would support her because the BNP is the major centrist party in the country. Even though the *Jamaat* helped the BNP to form a cabinet in 1991, Khaleda took pain to avoid identifying the orthodox Islamists as an ally. Led by several freedom fighters, the BNP was confident that it would be able to attract a broad spectrum of the Bangladeshis, including the Muslim identity sympathizers. The right-of-the-center BNP does better when it coalesces with Islamic groups, as it did 1991. The alliance also helps the Islamic parties. *Jamaat's* performance was miserable in 1996 when it contested on its own. Also, the BNP could not have emerged as the second largest party that year without the support of many who may be loosely described as believers in Muslim exclusiveness. Both the BNP and

Jamaat, following their post-election reckoning, have continued to cooperate. In 1999, the *Jamaat* joined the three-party anti-AL opposition alliance. The following year, the BNP-led four-party alliance—that included the *Jamaat* and *Islamic Oikkya* (Islamic Unity)—agreed to a distribution of the number of contested seats for each of the partners in the next elections. And Khaleda announced that all four alliance partners would be included in a future cabinet if this opposition front wins the elections.

As for the AL, the party disappointed the ardent secularists by its return to power in 1996: Hasina did not undertake a frontal assault on the BNP-initiated Bangladeshi nationalism. Also, she did not openly challenge the *Jamaat* leaders even though the acrimony between the 'pro-liberation' and 'anti-liberation' forces continued. In competing with BNP's synthesis of Islam and Bangla language, Hasina moved the AL towards the center and presented her party in 1996 as respecting the Muslim identity in the country. Hasina accepted the fundamentalist *Jamaat* as AL's partner during the 1994–1996 opposition movement. She performed *hajj* more than once and donned *hijab* (veil). One of the contributing factors for AL's defeat in the 1991 elections had been the rumor that the AL was pro-Indian. To counter that perception, Hasina mobilized her own semblance of 'Islamic front.' She reportedly advised her party activists not to abandon the 'mosques' to the Islamic groups and BNP.[5] During the 1996 election she promised not to overlook the Islamic traditions in Bangladesh. Hasina's Islamic posture embarrassed her secular cohorts. They feared that the AL, in its competition with the BNP, had abandoned its secular image that attracted the non-Muslim voters (*Jai Jai Din*, 1999). But the secular ideologues did not realize that there was a growing proliferation of religious identities worldwide, and what Hasina was doing was a pragmatic response to the changing realities. The AL leadership and their intellectual supporters were in a dilemma. On the one hand, the AL could force the secular logic in ending the difference between Bangladesh and India. On the other hand, the party could accept the *de facto* Muslim nationalism, which originally contributed to the division of India in 1947. Neither the AL leadership nor the intellectual establishment that supported them openly indicated that they wanted reunification with India. What they wanted to do was to continue as an independent but secular nation.

Conclusion

The reassertion of Muslim identity in Bangladesh has come a long way since the polity broke away from Pakistan in 1971. So far, the fear of Islamic extremism in Bangladesh has been grossly exaggerated. However, the Islamic parties on their own are not yet strong enough to challenge the secularists for political power in elections. In the meantime, they are forming alliances with other parties to gain further legitimacy and visibility. The Islamic groups have capitalized on the Muslim sentiment of the population, but they have been unable to reap any major political advantage for their party platform. Even though the Islamic parties will influence politics, they are unlikely to move forward as a major contender in the near future. The Bangladeshis are not yet ready for an Islamic party at the helm of the country! Yet, the yearning for Muslim nationalism will continue, and the secularists' drive to contain Islamic resurgence will fail. In fact, the antagonism from secular forces might even further energize the process of rekindling Muslim identity in

Bangladesh. The well-entrenched Islamic groups are the potent critics of Bangladeshi domestic and foreign policies. Islam produces a sense of commonality through a network of *masjids, madrassas,* and charitable institutions. The political strength of the Muslim nationalists   is reinforced through religious, spiritual, and moral exhortation. In a multicultural era people identify themselves by race, gender, and language. Indeed, many Bangladeshis identify themselves by districts, dialect, region, and even by sub-districts— and they are no longer ignored as primordial concerns. The majority of Bangladeshi Muslim nationalists wonder why they cannot demonstrate their Muslim contour in public life. It is that desire which will keep the Muslim identity quest alive though their organizational cohesion continues to be shaky.

The linguistic patriotism is also an undeniable reality in Bangladesh. It is an emotion that inspires major political groups, cultural establishments, intellectuals, leaders, and individuals that Muslim nationalists cannot ignore. Muslim consciousness and lingo-centric patriotism are the two parallel identities in Bangladesh for the foreseeable future, and their coexistence is the only realistic choice for a consensus in the civil society. The Muslim nationalists in general, and the Islamic groups in particular, have not yet specified their positions regarding pluralism in Bangladesh. They have to do more to establish that the search for Muslim identity is not just an obsolete sentimentality or obscurantism, and they are yet to convince others that it is not a metaphor for *communalism.* The strength of Muslim identity and the political ascendancy of Islamic groups are visibly feared by the secularists. One of their anxieties is that it will foment religious intolerance against the non-Muslims. But more disturbing is the prospect that the Islamic groups, in alliance with the centrist parties, have an appeal to a large number of voters who are generally inclined towards Muslim identity. Even if the Muslim nationalists want to be ruled by the *shari'a,* the religious minorities must not be forced to live under the Islamic legal system. But no perfect secular legal process is available either, both in the Western and non-Western countries (Salame, 1993). The secularists have, so far, failed to fully satisfy the religious and ethnic minorities in Bangladesh. Through their increasing contact with the centrist BNP and JP, the Islamic groups have no doubt become a factor in Bangladesh politics. However, the nature of the alliance between the Muslim groups and the centrist leadership is still tentative, and only time will tell how that relationship evolves.

Notes

1   In this chapter, Muslim identity, Muslim nationalism, and Muslim patriotism are used interchangeably as it is often difficult to delineate one from the other.

2   Sheikh Mujibur Rahman is known to have told the *Shangshod* that secular did not mean the end of religion (Husain, 1990, p. 98).

3   Interestingly, during the anti-colonial movement in British India, it was Kazi Nazrul Islam, a Bangali Muslim poet, who was more identified with nationalist struggle.

4   The author is grateful to Momtaz Ahmed for this information.

5   The author benefitted from his informal discussions with scholars and politicians during his 1995 trip to Dhaka, Bangladesh. Particularly interesting was a conversation with an Awami League member of the *Shangshod,* who wished to remain anonymous.

References

Ahad, Oli (1980), *Jatiya Rajniti, 1945–1975* (National Politics, 1945–1975), Cooperative Book Society: Dhaka (Bangladesh).

Ahmad, Abul Mansur (1986), *Kam Dame Kena, Beshi Dame Becha* (Buying Cheap, Selling High), Ahmed Publishers: Dhaka (Bangladesh).

Ahmed, Noman (1994), *NGO, Nastik and Murtad* (NGO, Atheist and Apostate), n.a.: Dhaka, (Bangladesh).

Ahmed, Rafiuddin (1988), *The Bengali Muslims, 1871–1906: A Quest for Identity*, Oxford University Press: New Delhi.

Ahsan, Syed Ali (1999), 'Bangladesh Culture and nationhood,' *The Independent*, Dhaka, February 2.

Bahadur, Kalim (1996), 'Muslim Identity in the Sub-Continent: An Overview,' *Comparative Studies of South Asia, Africa and the Middle East*, Vol. 16.

Banu, U.A.B. Razia Akhter (1992), *Islam in Bangladesh*, E. J. Brill: Leiden (The Netherlands).

Baxter, Craig and Syedur Rahman (1991), 'The Bangladesh Votes in 1991,' *Asian Survey*, Vol. 31, No. 8, August, pp. 683–693.

Baxter, Craig (1997), *Bangladesh: From Nation to a State*, Westview Press: Boulder, CO.

Chatterjee, Joya (1994), *Bengal Divided: Hindu Communalism and Partition, 1932–1947*, Cambridge University Press: Cambridge (United Kingdom).

Chateerjee, Joya (1996), 'The Bengali Muslim, A Contradiction in Terms: An Overview of the Debate on Bengali Muslim Identity,' *Comparative Studies of South Asia, Africa and the Middle East*, Vol. 16, pp. 16–24.

Chaudhury, Nirad C. (1987), *Thy Hand Great Anach! India 1921–1951*, Addison-Wesley: New York.

Chowdhury, Abdul Gaffar (1994), *Amra Bangali, Na Bangladeshi* (Are We Bangali or Bangladeshi), Aksharbritta: Dhaka (Bangladesh).

Daily Star (1999), Dhaka, internet edition, May 25.

Dixit, J.N. (1999), *Liberation and Beyond: Indo-Bangladesh Relations*, The University Press: Dhaka (Bangladesh).

Duara, Prasanjit (1991), 'The New Politics of Hinduism,' *The Wilson Quarterly*, Vol. 15, No. 11, Summer, pp. 42–50.

Government of Bangladesh (1972), *Constitution of the People's Republic of Bangladesh*, Government of Bangladesh Printing Press: Dhaka (Bangladesh).

Government of Bangladesh (1973), *Interim Education Report*, Government of Bangladesh Printing Press: Dhaka (Bangladesh).

Government of Pakistan (1972), *Report of General Elections, Pakistan 1970–1971*, Karachi (Pakistan).

Huntington, Samuel P. (1997), *The Clash of Civilizations: Remaking of the World Order*, Touchstone: New York.

Husain, Syed Anwar (1990), 'Bangladesh and Islamic Countries,' in Tepper, Elliot L. and Glen A. Hayes (eds.), *Bengal and Bangladesh: Politics and Culture on the Golden Bengal*, Michigan State University: East Lansing.

Independent (1999), Dhaka, internet edition, February 2 and May 7.

Jai Jai Din (1999), Dhaka, internet edition, February 23 to March 1.

Kabir, Bhuian Md. Monoar (1999), *Politics of Military Rules and the Dilemmas of Democratization in Bangladesh*, South Asian Publishers: New Delhi.

Kabir, Shariar (1995), *Bangladesh Maulabad O Shankahlogo Sampradya* (Bangladeshi Fundamentalism and Minority Community), n.a.: Dhaka (Bangladesh).

Khan, General Habib (1973), *Muslim Guerilla Faujer Char Nambar Ishtihar* (Muslim Guerilla Force's Number Four Leaflet), n.a.: Dhaka (Bangladesh).

Lelyveld, David (1994), 'The Fate of Hindustani: Colonial Knowledge and the Project of National Language,' in Breckenridge, Carol A. and Peter Van der Veer (eds.), *Orientalism and Post-Colonial Predicament*, Oxford University Press: Delhi.

Makeig, Douglas C. (1990), 'Identity, Aid and Security of Bangladesh and the Muslim World,' in Elliot, Tepper (ed.), *Bengal and Bangladesh: Politics and Culture on the Golden Delta*, Michigan State University: East Lansing.

Mishra, Pankaj (1998), 'A New Nuclear India,' *New York Book Review*, June 25, pp. 55–64.

Murshed, Tazeen M. (1997), 'The Quest for Legitimacy in Bangladesh,' *South Asia*, Australia, Vol. 20, No. 2, pp. 1–34.

Nag, Sajal (1999), *Nationalism, Separatism and Secessionism*, Rawat Publications: Jaipur (India).

Novak, James J. (1995), *Bangladesh: Reflections on the Water*, Indiana University Press: Bloomington.

Rashiduzzaman, Mohammad (1970), 'The Awami League in the Political Development of Pakistan,' *Asian Survey*, Vol. 10, No. 7, July, pp. 574–587.

Rashiduzzaman, Mohammad (1994), 'The Liberals and the Religious Right in Bangladesh,' *Asian Survey*, Vol. 34, No.11, November, pp. 974–990.

Rashiduzzaman, Mohammad (1997a), 'Political Unrest and Democracy in Bangladesh,' *Asian Survey*, Vol. 37, No. 3, March, pp. 255–267.

Rashiduzzaman, Mohammad (1997b), 'The dichotomy of Islam and development: NGOs, women's development and fatwa in Bangladesh,' *Contemporary South Asia*, United Kingdom, Vol. 6, No. 3, November, pp. 239–246.

Rashiduzzaman, Mohammad (1998), 'Bangladesh at 26: Encountering Bifurcated History and Divided National Unity,' *Journal of South Asian and Middle Eastern Studies*, Vol. 20, No. 3, Spring, pp. 54–74.

Said, Edward W. (1979), *Orientalism*, Vintage Press: New York.

Salame, Gharsan (1993), 'Islam and the West,' *Foreign Policy*, Vol. 90, No. 10, Spring, pp. 22–37.

Sangram (1997), Dhaka, internet edition, December 28.

Sen, Amartya (1995), 'Tagore and His India,' *The New York Book Review*, June 22, pp. 55–63.

Shahabuddin, Syed and Theodore P. Wright, Jr. (1987), 'India: Muslim Minority Politics and Society,' in Esposito, John L. (ed.), *Islam in Asia*, Oxford University Press: New York.

Shehabuddin, Elora (1999), 'Beware of the Bed of Fire: Gender, Democracy and the Jammat-i-Islami in Bangladesh,' *Journal of Women History*, Vol. 10, No. 4, Winter, pp. 148–171.

Siddiqi, Dina M. (1998), 'Taslima Nasreen and Others: The Contest over Gender in Bangladesh,' in Bodman, Herbert L. and Nayereh Tohidi (eds.), *Women in Muslim Societies: Diversity Within Unity*, Lynne Rienner Publishers: Boulder, CO.

Van Der Veer, Peter (1998), *Religious Nationalism*, Oxford University Press: Delhi.

Zaheer, Hasan (1994), *The Separation of East Pakistan*, Oxford University Press: Karachi (Pakistan).

Conclusion

Religion attempts to answer two important questions for humanity beyond the parameter of life. First, where did we come from? Second, what will happen to us after this life? Charles Darwin's theory of evolution answers the first question, but the creationists manage to resurface the debate periodically. In 1999, an archaeological discovery of an inscription referring to 'the House of David' served to authenticate the reign of King David in ancient Israel (Sheler, 1999, p. 52). The same year, the Kansas Board of Education voted six to four not to test students in the Kansas public schools about evolution. However, Kansas was not the first state to restrict the teaching of evolution. The issue can be traced back to the 1925 conviction of John Scopes in Tennessee for teaching evolution (Gould, 1999, p. 59; Marcus, 1999, p. 32). While the evolutionists have prevailed in the creation-evolution debate, science has yet to answer the second question. Ironically, the one thing certain after birth is death! And this is where religion is helpful in explaining the unknown. As human beings made progress in fathoming the mystery of nature, it was no longer appealing to worship the mountain, ocean, moon, and sun. Thus, God became an abstract entity, and polytheism gave way to monotheism. With the discovery of universal natural forces, furthermore, human rationality claimed autonomy from God. As reality was subsequently found to be relative, the very existence of God became subjective. And now genetic engineering promises humans they can play God! Yet, there is a lot that remains unknown. The much heralded Human Genome Project, launched in 1990, is really the beginning of a new era of exploring the mystery of life. With the Human Genome Project virtually completed, 'Proteomics'—decoding proteins— has already shifted attention from genes to proteins (Begley, 2001, pp. 52–53; Olson, 2001, p. 73). While human beings have managed to prolong life, death continues to be a reality in the final analysis. In the developing world, not blessed with scientific leaps, religion is very important in providing an answer about the 'eternal life.' And anchored in faith, religion does not require proof—a sine qua non for science. In drawing attention to the unknown eternity, religion invokes God in guiding human behavior on this earth. Unlike the West, the developing world does not temper religious emotions by a secular milieu.

This book began with the task of understanding the impact of religion on politics— particularly explosive behavior against the state. A few observations are in order. First, violence is not a monopoly of any religion or denomination. This study points not only to Islam in Algeria, Bangladesh, Chechnya, and Palestine, but also to Christianity in Haiti, Malawi, Mexico, and Nicaragua. Both Catholic and Protestant denominations are included in the above examples. Where Protestants eschewed violence, as in Haiti, Mexico, and Nicaragua, Catholics were the majority population in those countries. In addition to lacking a critical mass, the Protestant hierarchy in Haiti and Mexico discouraged retaliation even in the face of violence. The institutional restraint that is currently in place may be lifted with the coming of new converts. And that will compound the challenges facing the state. Leaving aside the Sufi order in Chechnya, the Sunni majority societies in Algeria, Bangladesh, and Palestine further undermine violence attributed to the Shi'ite sect of Islam. In fact, the majority of the case studies in The Fundamentalism Project involve countries with a predominantly Sunni population.

Second, in withdrawing its support from the ruling elite, religious institutions deny the state legitimacy and give momentum to opposition movements. What religion opposes is contingent upon the nature of the state in time and place. Thus, Christianity was a guiding force in challenging British colonialism in Malawi and Islam served the same role in opposing French colonialism in Algeria. At present, Islam is being invoked in resisting Russian domination in Chechnya and Israeli occupation in Palestine. While opposing external colonial domination *before* independence, a religious force can direct its energy against internal authoritarianism *after* independence. Religious forces opposed the Duvalier regime in Haiti, Banda's authoritarianism in Malawi, and the Somoza dictatorship in Nicaragua. At the end of the Somoza era, liberation theology challenged the authoritarianism of the Sandinista regime. The spirit of holy war that guided the National Liberation Front (FLN) against the French Government during the independence struggle came to haunt the FLN in postcolonial Algeria from within. While continuing to oppose Israel, *Harakat al-Muqawama al-Islamiyya* (HAMAS) adds a religious dimension to Palestinian internal dynamics.

Third, a crusading spirit of state secularism imposed on an unwilling population is counter-productive. Without access to legitimate channels for redressing grievances, religious opposition will feel compelled to resort to violence. Excessive anticlericalism prompted staunchly devout Catholic peasants to engage the Mexican Army in an insurgency warfare. Sandinista activities found support in grass roots Catholic movements in rural communities in Nicaragua. But in ignoring the Catholic sentiment after its Marxist Revolution, the Sandinista regime thereafter faced opposition from the country's Catholics. In Malawi, oppression against the Jehovah's Witnesses contributed to the Banda regime's downfall. While domestic religious opposition was on the defensive, international pressure helped to end Banda's dictatorship. After years of Marxist secularism during the former Soviet Union, Dzhokhar Dudayev was able to tap into Chechen Muslim sentiments in the secessionist struggle against Russia. State imposed secularism in post-independence Bangladesh has been quietly rolled back by successive administrations. However, the policy changes have rekindled identity debate between the secular and religious segments of the society. With democratic outlet curtailed, Algeria has witnessed a brutal armed conflict between the secular state and increasingly fractured religious groups. Allowed to participate in the democratic process, the religious organizations in Israel have found it prudent to avoid violence. While Israel has demonstrated a democratic tradition, such a tradition is lacking in contemporary Muslim countries. Of course there is no guarantee that religious groups gaining state power through democratic means will not impose religion 'from above' and end the democratic process itself (Miller (1993, p. 47). However, Talibans in Afghanistan, Ayatollahs in Iran, and Hasan al-Turabi in Sudan are not examples of democratic route to power. While some Muslim leaders have taken it upon themselves to decree *fatwa* (religious opinion), other Muslim groups have availed the judicial system (Weaver, 1998, pp. 41–42) and electoral process (Shadid, 2001, pp. 294–295).

Finally, whereas social and economic factors are necessary, they are not sufficient conditions for religious violence. For the latter to occur there must be, in addition, political leadership. Religious violence does not take place in a vacuum. Destitution and hopelessness without political efficacy creates frustration that makes people prone to violence. However, it is leadership that actually makes it an organized violence against the state. Liberation theology provided the environment for creating the religious based communities in rural Nicaragua. However, a crucial step was the appointment of new Catholic leadership in that country that reflected the changing mood in the Vatican. In fact, the appointment of Miguel Obando y Bravo to replace the pro-Somoza Archbishop in Nicaragua was decided in Rome. And that facilitated Fathers Fernando Cardenal and Uriel Molina to proceed with the Christian student movement which later supported the class struggle by the Sandinista National Liberation Front. Even though the Vatican tried to dissociate itself from Jean-Bertrand Aristide, one cannot deny the role of Aristide in the events in Haiti. In the process of opposing oppressive regimes, however, the religious hierarchy in both Nicaragua and Haiti experienced a bifurcation. Interestingly, the minority Protestants assiduously avoid politics and conflict in Haiti, Mexico, and Nicaragua. Where the Protestants are a majority, as in Malawi, they formed their own black churches. Resentful of European racism, these black churches incessantly opposed British colonialism. Whereas Landon Cheek, Emma DeLany, Charles Domingo were silenced, John Chilembwe was instrumental in organizing the revolt against the British authorities. Also, the word *amir* (commander) itself testifies to role of leaders in conflict strategies for the various armed religious groups in Algeria. And one has to consider the pivotal role of Mustapha Bouyali in establishing the Armed Islamic Movement in that country. To account for the militant dynamics within HAMAS, furthermore, attention must focus on the external leadership.

The above observations are far from general propositions, but provide a good starting point for future research. One task will be to keep the focus on examining the impact of religion on political violence. Rigorous case studies will facilitate the 'comparable-cases strategy' (Lijphart, 1988, p. 55). In that endeavor, it will be important to define 'explosive interactions' or to use a more suitable concept. The reference to violence is vague. In particular, there must be a clear yardstick to identify an event reaching an 'explosive' point. Do rock-throwing demonstrators meet the mark, or should the threshold be the use of bullets? Are injuries enough, or should death toll be the criterion? Another task is to expand the number of case studies in both time and space. Whereas Christianity had spread westward to Europe and the Americas from its birth-place in Palestine, Buddhism had traveled eastward across Asia from its origin in the foothills of the Himalayas Mountains. Yet, The Fundamentalism Project, in its five volumes, included only about two Christian and three Buddhist countries, compared to roughly three-fold that combined number for Muslim countries. Not only does Christianity have the largest following in the world, but also 60 percent of the Christians now reside in the developing world (Woodward, 2001, p. 48). The skewed focus on Islamic countries needs to be balanced by attention to the vast reservoir of Christian and Buddhist polities.

References

Begley, Sharon (2001), 'Solving the Next Genome Puzzle,' *Newsweek*, February 19, pp. 52–53.
Gould, Stephen J. (1999), 'Dorothy, It's Really Oz,' *Time*, Vol. 154, No. 8, August 23, p. 59.
Lijphart, Arend (1988), 'The Comparable-Cases Strategy in Comparative Research,' in Cantori, Louis J. and Andrew H. Ziegler, Jr. (eds.), *Comparative Politics in the Post-Behavioral Era*, Lynne Rienner Publishers: Boulder, CO.

Marcus, David L. (1999), 'Charles Darwin gets thrown out of school,' *U.S. News and World Report*, Vol. 127, No. 8, August 30, p. 32.

Miller, Judith (1993), 'The Challenge of Radical Islam,' *Foreign Affairs*, Vol. 72, No. 2, Spring, pp. 43–56.

Olson, Steve (2001), 'The Genetic Archaeology of Race,' *The Atlantic Monthly*, Vol. 287, No. 4, April, pp. 69–80.

Shadid, Anthony (2001), *Legacy of the Prophet: Despots, Democrats, and the New Politics of Islam*, Westview Press: Boulder, CO.

Sheler, Jeffery L. (1999), 'Is the Bible True?' *U.S. News and World Report*, Vol. 127, No. 16, October 25, pp. 50–59.

Weaver, Mary Anne (1998), 'Revolution by Stealth,' *The New Yorker*, June 8, pp. 38–48.

Woodward, Kenneth L. (2001), 'The Changing Face of the Church,' *Newsweek*, April 16, pp. 46–52.

Index